DEVELOPING
STANDARDS-BASED
REPORT CARDS

This book is dedicated to my dear friend and coauthor,

Jane M. Bailey.

While developing this book, our third book written together, Jane was diagnosed with cancer. She contributed to every aspect of the book but passed away before our work was completed. Jane was a dedicated wife, a proud mother, the most committed educator I have ever known, and the very best of friends. Her kindness, charm, and irrepressible spirit inspired everyone who knew her. In my life, I know only two other people who, in the face of such challenging adversity, showed comparable grace and courage: my mom and dad, Evelyn and Robert Guskey.

DEVELOPING
STANDARDS-BASED
REPORT CARDS

THOMAS R. GUSKEY
JANE M. BAILEY

CORWIN
A SAGE Company

For information:

 Corwin
A SAGE Company
2455 Teller Road
Thousand Oaks, California 91320
(800) 233–9936
Fax: (800) 417–2466
www.corwinpress.com

SAGE India Pvt. Ltd.
B 1/I 1 Mohan Cooperative
    Industrial Area
Mathura Road, New Delhi 110 044
India

SAGE Ltd.
1 Oliver's Yard
55 City Road
London EC1Y 1SP
United Kingdom

SAGE Asia-Pacific Pte. Ltd.
33 Pekin Street #02-01
Far East Square
Singapore 048763

Printed in the United States of America

Library of Congress Cataloging-in-Publication Data

Guskey, Thomas R.
Developing standards-based report cards/Thomas R. Guskey, Jane M. Bailey.
        p. cm.
Includes bibliographical references and index.
ISBN 978-1-4129-4086-3 (cloth)
ISBN 978-1-4129-4087-0 (pbk.)
    1. Report cards—United States. 2. Grading and marking (Students)—United States. 3. Education—Standards—United States. I. Bailey, Jane M., 1953- II. Title.

LB2845.7.G87 2010
371.27'2—dc22   2009035713

This book is printed on acid-free paper.

09   10   11   12   13   10   9   8   7   6   5   4   3   2   1

Acquisitions Editor:	Dan Alpert
Associate Editor:	Megan Bedell
Production Editor:	Eric Garner
Copy Editor:	Paula L. Fleming
Typesetter:	C&M Digitals (P) Ltd.
Proofreader:	Susan Schon
Indexer:	Kathy Paparchontis
Cover Designer:	Karine Hovsepian

Contents

About
the Authors

 **Thomas R. Guskey** is Professor of Educational Psychology in the College of Education at the University of Kentucky. A graduate of the University of Chicago's renowned Measurement, Evaluation, and Statistical Analysis (MESA) program, he served as director of research and development for the Chicago Public Schools and was the first director of the Center for the Improvement of Teaching and Learning, a national research center. The author of numerous award-winning books and over 200 articles and papers, Dr. Guskey has seen his work published in prominent research journals, such as *American Educational Research Journal, Educational Researcher,* and *Educational Measurement: Issues and Practice,* as well as *Educational Leadership, Kappan,* and *School Administrator.* Dr. Guskey served on the Policy Research Team of the National Commission on Teaching & America's Future and on the task force to develop the National Standards for Staff Development, and he recently was named a Fellow in the American Educational Research Association, one of the Association's highest honors. Dr. Guskey coedits the Experts in Assessment Series for Corwin and has been featured on the National Public Radio programs *Talk of the Nation* and *Morning Edition.* His most recent books include *Practical Solutions for Serious Problems in Standards-Based Grading* (2009); *Benjamin S. Bloom: Portraits of an Educator* (2006); *How's My Kid Doing? A Parent's Guide to Grades, Marks, and Report Cards* (2002); *Developing Grading and Reporting Systems for Student Learning* (with Jane Bailey, 2001); and *Evaluating Professional Development* (2000).

 **Jane M. Bailey** was Curriculum and Staff Development Coordinator for the Public Schools of Petoskey in northern lower Michigan. In addition to providing district leadership in the areas of curriculum and staff development, she served as special education and federal programs director. She had more than 20 years of experience in education in a variety of roles, including high school English teacher, special education consultant, high school principal, and staff development coordinator for an intermediate school district (regional service agency). She was coauthor of a chapter titled "Reporting Achievement at the Secondary Level: What and How" in *Communicating Student Learning*, the 1996 Yearbook of the Association for Supervision and Curriculum Development (ASCD). She was also coauthor with Thomas Guskey of *Developing Grading and Reporting Systems for Student Learning* (2001) and *Implementing Student-Led Conferences* (2001). She was on the executive board of the Michigan affiliate of the National Staff Development Council and consulted with school districts in the areas of assessment, grading, and school improvement.

1

Getting Started

You are about to take on one of the most difficult and challenging tasks in modern education: *Developing a standards-based report card!* Why is this task so difficult and challenging? Because while just about everyone today agrees that report cards need improvement and that grades should be based on clear standards for student learning, rarely do they agree on what those report cards should contain or how they should be constructed.

Efforts to develop a standards-based report card usually begin with great excitement and enthusiasm. Those charged with the task are familiar with the many inadequacies of current reporting forms and recognize the need for improvement. Before long, however, most find themselves embroiled in controversy and stymied in their efforts. Numerous unanticipated difficulties emerge, and discussions about the report card turn into heated debates. After suffering a series of setbacks and defeats, many simply give up on the task and return to the traditional reporting forms they have always used. Others persist in their efforts and end up with a new form that no one really likes but a few staunchly oppose.

Why is there so much controversy about the report card, and why should revising it be so hard? Although many factors undoubtedly contribute to these disputes, in most cases, it comes down simply to different groups wanting different things.

- Parents want a report card that offers more precise information about how their children are doing in school, but they want that information to be understandable and useful.

- Teachers want a report card that matches recent changes in their curricula and classroom assessments, but they do not want a form that requires a lot of extra time and effort to complete.
- Administrators want more consistency in grading, but they fear imposing changes that will add to teachers' workload or infringe on teachers' academic freedom.
- All these groups want a report card that is meaningful to students and facilitates learning, but few know precisely how that can be achieved!

Besides different groups wanting different things, it is not unusual to find members of the same group disagreeing about the kinds of changes that should be made. Teachers, for example, vary widely in their grading policies and practices. While most try to assign grades that they believe are fair and equitable, research shows that teachers differ tremendously in the sources of evidence they consider in determining students' grades. They also differ in the procedures they use for weighting that evidence. Studies show further that these disparities exist even among teachers who teach the same subject at the same grade level in the same school (Brookhart, 1993, 1994; Cizek, Fitzgerald, & Rachor, 1996; Kain, 1996; McMillan, Myran, & Workman, 2002)!

The Difficulty of Change

Clashes in perspective over the simplest reporting issues complicate the change process even further. Take, for example, the question of how often report cards should be distributed. Parents consistently say that they want report cards sent home more often. Every nine weeks is okay, but every six weeks would be better. More frequent reports help parents keep abreast of their child's progress in school. They also make it easier for parents to identify any difficulties their child may be experiencing so that immediate steps can be taken to remedy the problem (J. F. Wemette, personal communication relating the results of a parent survey on grading conducted by the North St. Paul–Maplewood–Oakdale Independent School District, MN, 1994).

Teachers, on the other hand, consistently argue for less frequent report cards. Every 9 weeks is okay, but every 12 weeks would be better. Teachers point out that completing report cards requires a lot of time and detracts from their instructional planning. The more time they spend recording grades and marks, the less time they have to design lessons and gather teaching materials. Some teachers also feel uncomfortable assigning grades based on information gathered over shorter periods (Barnes, 1985; Lomax, 1996).

Tradition further hampers change efforts. Despite tremendous advances in our knowledge of effective grading and reporting (see Allen, 2005; Brookhart, 2009; Guskey & Bailey, 2001; Haladyna, 1999; Marzano, 2000; O'Connor, 2009), report cards have remained largely unaffected. Especially at the secondary level, today's report cards look much like they did a century ago, listing a single grade or mark for each subject studied or each course taken (see Baron, 2000; Guskey, 2006b). The only significant change is that computers print report cards today while in years past, teachers filled them out by hand. We continue using these forms not because they have proven effective but simply because "we've always done it that way." Even parents dissatisfied with report cards can take some comfort in seeing a form that looks much like the one they received when they were students, two or three decades ago.

"WE'VE ALWAYS DONE IT THAT WAY!"

Once upon a time, a newlywed couple was preparing an evening meal of ham and potatoes. Before putting the ham in the pot for heating, the wife dutifully cut off the end of the ham, bone and all. Her new husband looked up from peeling the potatoes and asked why she did this, for it seemed to him that the practice wasted a lot of good ham. She replied, "My mother always did it that way."

"Does it make the ham taste better?" he asked.

"I don't know," replied the wife. "In my family, we've always done it that way."

Perplexed by this tradition, the husband set out to discover why his new wife's family cut off the end of the ham before cooking. So at the next family gathering, he asked his mother-in-law about the practice.

"My mother always did it that way," she answered.

"Does it affect the taste? Is it for health reasons?" he asked.

"I don't know," replied the mother-in-law. "In our family, we've always done it that way. Why don't you ask my mother?"

Continuing his inquiry, the husband next approached his wife's grandmother and asked her why she cut off the end of the ham before heating.

"When I first married," explained the grandmother, "we were very poor and owned little cookware. We had only one small pot. I cut off the end of the ham so that it would fit into our small pot."

"And do you still do that today?" asked the young man.

"Why no!" replied the grandmother. "I haven't done that for years. You waste a lot of good ham if you do."

Often in grading, we do much the same. We continue to use old policies and practices, not because of their proven merit but simply because "we've always done it that way" and never asked "why?"

Another factor that stifles report card change is that few educators have any formal training in grading and reporting. Nothing in their undergraduate preparation or professional development experiences gave them good information about effective grading and reporting practices (Allen & Lambating, 2001, Schafer, 1991). As a result, most have little understanding of the different reporting methods, the effects of different grading policies, or the advantages and shortcomings of different reporting forms (Stiggins, 1991, 1993, 1999). What knowledge they have is based on what was done to them: the grading policies and practices used by their teachers (see Guskey, 2006b). So even educators dissatisfied with their current report card typically lack clear direction in their improvement efforts.

Finally, as with so many aspects of education currently being "reformed," changing the report card often seems an added and unnecessary burden. Educators are working hard to articulate standards for student learning, define appropriate levels of student performance based on those standards, adapt instruction to help students with diverse learning needs meet those standards, and develop assessments to measure students' proficiency. The time required for this work and the complexity of the tasks involved make it exceedingly difficult to take on the additional challenge of revising the report card.

FACTORS THAT HINDER REPORT CARD CHANGE

1. Different groups want different things from the report card.

2. Report cards are based on tradition.

3. Educators have little formal training in grading and reporting.

4. Current demands for change in curriculum, instruction, and assessments seem more pressing than report card change.

The Need for Change

So with all these factors hindering efforts to change the report card, why take on this daunting task? We believe that there are three important reasons for making this change and for making it *right now.* First, a lot of current grading and reporting policies and practices are shamefully inadequate. We persist in using these ineffective practices and antiquated reporting forms simply because we have never thought deeply about the consequences of their many shortcomings and limitations. In working with educators to address these issues, however, we find that relatively small changes in grading practices and reporting forms can yield huge benefits for students, parents, and teachers alike. Modest, thoughtful adaptations can result in a multitude of important advantages for all groups involved.

Second, most report cards today are dreadfully misaligned with current reforms in teaching and learning. In recent years, educators have made great strides in developing standards for learning that clarify what they want students to know and be able to do. They also have created better and more authentic forms of assessment to measure students' proficiencies based on those standards. The one element not aligned with these important advances is the report card—the primary tool used to describe students' learning progress and achievement to parents and others.

Third, thoughtful and well-informed initiatives to develop new reporting forms frequently prompt discussions about other elements of schooling, which can be vitally important to students' success. When educators begin talking about what to report and how to report it, they also begin thinking about the clarity of state or district learning standards, the effectiveness of their instructional strategies, and the quality of their classroom assessments. In addition, they often become more conscientious about helping students learn well, earn high grades or marks, and gain confidence in learning situations.

Today we know more than ever before about effective grading and reporting practices. We have better information about what works and helps students and about what does not work and can even be potentially harmful. This knowledge base offers explicit direction for change efforts and provides guidance for making improvements. It also convinces us that we cannot wait any longer to put this knowledge into practice. For the sake of our students, improvements in grading practices and reporting forms are not just needed—they are imperative.

REASONS FOR CHANGING THE REPORT CARD

1. Many current grading practices and reporting forms are shamefully inadequate.

2. Report cards are misaligned with current reforms in teaching and learning.

3. Report card development often leads to a critical examination of standards, instructional goals, and assessments.

Why Standards Instead of Letter Grades?

Occasionally parents express skepticism about standards-based report cards. They believe that a traditional letter grade or percentage grade for each subject area on the report card works just fine, and they see no reason to change. Parents also understand letter grades, or at least believe that they do, because letter grades were used when they were in school. In addition, since most colleges and universities use letter grades and will probably continue to do so, parents want their children to become accustomed to letter grade systems so that they can successfully navigate within such systems when they reach that level.

As part of their improvement efforts, educators need to pay special attention to helping these parents understand the problems associated with traditional letter grades, as well as the benefits of moving to a standards-based system. Specifically, they need to help parents understand that when teachers assign a single letter grade or percentage to students for each subject studied or each course taken, they must combine many diverse sources of evidence into that one mark. This results in what researchers refer to as a "hodgepodge grade" that includes elements of achievement, attitude, effort, and behavior (Cizek et al., 1996; McMillan, 2001; McMillan et al., 2002). Even when teachers clarify the weighting strategies they use to combine these elements and employ computerized grading programs to ensure accuracy in their computations, the final grade remains a confusing amalgamation that is impossible to interpret and rarely presents a true picture of a student's academic proficiency (Brookhart, 1991, Cross & Frary, 1996; Guskey, 2002a). Researchers also contend that inclusion of these nonacademic factors in determining students' grades is responsible, at least in part, for the discrepancies frequently noted between students' grades and the students' performance on large-scale accountability assessments (Brennan, Kim, Wenz-Gross, & Siperstein, 2001, D'Agostino & Welsh, 2007; Guskey, 2006c; Welsh & D'Agostino, 2009).

This is not to imply that students' effort, responsibility, participation, punctuality, and other work habits are unimportant. Clearly they are. Teachers at all levels generally recognize the value of offering students, as well as parents, specific feedback on the adequacy of performance in these areas. A standards-based report card allows teachers to do precisely that by reporting on these nonacademic elements *separately*. As such, it provides parents with a clearer and more detailed picture of their child's academic performance in school along with information on other important school-related behaviors.

Furthermore, a standards-based report card breaks down each subject area or course into specific elements of learning. The "standards" within each subject area offer parents a more thorough description of their child's achievement. A single grade of C, for example, might mean a modest level of performance on each of five different learning goals or excellent performance on three goals but dismal performance on two others. Without the breakdown that standards-based reporting offers, this difference would be obscured. Standards-based grading provides a more comprehensive picture of students' academic progress by identifying specific areas of strength, as well as areas where additional work may be needed. It thus facilitates collaboration between parents and educators in their efforts to help students improve their performance.

As far as preparing students for colleges and universities, clearly the best preparation that any school can offer is to engage students in a rigorous and challenging curriculum and then do all that is possible to guarantee that students learn excellently what that curriculum includes. A standards-based report card identifies the specific learning goals within the curriculum so that appropriate rigor can be ensured. It also communicates more detailed information about student learning progress with regard to those goals to bring about higher levels of success. These distinct benefits serve to prepare students well, no matter what type of learning environment they enter after they leave school.

Guiding Premises

Before going forward in our discussion of how successfully to develop standards-based report cards, we need to clarify the premises that guide our work in this area. We will return to these premises frequently in later chapters because they provide the basis for many of the recommendations we offer. Our guiding premises include the following:

1. *Developing a standards-based report card is primarily a challenge in effective communication.* Regardless of the education level, the report card's purpose is to provide high-quality information to interested persons in a form they can understand and use. Rather than simply documenting student progress and quantifying achievement, the report card should communicate clear and unambiguous information about students' performance to parents, students, and others.

2. *Accurate interpretation is the key element in effective communication.* If parents and others cannot make sense of the information included in a report card, *it is not their fault.* Educators must design the report card to ensure that those who receive it understand the information it includes and find that information both helpful and meaningful.

3. *Consistency is essential to accurate interpretation.* Educators often use different words interchangeably to describe the same or similar concepts. This often results in unintended confusion and miscommunication. For example, most parents have difficulty distinguishing *achievement, competency, mastery,* and *proficiency.* Similarly, parents rarely understand how *standards, proficiencies, goals,* and *objectives* differ. In developing report cards, consistent terminology across subject areas and school levels greatly improves the clarity of communication and the accuracy of interpretations.

4. *Developing a successful report card involves a series of trade-offs.* Educators frequently try to accomplish too much with the report card and end up accomplishing very little. Simply put, no single reporting form can adequately serve all of educators' diverse communication needs. Success hinges, therefore, on recognizing the limitations of the report card and seeing it as part of a larger, multifaceted reporting system. Such a reporting system communicates multiple types of information to multiple audiences in different formats (see Guskey & Bailey, 2001).

5. *Report cards should be descriptive, not restrictive.* Regardless of its form, a report card should never limit or regulate teachers' instructional practices. Nor should it ever narrow or constrain the means teachers use to communicate with parents or others. As a communication tool, the report card should always serve to enhance teaching and learning, never to hamper or interfere with the process in any way.

6. *No report card is perfect.* Like instructional practices, the effectiveness of a report card depends largely on context. What works best in one school, with a particular group of educators who serve a particular group of students who come from a particular community, may not work equally well in another school. Success depends on appropriate adaptation to these contextual differences. So while we include lots of examples of report cards and reporting forms in this book, none should be considered an exemplary model. Instead, each should be taken

as one way, among many others, of meeting an important communication challenge.

7. *Developing a standards-based report card requires teamwork, broad involvement, and initial training or study.* We frequently ask school district leaders, "Who makes up the team charged with revising the report card?" and just as frequently their reply is, "Teachers and administrators from several schools and grade levels." But if the purpose of the report card is to communicate information about student learning primarily to parents and students, then two key groups are missing from the development team. In addition, development activities should be guided by our established knowledge base on standards-based grading and reporting, not by personal opinion or intuition. Therefore, teams charged with revising the reporting form should do extensive background reading and, if possible, participate in group training. Such training should be targeted at providing specific information on what works and what procedures are most likely to result in successful report card development and implementation.

These seven premises guide our work in developing standards-based report cards and shape our vision of what we hope this book will accomplish. They also provide the foundation from which we will address other critical issues. We encourage readers to keep these premises in mind as they consider each of the topics presented and each of the recommendations offered.

GUIDING PREMISES IN DEVELOPING STANDARDS-BASED REPORT CARDS

1. Developing a standards-based report card is primarily a challenge in effective communication.

2. Accurate interpretation is the key element in effective communication.

3. Consistency is essential to accurate interpretation.

4. Developing a successful report card involves a series of trade-offs.

5. Report cards should be descriptive, not restrictive.

6. No report card is perfect.

7. Developing a standards-based report card requires teamwork, broad involvement, and initial training or study.

Our Purpose

We prepared this book so that educators involved in the complicated work of developing standards-based report cards would have a coherent and logical framework from which to approach this challenging task. Since our primary focus is standards-based grading and reporting at the elementary, middle, and high school levels, we consider school leaders and teachers at these levels to be our primary audience. As part of their professional responsibilities, these educators must collect evidence on student achievement and performance, evaluate that evidence, and then communicate the results of their evaluations to others through a variety of means, report cards being the most obvious. We also recognize, however, that many others have important roles in this process as well, including parents, district administrators, community members, and students themselves. Thus, these groups represent important audiences for this work, too.

We hope that the framework described in these pages helps these diverse groups develop a deeper and more thoughtful understanding of the various aspects of grading and reporting. We also hope that it helps clarify the challenges involved in revising the report card or in developing an entirely new form. The context-specific nature of these challenges makes it impossible to recommend a single set of "best" policies and practices or even to present what we might consider an "ideal" report card. Nevertheless, we remain convinced that having a practical framework for approaching these development challenges will result in better, more meaningful, and more educationally sound report cards that benefit everyone.

Our Organizational Scheme

We have organized this book based on what we believe to be the essential steps involved in developing an effective standards-based report card. These steps relate to the issues that we believe are most crucial in the development process but also the most troublesome.

In Chapters 2 and 3, we focus on defining essential terms and purposes. We describe the importance of defining standards and explaining the purpose of standards-based reporting. Although a lot of excellent work has been done in recent years to articulate standards for student learning, reporting students' progress and achievement based on standards requires new perspectives and a new orientation.

Next, in Chapters 4 through 7, we turn to a series of crucial questions that need to be addressed in the process of developing standards-based report cards. We stress that while there are no right or wrong answers to these questions, the consequences of the decisions made at each step will have profound implications for everything that follows. For this reason, consensus must be sought at each step so that successful progress can be maintained. Some of these decisions are relatively straightforward, such as how often report cards will be completed and sent home. Others are much more complicated. For example, deciding what specific standards will be included on the report card and what labels will be used to describe different levels of student performance is likely to require lengthy discussion. We also will look at the distinctive conditions of reporting on the performance of students with special needs and those with exceptional talents and abilities.

Finally, in Chapters 8 and 9, we turn to the process of piloting and revising newly developed reporting forms and procedures for building a unified reporting system. The report card represents but one of a variety of useful tools for communicating information about student progress and achievement to parents and to others. Success in implementing a standards-based report card often depends on how well the report card is integrated within that comprehensive reporting system. So in this section, we offer specific suggestions for ensuring that successful integration.

Obviously, the issues considered in these pages are highly diverse. Our intent in addressing this broad array of issues is not to offer a comprehensive treatise on grading and reporting student learning. Rather, we hope to provide a thoughtful analysis of the most basic issues that need to be considered in successfully developing and implementing standards-based report cards.

In our work with schools across the United States and Canada and in Europe, Asia, and Australia, we have seen several highly successful efforts to develop standards-based report cards, along with numerous failures. We also have seen widely varied schools and school systems encounter many of the same dilemmas and pitfalls. In this book, we address those dilemmas and problems head-on in hopes of helping more schools and school systems succeed. We believe that approaching the change process with deliberateness, thoughtfulness, honesty, and a sense of fairness to all can lead to lasting improvements. The key to success, however, rests in maintaining a laserlike focus on effective communication and the clear intention of all educators to enhance student learning.

Our Hope

The issues involved in grading and reporting are far too diverse and much too complex to be addressed with simple ideas or strategies. Success depends largely on the ability of educators to approach the process with sensitivity, understanding, and a true sense of purpose. Our intent, therefore, is not to offer "the one correct way" to develop a standards-based report card. Rather, we hope to show that thoughtfully planned development efforts can succeed in any context and that specific and practical ideas are available for achieving such success.

To serve that purpose, we hope this book does not just sit on someone's office bookshelf or in a professional library. Instead, we would like to see it passed around among educators, used and reused, analyzed and debated. We hope it finds its way into undergraduate education courses to help those preparing to become teachers develop a deeper understanding of grading and reporting issues. It might even become the focus of study groups and faculty retreats where the ideas we present are questioned and discussed. We would like to find well-worn, coffee-stained copies of the book in teachers' lounges, with dog-eared pages and notes scribbled in the margins, where it becomes the basis for brief conversations and extended planning sessions.

We also hope readers will take an active, reflective, and perhaps even skeptical approach to the ideas we present. As a result, we hope it simulates further inquiry and purposeful action. Most important, we hope this book prompts the development of better standards-based report cards that school leaders, teachers, parents, students, and others consider true models of effective communication.

2

The Importance of Standards

The essential first step in developing a standards-based report card is to clarify what we mean by *standards* and why they should be used as a basis for reporting on student learning. This definition and rationale provide the foundation for our development work. So in this chapter we will define *standards*, describe crucial understandings related to a standards-based approach, and outline the essential steps involved in developing a report card based on standards for student learning.

Defining *Standards*

In simplest terms, standards in education are the goals of teaching and learning. They describe precisely what we want students to know and be able to do as a result of their experiences in school. Standards specify the particular knowledge, skills, abilities, and dispositions that we hope students will gain through interactions with teachers and fellow students in school learning environments.

Most standards include two components. First, they describe specific elements of *content*. That is, they represent *what we want students to learn*. Standards identify the particular knowledge students are expected to acquire as a result of their involvement in instructional activities. Second, they describe levels of *performance*. In other words, standards also indicate *what we want students to be able to do* with what they learn. These levels of performance typically relate to specific student behaviors. In some cases they might involve simply knowing particular information, such as mathematics facts or scientific principles. In other instances, they might describe higher-level cognitive processes, such as the ability to solve complex problems, conduct and analyze the results from scientific experiments, or compose meaningful stories.

On the surface, the process of developing standards might appear relatively simple and straightforward. After all, educators should certainly know what learning goals they want students to attain. Teachers especially should have clear ideas about what they want their students to know and be able to do as a result of planned instructional activities. But those engaged in developing standards for student learning typically find the process to be far more complicated and much more difficult than they ever anticipated. The clearer we make our instructional goals, the easier they are to judge and criticize. Clarifying standards also can lead to educational and political controversies that challenge even the most well-intentioned educators.

Despite the challenges, the logic and utility of focusing on student learning standards has proven extraordinarily powerful. The knowledge, skills, and abilities that educators expect students to acquire have become the foundation for aligning entire educational systems (Murphy, 2006). Thoughtfully developed standards offer direction to reform initiatives by providing consensus about what students should learn and what skills they should acquire. Standards also bring much needed focus to curriculum development efforts and provide the impetus for fashioning new forms of student assessment.

Educators at all levels have generally welcomed the idea of having clearly articulated educational standards. The release of the first set of standards by the National Council of Teachers of Mathematics in 1989 was greeted with unprecedented optimism. Soon after, other professional organizations followed suit. The National Council for the Social Studies (1994), National Academy of Science (1996), National Council of Teachers of English (1996), and the American Council on the Teaching of Foreign Languages (1996) all developed standards in their respective disciplines. States and provinces also took up the task, and today, nearly all have identified specific standards for student learning.

Implementing standards-based reforms has not come easily, however. As we mentioned earlier, the process can be enormously complex and highly political, especially when it involves individuals with different world views that reflect divergent perspectives on the goals of schooling. In addition, because of the dynamic nature of our society and the world, the process is continuously evolving. The learning goals and standards we establish today are unlikely to be adequate five years from now and will surely be antiquated ten years hence. Nevertheless, just about everyone today recognizes the essential nature of this process for effective teaching and learning at every level of education.

Five Essential Understandings

The effective implementation of standards-based reforms depends largely on educators' recognition of five essential understandings (Guskey, 1999, 2005). These understandings provide an historical and theoretical basis for efforts designed to help all students achieve at high levels. They also serve to guide educators as they work to improve their effectiveness. While none of these understandings is especially novel or complex, each has important implications for how we go about helping students achieve established educational standards. Each also has profound implications for standards-based reporting.

1. Standards Are Not New

Many educators believe the push to define standards and clarify learning goals is a recent phenomenon in education. The dominant educational theme of the last two decades certainly has been to "get serious about standards" (National Commission on Teaching and America's Future, 1996). But the importance of well-defined learning goals has been recognized for decades—we just have not done much about it.

More than a half century ago, renowned educator Ralph W. Tyler (1949) stressed that prior to teaching anyone anything, two fundamental questions must be addressed: (1) What do we want students to learn and be able to do? and (2) What evidence would we accept to verify that learning? As Tyler put it,

> if an educational program is to be planned and if efforts for continued improvement are to be made, it is necessary to have some conception of the goals being sought. These educational objectives become the criteria by which materials are selected, content is outlined, instructional procedures are developed and tests and examinations are prepared. All aspects of the educational program are really means to accomplish these basic educational purposes. (p. 3)

As self-evident as this may seem, Tyler (1949) also pointed out that most decisions regarding curriculum and instruction in schools are not based on student learning. Instead, they are based on *time.* We tend to worry more about what content should be covered in the time available than about what students learn and acquire. As a result, we cannot say with certainty what the graduates of our schools have learned and are able to do. All we know for sure, argued Tyler, is how much time they spent in the school environment.

Tyler further emphasized that the best evidence of teaching effectiveness comes not from what teachers do but from what their students are able to do. In other words, teaching and learning must be intrinsically linked. For a teacher to suggest, "I taught it to them, they just didn't learn it," was to Tyler as foolish as saying, "I sold it to them, they just didn't buy it." It would be like saying, "I taught this fellow to swim, even though every time he jumps in the water, he still sinks." Tyler stressed that teaching is not something that one can do alone in the wilderness—not even if curriculum frameworks, textbooks, and lesson plans are carried along!

Thoughtfully addressing these fundamental questions has *always* been essential to the effectiveness of the teaching and learning process. Once decisions are made about the goals of learning, educators must then implement high-quality instructional activities to help all students achieve those specified goals.

2. Standards Reflect Our Philosophy of Schooling

Standards-based reforms become particularly complicated when those involved in the reform process hold different philosophies of schooling. These philosophies reflect not only what we value as individuals but also what we hope for and value as learning communities and as a society (Sirotnik, 2002). When philosophies differ, the goals being sought differ, and so do approaches for achieving those goals. Again, Ralph Tyler (1949) pointed out:

> A fundamental first step in the process of defining our educational goals is to make our philosophies of schooling clear. . . . Should the school develop young people to fit into the present society as is, or does the school have a revolutionary mission to develop young people who will seek to improve the society? . . . How these questions are answered affects the educational goals we select. If the school believes its primary function is to teach people to adjust to society, it will strongly emphasize obedience to the present authorities, loyalty to the

present forms and traditions, skills in carrying on the present techniques of life. Whereas if it emphasizes the revolutionary function of the school it will be more concerned with critical analysis, the ability to meet new problems, independence and self-direction, freedom, and self-discipline. (pp. 35–36)

Philosophical conflicts about the traditional or revolutionary functions of schools are at the heart of many current debates regarding learning goals and standards. To move ahead with standards-based reforms, we must clarify these philosophical differences and help all concerned groups, as members of a shared learning community, to reach meaningful compromise and functional agreement. We also must work to bring a shared vision of success to improvement efforts by uniting various stakeholders in the process: parents, teachers, administrators, board members, and community leaders. Only when we agree on what we want to accomplish and the value of the goals we are striving to attain can true success be achieved.

3. Ideas Are More Important Than the Terminology We Use

Another problem thwarting standards-based reforms is the tangled thicket of terminology involved. Educators' confusion about this terminology and the arguments stemming from that confusion squander precious time and detract from the important work that needs to be done.

We became acutely aware of the problems associated with terminology several years ago while working with a school district's curriculum development committee. This group of dedicated educators spent an entire morning debating the differences among *standards*, *goals*, and *objectives*. To help resolve the debate and hopefully bring new focus to their discussion, we wrote a simple statement on a sheet of paper. Our statement began with the phrase "The student will be able to . . ." We then added the ever-popular, performance-oriented verb *demonstrate*, and we ended the statement with some elements of content. Finally, we shared our statement with the group and asked if they would consider the statement to be a(n):

a. Standard

b. Goal

c. Objective

d. Competency

e. Outcome

f. Benchmark

g. Proficiency

h. Target

i. Performance

j. Expectation

k. Aspiration

l. New Year's Resolution?

What we intended as a tongue-in-cheek gesture served only to extend their debate! Frustrated, we left the room with our statement in hand and walked down the hall to the cafeteria where the students were having lunch. There we shared our statement with ten high school students and asked them the same question. But unlike the teachers and school administrators on the curriculum development committee, who were unable to reach consensus, every student gave us the same answer: "Who cares?"

To make meaningful progress, we must maintain an unwavering focus on learning and learners and avoid these senseless battles over terminology. Especially in dealing with standards, we need to keep discussions centered on what students should learn, what they should be able to do, and what evidence best reflects that learning. The particular labels we attach to those things really do not matter. Distinctions in terminology that facilitate communication and promote understanding should be noted and used with consistency. But the confusion and distraction that different terminology can cause must be kept in check so that precious energy is not wasted and improvement efforts do not get sidetracked.

4. Good Ideas Can Be Implemented Poorly . . . or Not at All

Most states' and provinces' standards for student learning are outlined in a series of curriculum frameworks or documents labeled "content and/or performance standards." These frameworks typically consist of large notebooks that are color coded by grade level or subject area. State and school district curriculum directors take great pride in these documents and display them prominently at meetings and conferences. What they rarely consider, however, is whether or not teachers actually use these documents or find them helpful when planning their instruction.

To make a real difference in the classroom practices of teachers and improve student learning, curriculum frameworks *must* be linked to specific procedures for implementation. Without clear guidance for implementation, these documents will likely end up in the same place as did the curriculum guides developed in the 1970s. Like the frameworks of today, those curriculum guides were carefully designed, color coded by level, and the pride of curriculum directors. But because little attention was paid to how they could be practically and efficiently used, most were left in desk drawers or on bookshelves where they did little more than gather dust, while teachers continued to teach using whatever textbooks and materials were available.

An essential aspect in the design of any curriculum is consideration of how it will be implemented (Joyce, 1993). This involves the difficult task of bridging the sometimes wide and deep chasm between the goals we set for student learning and prevailing policies and practices. Professional development that centers on the knowledge and skills teachers and school leaders must have to implement new educational standards must be incorporated in all improvement plans (Guskey & Yoon, 2009; Yoon, Duncan, Lee, Scarloss, & Shapley, 2007). These experiences will provide educators with the time and direction they need to adapt available textbooks and other materials for instruction on the standards. They will help teachers see that textbooks are just one resource to be used in implementing standards and that, in many cases, textbooks do not match well the standards outlined for a particular grade level or course. Educators also need time and professional guidance to identify and then appropriately use new materials and resources. Regardless of the work that goes into the specification of standards for student learning, the true value of this work will be evident *only* when accompanied by high-quality implementation.

5. Success Hinges on What Happens at the Classroom Level

Studies of change convincingly show that success in any change effort *always* hinges on what happens at the smallest unit of the organization (Senge, 1990). To educators, this means that success in improvement efforts based on standards will *always* hinge on what happens at the classroom level. The hard lesson learned from analyses of the various waves of education reform is that it matters little what happens at the national, state/provincial, or even district level. Unless positive change takes place at the school and classroom levels, improvement is unlikely. As Cooley (1997) lamented:

> I have concluded that most educational reform takes place in our literature and on the pages of *Education Week*, not in schools and classrooms. . . . It seemed to me that all this talk about waves and waves of reforms really refers to trends in the reform literature, not changes that are really taking place in real schools. Of course, that's true of waves. They tend to be highly visible at the surface, but do not affect what's going on down in the lower depths. (p. 18)

Improvement in education means one simple thing: more students learning better. And the only level at which student learning generally takes place is in classrooms. Judged by the criterion of classroom impact, however, most educational reforms have a poor record of success (Sarason, 1990). Even with reforms that include the development of high-level learning standards for students paired with performance assessments on which teachers are held accountable for results, changes in classroom practice remain relatively modest (Guskey, 1994c, 1999). Significant change at the classroom level is tied more directly to the provision of ongoing, job-embedded, high-quality professional development (Garet, Porter, Desimone, Birman, & Yoon, 2001; Guskey, 1994b, 2009a; Guskey & Huberman, 1995; Guskey & Yoon, 2009; Lieberman, 1995).

Standards that clarify what students should learn and be able to do as a result of their experiences in school are vitally important. They provide essential focus and direction in reform efforts at all levels. But clearly specified goals are just the first step in the improvement process. If these efforts are to result in significant improvements in student learning, serious attention must be given to their intended impact on classroom practice and the conditions necessary for change at that level.

FIVE ESSENTIAL UNDERSTANDINGS REGARDING STANDARDS

1. Standards are not new.

2. Standards reflect our philosophy of schooling.

3. Ideas are more important than the terminology we use.

4. Good ideas can be implemented poorly . . . or not at all.

5. Success hinges on what happens at the classroom level.

Standards-Based Report Card Development Levels

The challenges involved in developing a standards-based report card can frustrate the most dedicated educators, despite their good intentions. Success requires thoughtfulness, perseverance, and, most important, a systematic plan. Creating that plan involves six development levels:

1. Defining the purpose

2. Developing the reporting standards

3. Addressing essential steps in development

4. Establishing performance indicators

5. Developing the reporting form

6. Pilot testing and revision

Each of these levels is vitally important. In addition, success at each level depends on the success achieved at all preceding levels. If the process breaks down at any point along the way, no further progress can be expected.

Following is a brief description of each of these essential levels. In forthcoming chapters, we will consider the crucial aspects of each level in greater detail and outline a set of essential questions to be addressed at each level. We also will offer specific suggestions for ensuring success.

1. Defining the Purpose

The primary reason so many educators fail in their efforts to develop standards-based report cards is that they charge ahead, changing their reporting method without first clarifying the report card's purpose. Before any revision can be planned and any development work begun, the purpose of the report card must be made clear. This involves reaching consensus about what information to include in the report card, who is the primary audience for that information, and, ideally, how that information should be used. The process of making these decisions will be our focus in Chapter 3.

Other practical issues related to the report card's purpose will need to be considered as well. In particular, developers will have to address questions such as these: How often will report cards be completed and sent home? Will the report card be mailed directly to parents or guardians, or will it be distributed in school and carried home by students? Will parents be expected to sign the report card and then have their child return the report card or some portion of it to school? Whom should parents contact if they have questions or concerns? Will students be asked to respond to the report card? What steps should be followed if students have questions or concerns?

While these questions may appear to be easy to address, the process of deciding the report card's purpose and resolving procedural issues can prove extremely challenging. Serious debates often arise that can significantly forestall development. As difficult as this process might seem, however, deciding the report card's purpose remains the essential first step. All of the other crucial decisions that follow regarding reporting format, frequency of reporting, descriptions of the standards, the symbols or marks used, and the like become much easier when consensus about the report card's purpose is reached at the beginning of development process.

2. Developing the Reporting Standards

The standards for student learning outlined in the curriculum frameworks of most states and provinces today are too many in number and too complicated in their wording to be included verbatim on the report card. Reports that include all of these detailed standards tend to overwhelm parents and students with too much information and severely diminish the report card's value as a communication tool. Furthermore, reporting on all of these detailed standards typically creates a bookkeeping nightmare for teachers. To resolve these dilemmas, educators must develop *reporting standards* that are specific enough to communicate the knowledge and skills students are expected to acquire but not so detailed that they lose their utility when shared with parents. In some cases, developing reporting standards requires combining more narrowly defined standards into broader groupings or categories that meaningfully summarize students' performance. In other cases, it involves rewording the standards, using clearer and more parent-friendly language. Identifying reporting standards will be our focus in Chapter 4.

Always keep in mind when developing a standards-based report card that the primary goal is effective communication. This means that educators must strive to offer enough information of sufficient detail to communicate plainly how well students are performing in relation to well-defined learning goals. But at the same time, they must be careful not to confuse parents with information the parents do not understand and do not know how to use. Furthermore, educators must take special care to ensure that essential cognitive or achievement goals are kept distinct from specific aspects of students' behavior—such as effort, responsibility, punctuality, participation, respect for classmates, and the like—which also may be considered important goals in the teaching and learning process.

3. Addressing Essential Steps in Development

After identifying the major learning goals or standards to be used in reporting, educators need to take a series of essential steps in developing standards-based report cards. These steps correspond to crucial questions that must be addressed and answered to ensure success in the development process. In Chapters 5 and 6, we describe these crucial questions and offer specific recommendations for answering each one.

4. Establishing Performance Indicators

With the crucial questions about development answered, we next turn to establishing specific performance criteria for demonstrating mastery or proficiency on the included reporting standards. These criteria help clarify expectations for student performance and allow educators to determine more precisely whether or not students are meeting those expectations.

Because reaching mastery or proficiency is not an all-or-nothing process but instead involves helping students progress from relatively modest levels to highly competent levels of performance, graduated levels of performance, or benchmarks, must be articulated. These levels are sometimes labeled "learning progressions" (Heritage, 2007). They help teachers locate students' current levels of performance on the continuum along which students are expected to progress. Identifying these levels typically requires determining three or four identifiable steps in students' progress toward mastery of each standard. In addition, meaningful labels must be attached to each of these levels or steps to describe aptly students' learning progress to their parents, to the students themselves, and to others. The best way to communicate the meaning of these levels, of course, is to match each level with specific examples of students' work. We will see how the adage "A picture is worth a thousand words" proves to be particularly appropriate in this case. Chapter 6 describes the process of identifying and labeling levels of performance.

5. Developing the Reporting Form

With the standards clarified and graduated levels of performance set, educators can then turn their attention to developing a reporting form that clearly and accurately communicates information about student achievement and learning progress. Some of the essential questions that need to be addressed at this stage include these: What marks or performance indicators will be used? Will both progress and achievement be noted and, if so, how? Should specific reporting forms be developed for each grade level, or should a more general form be developed that would be appropriate across several grade levels? In addition, the implications for crucial transition points in the school curriculum will need to be considered, such as from primary to elementary, elementary to middle school, and middle school to high school. Important issues related to the involvement of parents and students in the development process also must be reviewed. These vital issues will be our focus in Chapter 7.

6. Pilot Testing and Revision

Regardless of the care and thoughtfulness that goes into the development process, initial versions of standards-based report cards are never perfect. Nearly all have unanticipated flaws that can lead to miscommunication and misunderstandings. Pilot testing the new form is one of the best ways to identify these shortcomings so that appropriate revisions can be made. These trial implementations must be conducted with skill and sensitivity, however, to avoid unnecessary conflicts and disputes. Chapter 8 describes the essential steps in this process and ways to ensure the involvement of important constituents to guarantee high levels of success.

STANDARDS-BASED REPORT CARD DEVELOPMENT LEVELS

1. Defining the purpose

2. Developing reporting standards

3. Addressing essential steps in development

4. Establishing performance indicators

5. Developing the reporting form

6. Pilot testing and revision

Summary

Attending to the ideas described here will not lessen the challenge involved in developing an effective standards-based report card. Carefully following these steps, however, will help ensure that development efforts remain focused on the issues most vital to success. The five essential understandings about standards and the six general steps involved in developing standards-based report cards provide the basis for achieving success and avoiding the pitfalls that have wrecked so many well-intentioned development efforts.

3

Defining the Purpose

Having defined what we mean by *standards* and why they offer the basis for improving the way we report on student learning, we now turn our attention to clarifying the purpose of the report card. All of the crucial decisions that need to be made in constructing a standards-based report card will be based on its purpose. In addition, all of the development tasks outlined in later chapters will relate back to the report card's purpose. No other decision will be more important or more fundamental to everything we do.

Although defining the purpose of the report card may at first appear to be an easy task, rarely is that the case. As we described in Chapter 1, different groups often want different things, and consensus can be difficult to reach. Nevertheless, for the report card to have meaning, all groups must be able to interpret the information it includes in the same manner (Seeley, 1994). This can happen only when everyone is clear about the report card's purpose.

Nearly every failed effort to revise the report card that we know of can be traced to the lack of a well-defined and commonly understood purpose. Developers who do not agree on why they are revising the report card or precisely what they want to achieve frequently try to accomplish too much with this single reporting device. Often they attempt to create a report card that serves multiple purposes to meet the diverse needs of all groups involved. This inevitably results in a report card that serves no purpose well and leaves everyone dissatisfied (Austin & McCann, 1992).

In this chapter, we explore the essential issues that need to be considered when defining the purpose of the report card and how to address those issues with precision, thoughtfulness, and sensitivity. We then describe the implications of the chosen purpose for the development activities that lie ahead. Finally, we examine multiple reporting purposes and the advantages of a comprehensive and multifaceted reporting system.

Purpose Options

Differences abound regarding the purpose of the report card—and so too do explanations for those differences. Some suggest that the differences stem from conflicting opinions held by different groups about the report card's intended audience. Others argue that these differences run much deeper, arising from fundamental tensions in values and educational philosophies. One side points to the need to discriminate and differentiate levels of student performance to make accurate decisions about what students have achieved. The other side emphasizes the desire to treat all students as capable of high levels of performance (Hiner, 1973; Trumbull, 2000). These tensions can be particularly problematic in developing standards-based report cards because the process usually begins from the premise that all students can and should learn well (Bloom, 1976; Guskey, 2006a).

In studies of grading, researchers have asked educators questions such as "What is the purpose of grading?" and "Why do we have report cards, transcripts, and other reporting devices?" Responses to these questions generally fall into six broad categories (see Airasian, 2001; Feldmesser, 1971; Frisbie & Waltman, 1992; Guskey & Bailey, 2001; Linn, 1983):

1. *To communicate information about students' achievement to parents and others.* Report cards provide parents and other interested persons (e.g., guardians, relatives, etc.) with information about their child's achievement and learning progress in school. To some extent, they also serve to involve parents in the educational process.

2. *To provide information to students for self-evaluation.* Report cards offer students information about the level and adequacy of their academic achievement and performance in school. As a feedback device, reports can also serve to redirect and hopefully improve students' academic performance.

3. *To select, identify, or group students for certain educational paths or programs.* Report card grades are a primary source of information

used to select students for special programs. High grades typically are required for entry into gifted education programs and honors or advanced classes, while low grades are often the first indicator of learning problems that result in students' placement in special needs programs. Report card grades on transcripts are also used as a criteria for entry into colleges and universities.

4. *To provide incentives for students to learn.* Although many educators debate the idea, extensive evidence shows that report card grades and other reporting methods are important factors in determining the amount of effort students put forth and how seriously they regard any learning or assessment task (Brookhart, 1993; Cameron & Pierce, 1994, 1996; Chastain, 1990; Ebel, 1979; Natriello & Dornbusch, 1984).

5. *To evaluate the effectiveness of instructional programs.* Comparisons of report card grades and other reporting evidence frequently are used to judge the value and effectiveness of new programs, curricula, and instructional techniques.

6. *To provide evidence of students' lack of effort or inappropriate responsibility.* Report card grades and other reporting devices are used to document unsuitable behaviors on the part of certain students, and some teachers threaten students with poor grades to coerce more acceptable and appropriate behavior.

MAJOR PURPOSES OF REPORT CARDS

1. To communicate information about students' achievement to parents and others

2. To provide information to students for self-evaluation

3. To select, identify, or group students for certain educational paths or programs

4. To provide incentives for students to learn

5. To evaluate the effectiveness of instructional programs

6. To provide evidence of students' lack of effort or inappropriate responsibility

---

While all of these purposes may be considered legitimate, educators seldom agree on which purpose is *most* important. In workshops and seminars on grading and reporting, for example, we frequently ask participants to rank order these six purposes in terms of their importance. In almost every case, some portion of the group ranks each one of the purposes as first—even when the group consists of teachers and school leaders from a single school. And that is precisely the problem.

When we do not agree on the report card's primary purpose, we often attempt to develop a reporting device that addresses *all* of these purposes and typically end up achieving none very well (Austin & McCann, 1992; Brookhart, 1991; Cross & Frary, 1996). The simple truth is that no single reporting device can serve all of these purposes well. In fact, some of these purposes actually run counter to others.

Suppose, for example, that the educators in a particular school or school district strive to have all students learn well. Suppose, too, that these educators are highly successful in their efforts and, as a result, nearly all of their students attain high levels of achievement and earn high grades. These very positive results pose no problem if the purpose of the report card is to communicate information about students' achievement to parents and others or to provide information to students for the purpose of self-evaluation. The educators from this school or school district can be proud of what they have accomplished and can look forward to sharing those results with parents and students.

This same outcome poses major problems, however, if the purpose of report card grades is to select students for special educational paths or to evaluate the effectiveness of instructional programs. To use grades for selection or evaluation purposes requires variation in the grades— and the more variation, the better! For these purposes, it is best to have the grades dispersed across all possible categories to maximize differences among students and programs. How else can appropriate selection take place or one program be judged better than another? But if all students learn well and earn the same high grades or marks, there is no variation. Determining differences under such conditions is impossible. Thus, while one purpose is served well, another purpose clearly is not.

Leading Discussions About Purpose

Discussions about the purpose of a standards-based report card must have four essential features: they must be *focused, informed, inclusive,* and *purposefully led.*

Focused. Participants must concentrate on the task at hand and not allow discussions to become complaint sessions about past injustices and misguided practices. Nearly everyone has had a negative personal experience with grading that involved biased or unfair treatment by a teacher or professor (see Guskey, 2006b). While important, these personal issues should not be allowed to divert attention from the specific task of clarifying the intent and purpose of the report card.

Informed. Discussions should be guided by research evidence and the established knowledge base on effective grading and reporting practices, rather than by emotions, opinions, or intuitions. Several useful resources for this knowledge base are listed in the box below.

USEFUL RESOURCES ON GRADING AND REPORTING

Azwell, T., & Schmar, E. (Eds.). (1995). *Report card on report cards: Alternatives to consider.* Portsmouth, NH: Heinemann.

Brookhart, S. M. (2009). *Grading* (2nd ed.). Upper Saddle River, NJ: Pearson Merrill Prentice-Hall.

Brookhart, S. M., & Nitko, A. J. (2008). *Assessment and grading in classrooms.* Upper Saddle River, NJ: Pearson Education.

Freedman, M. K. (2005). *Grades, report cards, etc. . . . and the law.* Boston: School Law Pro.

Guskey, T. R. (Ed.). (1996a). *Communicating student learning: 1996 yearbook of the Association for Supervision and Curriculum Development.* Alexandria, VA: Association for Supervision and Curriculum Development.

Guskey, T. R. (2002b). *How's my kid doing? A parent's guide to grades, marks, and report cards.* San Francisco: Jossey-Bass.

Guskey, T. R. (Ed.). (2009b). *Practical solutions for serious problems in standards-based grading.* Thousand Oaks, CA: Corwin.

Guskey, T. R., & Bailey, J. M. (2001). *Developing grading and reporting systems for student learning.* Thousand Oaks, CA: Corwin.

Haladyna, T. M. (1999). *A complete guide to student grading.* Boston: Allyn & Bacon.

Hargis, C. H. (2003). *Grades and grading practices: Obstacles to improving education and to helping at-risk students* (2nd ed.). Springfield, IL: Charles C Thomas.

Marzano, R. J. (2000). *Transforming classroom grading.* Alexandria, VA: Association for Supervision and Curriculum Development.

O'Connor, K. (2007). *A repair kit for grading: 15 fixes for broken grades.* Portland, OR: Educational Testing Service.

O'Connor, K. (2009). *How to grade for learning K–12* (3rd ed.). Thousand Oaks, CA: Corwin.

Stiggins, R., & Knight, T. (1997). *But are they learning? A commonsense parent's guide to assessment and grading in schools.* Portland, OR: Assessment Training Institute.

Trumbull, E., & Farr, B. (Eds.). (2000). *Grading and reporting student progress in an age of standards.* Norwood, MA: Christopher-Gordon.

Walvoord, B. E., & Anderson, V. J. (1998). *Effective grading: A tool for learning and assessment.* San Francisco: Jossey-Bass.

Wormeli, R. (2006). *Fair isn't always equal: Assessing and grading in the differentiated classroom.* Portland, ME: Stenhouse.

As we described in Chapter 1, becoming informed also may require participation in group training or study sessions centered on providing detailed information about what works in grading and reporting and what procedures are most likely to result in successful development and implementation of standards-based report cards.

Inclusive. Various stakeholder groups must be involved so that their voices are heard and their concerns made clear. Excluding any group that has vital interests in the format and structure of the report card, along with the information it includes, will most certainly sabotage change or reform efforts. While all stakeholder groups may not be involved at every stage in the development process, all groups should have input at critical stages so that their perspectives can be considered and their support gained.

The size of the discussion group also must be given serious consideration. Groups that are too large are easily diverted by peripheral issues and seldom reach consensus on any decision. Groups that are too small may be perceived as exclusionary and dictatorial. A crucial balance must be struck, therefore, between broad-based and representative involvement on one hand and manageable efficiency for group work on the other. A group of 15 to 20 persons representing teachers, school leaders, district representatives, and parents might work very well, for example. A group of 40 persons drawn from those same stakeholder groups probably would not.

Purposefully Led. Ensuring that these discussions remain focused, informed, and inclusive requires strong and determined leadership. Cooperation and effective teamwork occur only when accompanied by purposeful and intentional facilitation. In the absence of such leadership, teams sometimes reinforce inadequate practices and collaborate to resist significant change (Corcoran, Fuhman, & Belcher, 2001). Strong leaders make certain that development teams maintain their direction, remain true to their purpose, and stay mindful of the vital importance of their work.

**DISCUSSIONS ABOUT THE PURPOSE
OF THE REPORT CARD MUST BE . . .**

1. Focused	3. Inclusive
2. Informed	4. Purposefully led

Key Questions in Defining the Report Card's Purpose

Three key questions need to be answered by any group in defining the purpose of a standards-based report card: (1) What information will be communicated in the report card? (2) Who is the primary audience for the information? and (3) What is the intended goal of that communication? or How should that information be used? After these key questions about the purpose are answered, other critical issues about the form and structure of the report card become much easier to address and resolve.

What Information Will Be Communicated in the Report Card?

While other types of report cards and reporting devices often contain widely varied data, the information included in a standards-based report card is quite specific. In particular, three types of information must be incorporated:

1. The explicit standards or learning goals students are expected to meet

2. Each student's level of progress or proficiency in meeting those standards

3. The adequacy of that level of progress or proficiency at the time of reporting

In other words, a standards-based report card should clearly communicate what we want students to learn and be able to do, how well they are doing those things, and whether or not that level of performance is in line with our expectations at this time in the school year.

As we stressed earlier, reporting based on standards or learning goals requires a crucial balance. The standards included on the report card must be specific enough to communicate the knowledge and skills we want students to gain but not so detailed that they lose their meaning and utility when shared with parents and others. This means the reporting standards included on the report card must be relatively few in number but also clear, unambiguous, and expressed in language that parents and others can understand. For example, while few parents are likely to understand the meaning of a standard labeled "Develop phonemic awareness," most would know what it means to "Understand the relationship between letters and sounds." As we will describe in the next chapter, this clarification process sometimes requires developers to synthesize 20 or more grade-level learning standards in each subject area into 4 to 6 broader reporting standards that convey meaningful information that parents can both comprehend and use.

In addition, a standards-based report card must identify every student's level of achievement with regard to each standard. That is, not only must the expectations for student learning be clear, but so too must be each student's level of progress in meeting those expectations. As we explained in Chapter 2, achieving this clarity usually requires identifying three or four explicit steps that describe students' progress toward mastery or proficiency on each standard, along with specific examples drawn from students' work that represent each step or level.

The third type of information that must be included in a standards-based report card, and the one most often neglected, is an honest appraisal of the adequacy of each student's level of performance at this time in the school year. Parents frequently criticize standards-based report cards because in many cases such report cards do not communicate the *adequacy* of students' performance. Parents and others certainly want to know how well the child is doing, but they also want to know whether or not that level of performance is in line with the teacher's and school's expectations. If it is not, then they want to know what they can do to help so that minor learning difficulties can be remedied before they become major learning problems. In Chapter 4, we will describe how this often requires a "two-mark system," in which the first mark denotes the student's level of progress with regard to the standard and the second mark indicates whether that level of progress is on target, advanced, or behind what we would expect at this time in the school year.

KEY QUESTIONS IN DEFINING THE PURPOSE OF STANDARDS-BASED REPORT CARDS

1. What information will be communicated in the report card?

2. Who is the primary audience for that information?

3. How should that information be used?

Who Is the Primary Audience for That Information?

The second question considered in defining the purpose of the report card is the primary audience for the included information. Again, while the audience for other types of reporting devices tends to vary, the audience for a standards-based report card is likely to be (1) parents or other adults, such as guardians or relatives, and/or (2) the students themselves.

Elementary educators rarely debate this matter. For them, the primary audience is definitely parents, guardians, and other adults. Because of the nature of most elementary classrooms, teachers regularly communicate with their students about each individual's learning progress. They let students know when they are doing well and when additional work or effort may be needed. Report cards are designed to bring parents up-to-date and keep them abreast of their child's achievement and learning progress in school.

When queried about the purpose of the report card, parents express similar consistency in their perspectives: they believe the report card is for them. Parents see report cards as their primary communication link with teachers and the school regarding their child's learning progress. Why else would they be asked to sign the report card to ensure that they received it?

Middle-grade and secondary-level educators tend to be more divided. Many believe, like elementary educators, that the primary audience is parents. To these educators, report cards serve to inform parents and other adults about their children's academic performance. Other secondary educators argue, however, that older students should be taking increased responsibility for their own achievement and accomplishments in school (see Guskey & Anderman, 2008). For these educators, report cards serve to inform students about their teachers' formal judgments of how well they have met established learning goals and expectations.

In some cases, educators decide that the primary audience is *both* parents and students. While completely appropriate, this heightens the communication challenge. Under these conditions, specific steps must be taken to ensure that both parents and students understand the information included in the report card and can use it to guide improvements when needed.

How Should That Information Be Used?

Finally, the purpose of the report card should offer guidance regarding how the included information ought to be used. In other words, the report card communicates *with intent*. Obviously, the best use of that information will depend on the primary audience. The report card may, for example, provide parents and others with information about their children's academic strengths and weaknesses so that successes can be celebrated and specific steps can be taken to remedy any difficulties. For students, it might recognize their accomplishments and identify areas where additional study is needed. The key point is that rather than offering a culminating, final evaluation, the report card should be seen as part of a continuous and ongoing reporting process. Above all, the report card communicates information to facilitate improvements in student learning.

THE IMPORTANCE OF PURPOSE: A REAL-LIFE EXAMPLE

In one school district where we worked, a representative team of teachers, administrators, support personnel, and parents began the task of developing a new elementary school standards-based report card. When we suggested the team should begin by writing a clear statement of purpose for the report card, we heard groans and comments such as "Oh, no, how long is *this* going to take?" "No way am I going to spend time arguing over wording like we did when we wrote a mission statement 15 years ago!" and "Can't we just start on the report card? Why do we have to spend time doing this?"

As team leaders, we persevered. We assured the team that we would not quibble endlessly over each word and that the important work of defining a purpose would serve us well later in the process. We set a time limit of one hour to complete the task and, as leaders, monitored the group's work. At the end of an hour, the team had written a succinct, clear statement of purpose.

During a later team meeting, members were discussing what marks or labels should be used to communicate student progress and how many levels should be included. Some educators wanted to use a four-mark system, while others preferred three marks. Still others said, "Two marks are sufficient: students either meet the standard or they don't. A simple yes/no for each standard should be clear enough."

One parent then questioned how the marking system would address students who did more than simply meet the standard, achieving at a higher level. Another questioned how his special education student's progress would be conveyed. This led to further disagreement about the marking system. Some favored terms like "outstanding, good, fair, and poor." Others argued that a number system, such as "4, 3, 2, and 1," would be easier to interpret and less emotionally charged than other labels.

Sensing frustration and a loss of group focus, we called a time-out and asked the team to review the purpose statement written earlier. It said: "The purpose of this report card is to communicate current information on student progress in achieving standards to parents and to students in order to promote learning." Once the team had reviewed their purpose, the nature of the discussion quickly changed. We recorded the following comments:

"If we're going to communicate student progress, the kids have to understand the marking system. It can't seem punitive, and whatever wording we choose has to encourage learning."

"Our point with this report card is to use standards as a basis for reporting. So kids are either progressing well toward the standard, or they're just not making it. Two marks seem sufficient."

"Yes, but some kids progress slowly. They're making progress toward the standard but perhaps not as rapidly as we'd like. Our purpose says we want to promote learning. If we just tell a student, 'You haven't met the standard,' he or she might get discouraged. How about adding a third level that says, 'Making progress'?"

"But as a parent, I want to know if my child is likely to meet the standards teachers have set on time. Is she progressing well enough to keep up with the rest of the class? Will she be ready for the next grade level at the end of the year? I need to know if 'making progress' means she's on target and likely to make it or if she needs help to keep on track."

As seen in this example, the nature of the group's discussion quickly changed once they reviewed their agreed-upon purpose. Within a few hours, the group had designed the major elements of the new report card. They chose a four-mark system using both numbers and descriptors, and they built in a section for narrative comments in each subject area where the adequacy of progress could be described. The report card this team designed was favorably received by teachers and parents and is still being used today.

Making the Purpose Clear

To clarify the purpose of a standards-based report card to everyone involved, we recommend that the purpose be printed directly on the report card. In a special box on the front of the card or at the top of the first section, the purpose of the report card should be spelled out in bold print. This helps identify the report card's intent, the information it includes, and its targeted audience. The explicit statement also helps minimize miscommunication and misinterpretation.

Statements of purpose can vary as widely as the report cards themselves. A highlighted box on the front of the report card might include a statement such as this:

EXAMPLE 1
STATEMENT OF PURPOSE

The purpose of this report card is to describe students' learning progress to their parents and others, based on our school's learning expectations for each grade level. It is intended to inform parents and guardians about learning successes and to guide improvements when needed.

This statement tells the specific aim of the report card, for whom the information is intended, and how that information might be used.

Here is another example of a purpose statement for a standards-based report card:

> ### EXAMPLE 2
> ### STATEMENT OF PURPOSE
>
> The purpose of this report card is to communicate with parents and students about the achievement of specific learning goals. It identifies students' levels of progress with regard to those goals, areas of strength, and areas where additional time and effort are needed.

This statement identifies both parents *and* students as recipients of the report card's information. Middle school and high school report cards often use this approach. The second part of the statement also makes clear how the information should be used.

In instances where educators decide that the primary audience for the report card is students, the statement of purpose would reflect that decision. An example might be as follows:

> ### EXAMPLE 3
> ### STATEMENT OF PURPOSE
>
> The purpose of this report card is to inform students of teachers' judgments of their academic performance in each of their classes. Grades reflect how well students have met the established learning goals in each class, areas of outstanding performance, and areas where additional effort is required.

The statement of purpose that works best will vary depending on the context. Differences across education levels also are not uncommon. The purpose of an elementary report card, for example, may differ slightly from that of a middle school or high school report card. At all levels, however, it is essential that the purpose be clearly stated to everyone involved in the grading and reporting process—teachers, parents and guardians, students, and administrators—so that all understand its intent and can use it appropriately.

Method Follows Purpose

We cannot emphasize strongly enough the essential nature of defining the report card's purpose. As we noted earlier, all of the other crucial decisions that need to be made regarding the design, format, and structure of a standards-based report card will be based on this basic definition of purpose.

Recall the adage from architecture that "form *follows* function"? The same holds true regarding the report card: method *follows* purpose. Many efforts to develop standards-based report cards fall apart and eventually fail because developers charge ahead, changing the reporting method without first resolving the core issue of purpose. Before any development work can begin and any meaningful reporting form constructed, the purpose of the report card must be made clear.

FOR ALL STANDARDS-BASED REPORT CARDS . . .

Method follows purpose!

Purpose Determines the Development Process

We also need to keep in mind the first Guiding Premise we discussed in Chapter 1: *Developing a standards-based report card is primarily a challenge in effective communication.* While the purpose of a standards-based report card may vary from one setting to another, it still serves primarily as a tool for communication. As such, those who receive the report card (i.e., parents, guardians, other adults, and/or students) must be able to understand the information it includes. If they cannot make sense of the report card, the fault is not theirs. The fault lies instead with the report card itself and with those who developed it.

Every developmental step considered from this point on will build on our defined purpose. Who will be involved in the development process, what format the report card will take, what information it will include, and who will review draft versions—all will be based on the purpose. Referring to the defined purpose also will help resolve debates and settle the occasional arguments that inevitably arise.

If, for example, a school staff decides that the primary purpose of its report card is to communicate to parents and others information about students' achievement status, then parents must be able to understand that information, interpret it correctly, and use it appropriately. This also means that parent representatives need to be involved in the development of the report card and most certainly should be given opportunities to offer suggestions and feedback on its implementation. If parents find the report card too complicated to understand or if they cannot interpret or make sense of the information it includes, then that report card clearly has not met its purpose.

On the other hand, if a school staff decides that the primary purpose of its report card is to provide students with information they can use for self-evaluation, then student representatives need to be involved at some stage in both the development and implementation of the report card. Not only must they understand the information contained in the report card, they also need to be given guidance and direction on how to use that information. If students find the report card ambiguous and confusing, or if they cannot make use of the information it includes, then again, the report card clearly is not serving its intended purpose.

Defending the fairness, adequacy, and appropriateness of the grades or marks recorded on the report card also must be done in relation to the defined purpose. When challenged to defend the grades they assign, educators sometimes describe the precision of their mathematical calculations or point out that all students' grades were determined through identical procedures. But consistency in the application of an inadequate or corrupt process is never an adequate defense (see Guskey, 2001b, 2002a)! Instead, grades must be defended with evidence based on their defined purpose, regardless of the mathematical procedures used or the uniformity of their application.

Serving Multiple Purposes Requires a Comprehensive Reporting System

Grading and reporting procedures *must* be tailored to fit specific purposes. Expecting any report card, standards based or otherwise, to satisfy multiple purposes is not only unwise, it may be perilous. As we mentioned earlier, this is precisely why so many report card reform initiatives fail miserably. Either they attempt to serve too many purposes with this single reporting tool, or they expect that single tool to serve purposes for which it is ill suited (Allison & Friedman, 1995; Pardini, 1997).

At the same time, we must remember that reporting procedures often need to serve multiple purposes. In most cases, for example, they must accomplish both *formative* and *summative* purposes. Formative reports address the questions: "How are things going at this time, and what improvements are needed?" Summative reports address a more culminating question: "Have the course or grade level standards or goals been met?" (Reedy, 1995). Because no single reporting tool can serve all of these diverse purposes well, the most successful reform initiatives typically focus on developing a comprehensive, multifaceted *reporting system* (Guskey & Bailey, 2001).

A reporting system includes multiple reporting tools, each with its own explicit and well-defined purpose. The specified purpose of each tool guides its development, determines its format, and establishes the criteria by which its effectiveness will be judged. For instance, a particular school or school district's reporting system might include a standards-based report card, standardized assessment reports, planned phone calls or e-mail messages to parents, monthly progress reports, school open houses, newsletters to parents, portfolios or exhibits of students' work, and student-led conferences. The integrated combination of these various reporting tools, each designed to serve a specific purpose, would comprise that school or school district's comprehensive reporting system.

Developing a reporting system helps solve many reporting problems. Recall, for example, our earlier discussion about how parents consistently indicate that they would like to receive report cards more frequently (Wemette, personal communication, 1994)? Our interviews with parents reveal, however, that most do not necessarily want report cards sent home more often. Rather, they simply want to receive more regular information about their child's learning progress and behavior in school. Because parents perceive report cards as the primary and sometimes only source of such information, most indicate by default that they want to receive them more often. However, a reporting system that includes multiple reporting tools can address this parental concern and, if well designed, can offer parents precisely the kind of information they want and need.

Focus on a "Reporting System"

Developing a successful reporting system begins with considering the specific reporting purposes we want to serve. Just as was true with the report card, this means deciding what information we want to communicate, who is the primary audience for that information, and how would we like that information to be used. Once our purposes are clarified, we can then select the tool or tools that best serve those purposes.

Some of the reporting tools included in many schools' and school districts' reporting systems are listed in the box below (see Guskey & Bailey, 2001). In Chapter 9, we will describe in detail how each of these tools can be used to complement standards-based report cards.

Too often, educators become enamored with particular reporting tools and move ahead in their development and implementation without considering thoroughly the purpose they want those tools to serve. They start off saying, "Let's change the format of our school open house," or "Let's have students develop portfolios," without ever considering why they are doing it or what purpose they hope to accomplish. Just as was true with report card reform, such efforts inevitably fail. To succeed, change needs to be intentional and purposeful. Form must always *follow* function. Process, method, and format must always *follow* purpose. Decisions about purpose must always come first.

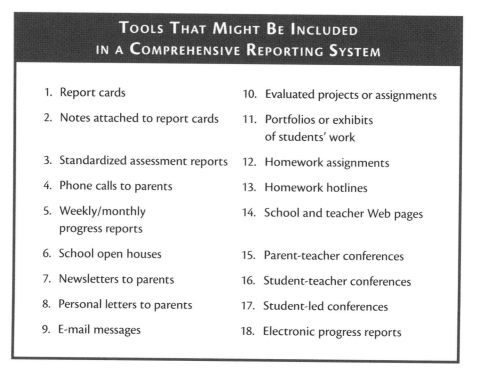

TOOLS THAT MIGHT BE INCLUDED IN A COMPREHENSIVE REPORTING SYSTEM

1. Report cards
2. Notes attached to report cards
3. Standardized assessment reports
4. Phone calls to parents
5. Weekly/monthly progress reports
6. School open houses
7. Newsletters to parents
8. Personal letters to parents
9. E-mail messages
10. Evaluated projects or assignments
11. Portfolios or exhibits of students' work
12. Homework assignments
13. Homework hotlines
14. School and teacher Web pages
15. Parent-teacher conferences
16. Student-teacher conferences
17. Student-led conferences
18. Electronic progress reports

Summary

Perhaps the most important step in developing a standards-based report card is defining its purpose. But making the report card's purpose clear and explicit is never an easy task. Different groups often want different things, and consensus can be difficult to reach. Nevertheless, reaching consensus is essential to success.

Three key questions need to be addressed in defining the purpose of standards-based report cards. These include (1) What information will be communicated in the report card? (2) Who is the primary audience for the information? and (3) How should that information be used? Once these key questions are answered, other critical issues regarding the form and structure of the report card become much easier to address and resolve.

Educators often want reporting procedures to serve multiple purposes. Because no single reporting tool can serve all purposes well, meeting varied goals typically requires development of a comprehensive and multifaceted reporting system. Such a system includes multiple reporting tools, each with its own specific and well-defined purpose. The purpose of each tool then guides its development, determines its format, and establishes the criteria by which its effectiveness will be judged.

4

Developing
Reporting Standards

In Chapter 2, we described the importance of defining and clarifying the meaning of *standards* as the first step in developing a standards-based report card. Chapter 3 focused on determining the report card's purpose as part of a larger reporting system and described how the purpose provides the basis for all the development tasks that follow. In this chapter, we turn to procedures for identifying *reporting standards*, the next essential step in building a standards-based report card. Reporting standards provide the basis for communicating meaningful and understandable information about students' performance and achievement in school.

Reporting Standards

Although many words might be considered synonymous with *standards*—including *goals*, *objectives*, *outcomes*, *competencies*, and *proficiencies*—their meaning in educational settings is quite specific. Standards describe what students should know and be able to do as a result of their experiences in school. In other words, standards identify the specific knowledge, skills, abilities, and dispositions that we hope students will gain through interactions with teachers and fellow students in school learning environments.

As we stressed in Chapter 2, most modern standards for student learning include two components. First, they describe particular elements of *content;* that is, what specific knowledge students are expected to acquire as a result of their involvement in instructional activities. Second, they describe levels of *performance* in relation to that knowledge; that is, what students are expected to do with what they learn. These levels of performance usually depict particular student behaviors. They might convey a relatively simple skill, such as knowing specific facts in mathematics or science. Or they might describe more complex cognitive processes, like the ability to reason logically, analyze data, or solve multipart problems.

The curriculum frameworks developed by educators at the national, state/provincial, and district levels typically classify standards for student learning along multiple dimensions of both content and performance. These frameworks often serve as excellent tools for teachers as they plan instructional units and design classroom assessments. Rarely, however, do they provide an appropriate basis for *reporting* on student learning. Most curriculum frameworks include far too many standards described in too much detail and in language that is far too complicated for most parents and students to understand.

To develop an effective standards-based report card, educators must keep in mind the distinction between the content and performance standards defined for curriculum and instructional purposes and the reporting standards developed for the purpose of communicating information about student learning to parents, students, and others. The best reporting standards are precise enough to communicate the knowledge and skills students are expected to acquire but not so detailed that they lose their significance and usefulness when shared with parents and students. Furthermore, reporting standards must be expressed in parent-friendly language so that parents and students alike understand exactly what they mean.

Perhaps most important, the best reporting standards are limited in number to facilitate their utility as tools for improvement. As we will emphasize again in the next chapter, four to six reporting standards in each subject area generally work best for a standards-based report card. Breaking down each subject area into four to six reporting standards helps clarify precisely enough what students are expected to learn and be able to do but does not overwhelm parents and students with unnecessary detail.

We are not certain as to why four to six reporting standards work best. We suspect that it may be due to our human capacity to retain meaningful information. In a classic paper published in 1956, George A. Miller observed that individuals can hold only a small number of "chunks" of information in what we now understand to be the "working memory." He estimated the capacity of chunks for most people to be about seven, depending on the type of information involved. Memory expert Nelson Cowan revisited Miller's seminal work more recently (Cowan, 2000) and estimated the capacity of most individuals' working memory for new information to be only four chunks. Keeping the number of reporting standards in a subject area at four to six therefore may facilitate memory and help both parents and students maintain a clearer focus on improvement efforts. This research also provides strong evidence to support the saying "Less is more." The less you overload parents with extraneous information, the more helpful and useful that information is likely to be.

Furthermore, the use of four to six reporting standards significantly lessens the reporting burden for teachers. To record information on every student's learning progress on 34 language arts standards and 27 mathematics standards—not to mention the standards in science, social studies, art, music, and physical education—creates a bookkeeping nightmare for teachers. The use of four to six reporting standards in each subject area makes the task much more manageable. The box below summarizes some of the major differences between curriculum framework standards and reporting standards.

DIFFERENCES IN STANDARDS

Curriculum Standards	*Reporting* Standards
1. Designed for Planning Instruction and Assessments	1. Designed for Reporting on Student Learning
2. Many in Number (10–50 per subject)	2. Relatively Few in Number (usually 4–6 per subject)
3. Highly Specific	3. Broad and More General
4. Complicated and Detailed	4. Clear and Understandable
5. Expressed in Complex, Educator Language	5. Expressed in Parent-Friendly Language

The Development Process

Developing reporting standards typically requires combining or synthesizing more narrowly defined curriculum framework standards into broader categories that expressively summarize students' performance. Many curriculum frameworks already sort standards into these broader categories and label them *strands*, *domains*, or *areas of study.* If these categories are clear, concise, and understandable, they may serve well as a basis for identifying reporting standards.

Several resources offer educators guidance in developing these broader categories. One resource that we have found useful is the Mid-Continent Research for Education and Learning (McREL) 2007 standards project entitled *Content Knowledge: A Compendium of Standards and Benchmarks for K–12 Education* (4th edition). The purpose of McREL's standards project is "to address the major issues surrounding content standards, provide a model for their identification, and apply this model in order to identify standards and benchmarks in the subject areas" ("Purpose of This Work: The Standards Project").

McREL's standards project offers an excellent resource to educators who are designing reporting standards because the standards for each subject area are identified by strand or major topic area. This type of category listing helps simplify the process of synthesizing multitudes of highly specific curriculum standards into more manageable and understandable reporting standards.

If clear and relatively few in number, strand or category labels may serve well as reporting standards. In our experiences developing standards-based report cards, however, we find that those curriculum framework categories often need to be reworded to use simpler and more parent-friendly language. Student learning standards for mathematics, for example, are frequently grouped into categories or strands such as the following.

MATHEMATICS CURRICULUM STRANDS

A. Number Sense and Numeration	D. Data Analysis and Statistics
B. Patterns, Functions, and Relationships	E. Algebraic Thinking and Operations
C. Measurement and Geometry	F. Probability

The breakdown process has the additional benefit of providing teachers with direction as they analyze specific instructional goals and plan appropriate instructional activities. It also guides them in describing the explicit levels of performance that they want to help students acquire.

In addition, most curriculum frameworks offer further detailed information on each curriculum strand. Table 4.1 shows an example of some of the precise student performances or proficiencies associated with each mathematics strand or category.

Table 4.1 Mathematics Curriculum Standards by Strand

	Mathematics Curriculum Standards By Strand					
Specific Proficiency	*Number Sense and Numeration*	*Patterns, Functions, and Relationships*	*Measurement and Geometry*	*Data Analysis and Statistics*	*Algebraic Thinking and Operations*	*Probability*
	Know the meaning, notation, and place value of numbers.	Identify and use patterns.	Identify, describe, and construct basic shapes and solve problems.	Collect, organize, and present data (including charts, graphs, and tables).	Know and use variables, write expressions and equations, and combine like terms.	Know and use probability to solve problems.
	Know the different uses of numbers.	Identify and describe variations in patterns.	Identify the location of objects and describe spatial relationships.	Describe and interpret data.	Solve algebraic expressions.	Determine the likelihood of an event.
	Identify relationships among numbers.	Construct patterns.	Measure objects (including length, perimeter, area, and volume), time, temperature, and money.	Make inferences and predictions using data.	Use algebra to express and solve problems.	Predict outcomes.
	Demonstrate fluency with number operations and estimation.		Choose appropriate measurement tools and use them accurately.			Solve problems that involve scheduling and sequencing.

The challenge in designing a good standards-based report card is in moving from the curriculum standards teachers are accustomed to using on a daily basis to the reporting standards that will most help parents or others make sense of students' performance in a given subject area. Reporting standards *must* be expressed in parent-friendly (or student-friendly) language. In some contexts, we might use the titles of the six strands or categories in Table 4.1 as reporting standards. There are only six, they are relatively clear, and they probably make sense to many parents. But a few modest revisions might make them even better. For example, some parents might not know exactly what "Number Sense and Numeration" means. Renaming this category "Basic Facts and Computations" could make its meaning clearer. Similarly, because the "Probability" standards are likely to be closely linked to those included in "Data Analysis and Statistics," these two categories could be easily combined. "Patterns, Functions, and Relationships" could be rephrased more simply as "Number Patterns and Relationships" and "Algebraic Thinking and Operations" as "Algebraic Concepts." A revised, more parent-friendly set of five reporting standards might read as follows.

MATHEMATICS REPORTING STANDARDS

A. Basic Facts and Computations   D. Probability and Statistics

B. Number Patterns and Relationships   E. Algebraic Concepts

C. Measurement and Geometry

A second challenge for educators developing a standards-based report card is the amount of detail to include for each reporting standard. Again, Table 4.1 is a typical example of the type of language educators use to outline and clarify more "specific proficiencies" for major mathematics curriculum areas or strands. For teachers, a list of these specific proficiencies may help them organize information in their grade book or prepare checklists to keep track of students' progress in meeting major learning goals. Parents, however, may find such detail confusing. Always remember that the primary goal of the report card is effective communication. Therefore, above all else, the selected reporting standards must clearly communicate to parents and others what students are expected to learn and are able to do. Too much detail can detract from the effectiveness of that communication.

At the same time, it is important to keep in mind what we said earlier about understanding the context and audience for the report card. In some school contexts, parents and others may find the language of the "specific proficiencies" for the mathematics curriculum standards shown in Table 4.1 to be perfectly clear. In other contexts, however, parents may find it difficult to understand. A simplified version of the mathematics curriculum standards, as they relate to proficiencies but reduced in number and written in more parent-friendly language, is illustrated in Table 4.2.

Table 4.2 Mathematics Reporting Standards With Accompanying Detail

Mathematics Reporting Standards With Accompanying Detail				
Basic Facts and Computations	*Algebra*	*Geometry*	*Measurement*	*Probability and Statistics*
Know basic math facts and perform operations proficiently.	Understand and apply basic algebra to solve problems.	Know and identify different geometric shapes.	Identify different forms of measurement.	Collect, organize, analyze, and present data.
Make mental calculations and reasonable estimates.	Solve equations and inequalities using algebraic principles.	Use geometry correctly to solve problems.	Measure objects (including length, perimeter, area, and volume), time, temperature, and money.	Predict the probability of events.
Use appropriate strategies to solve problems.			Apply appropriate techniques and tools to measure accurately.	

To illustrate further the differences between curriculum standards and reporting standards, we turn to another important subject area—English or language arts. Language arts standards are typically divided into broad categories, or strands. While the strands or domains in mathematics usually relate to different subtopics, in language arts they more often describe different subskills or means of expression. For example, the language arts standards established in many curriculum frameworks include strands similar to these.

ENGLISH LANGUAGE ARTS CURRICULUM STRANDS	
A. Reading	D. Speaking
B. Writing	E. Viewing and Media
C. Listening	

Within each strand, there may be more specific content standards. Table 4.3 shows an example based on a compilation of standards documents in English language arts from several organizations, states, and provinces.

Table 4.3 English Language Arts Curriculum Standards by Strand

	English Language Arts Curriculum Standards by Strand				
	Reading	*Writing*	*Listening*	*Speaking*	*Viewing and Media*
Specific Proficiency	Use reading skills and strategies to understand and interpret a variety of fiction and nonfiction texts.	Use the writing process effectively.	Employ listening skills for a variety of purposes.	Use speaking strategies to convey information.	Understand characteristics and components of the media.
	Comprehend grade-level text, fiction, and nonfiction.	Use grammatical and mechanical conventions correctly in writing.	Comprehend and retell information from listening.	Adapt speaking strategies based on intended audience.	View and comprehend information from a variety of visual sources.
	Read fluently.	Gather, use, and organize information for research purposes.	Use active listening skills in classroom situations.	Use correct grammar while speaking.	
		Write for a variety of purposes.			

To simplify these English language arts content standards for reporting purposes, we might use language more similar to that in Table 4.4.

Table 4.4	English Language Arts Reporting Standards With Accompanying Detail

English Language Arts Reporting Standards With Accompanying Detail				
Reading	*Writing*	*Listening*	*Speaking*	*Viewing and Media*
Sound out (decode) unknown words.	Apply the writing process effectively in different situations.	Listen and gain information accurately.	Speak appropriately to different audiences.	View and understand information from multiple sources (e.g., TV, radio, Internet, etc.).
Read smoothly and fluently.	Use correct grammar and spelling.	Respect others by listening actively.	Use correct grammar while speaking.	
Comprehend what is read.	Write well for different purposes and audiences.			
Read for information.	Research and report information.			

To be meaningful and effective, reporting standards must be clear, concise, and readily interpretable. Several modern volumes offer educators guidance on developing standards that meet this critical balance (e.g., Gronlund, 2000, 2006; Wiggins & McTighe, 2005). Two of the best resources available, however, are the classic works *Basic Principals of Curriculum and Instruction* by Ralph W. Tyler (1949) and *Evaluation to Improve Learning* by Benjamin S. Bloom, George F. Madaus, and J. Thomas Hastings (1981).

We always must keep in mind that our primary goal in developing a standards-based report card is effective communication. Context is always vitally important. Educators in all settings must consider their audience when designing a reporting form. Reporting standards should offer enough information of sufficient detail to communicate how well students are performing in relation to explicit learning goals. At the same time, they should not overwhelm parents with unnecessary detail or confuse parents with information they can not understand or do not know how to use. Inundating parents and others with information that does not make sense or that they cannot use defeats the purpose of reporting. The primary goal is to present information about students' performance and achievement in school to parents and others in a form that they find both useful and meaningful.

Three Types of Learning Goals

Most curriculum framework standards describe cognitive or academic learning goals. These form the core of every school's curriculum and are the basis of most teachers' instructional planning. Some believe that schools should focus on goals that are *s*pecific, *m*easurable, *a*ttainable, *r*elevant, and *t*imely, or SMART goals (Doran, 1981; O'Neill & Conzemius, 2005). Others might argue that it would be just as valuable to have goals that are *d*oable, *u*nderstandable, *m*anageable, and *b*eneficial—that is, DUMB goals—or those that are *s*pecific, *t*imely, *u*nderstandable, *p*owerful, *i*ntelligent, and *d*oable—STUPID goals. Those acronyms are unlikely to catch on, however.

When assigning grades or marks to students' performance, teachers frequently consider goals other than those associated strictly with cognitive or academic areas. These other goals often relate to student behaviors associated with traits such as responsibility, cooperation, respect, or effort. Occasionally, such goals relate to students' work habits and consider things such as completion of homework, class participation, punctuality in turning in assignments, or the appearance and neatness of students' work.

The different learning goals that teachers consider in grading can generally be classified into three broad categories (see Guskey, 2004, 2006c; Guskey & Bailey, 2001; Guskey & Jung, 2006). These categories, in turn, correspond to three distinct types of reporting standards.

1. **Product goals** describe the major cognitive and academic learning outcomes being sought. They provide the foundation for standards-based reporting, as well as all standards-based approaches to teaching and learning (Stiggins, 2008b). Product goals center on *what* students should know and be able to do at a particular point in time. Grades or marks based on product goals are usually determined from the results of students' performance on summative examinations; final products such

as reports, projects, or exhibits; overall assessments; and other culminating demonstrations of learning.

2. **Process goals** focus on learning activities and classroom behaviors rather than on specific learning outcomes. They derive from the belief that grading and reporting should reflect not just the final results but also *how* students got there. In other words, process goals consider how students behave while they are learning. Some researchers consider these goals to be "enabling behaviors or traits" (McMillan, 2001). Responsibility, effort, study skills, work habits, homework completion and quality, class participation, punctuality in turning in assignments, attendance, and other similar aspects of learning all relate to process goals.

3. **Progress goals** consider how much students *gain* from their learning experiences. They relate not necessarily to where students are but to how much improvement has been made over a period of time. Other names for progress goals include "learning gain," "value-added learning," and "educational growth and development."

Some educators distinguish between *progress*, which they measure backward from a final performance standard or goal, and *growth*, which is measured forward from where a student begins on a learning continuum (see Wiggins, 1996). We believe, however, that if improvement is judged on the basis of well-defined and credible learning standards that include graduated levels of performance or a specified learning progression, *progress* and *growth* can be considered synonymous.

Because progress goals focus on how far students have come over a period of time, grades or marks based on progress goals can be highly individualized among students. Most of the current research evidence on progress goals comes from studies of students involved in individually or differentially paced instructional programs (Esty & Teppo, 1992) and those enrolled in special education (Gersten, Vaughn, & Brengelman, 1996; Ring & Reetz, 2000).

**TYPES OF LEARNING GOALS USED
IN DEVELOPING REPORTING STANDARDS**

1. Product goals

2. Process goals

3. Progress goals

Because of concerns about student motivation, self-esteem, and the social consequences of grading and reporting, most teachers base their grading procedures on some combination of these three types of learning goals (Brookhart, 1993; Frary, Cross, & Weber, 1993; Friedman & Manley, 1992; Nava & Loyd, 1992; Stiggins, Frisbie, & Griswold, 1989). In many cases, they combine elements of product, process, and progress into a single grade or mark. Evidence indicates that teachers also vary the goals they consider from student to student, taking into account individual circumstances (Bursuck et al., 1996; Natriello, Riehl, & Pallas, 1994; Truog & Friedman, 1996). Although they do this in an effort to be fair, the result is a "hodgepodge grade" that includes components of achievement, effort, and improvement (Brookhart, 1991; Cross & Frary, 1996). Interpreting the grade or report card thus becomes extraordinarily difficult, not only for parents but also for administrators, community members, and even the students them-selves (Friedman & Frisbie, 1995; Waltman & Frisbie, 1994). A high grade or mark, for example, might mean the student knew what was intended before instruction began (product), did not learn as well as expected but tried very hard (process), or simply made significant improvement during the time considered (progress).

Conflicts in Reporting on Different Learning Goals

Recognizing these interpretation problems, most researchers and measurement specialists recommend the exclusive use of product goals in determining the grades or marks assigned to students' per-formance. They point out that the more process and progress goals come into play, the more subjective and biased grades can become (Ornstein, 1994). How can a teacher know, for example, how difficult a task was for students or how hard they worked to complete it?

Many teachers point out, however, that if they base grades or marks on only product goals, some high-ability students may receive high grades with little effort, while the hard work of less talented students goes unacknowledged. Consider, for example, two students enrolled in the same physical education class. The first is a well-coordinated athlete who can perform any task the teacher asks with-out putting forth serious effort—and typically does not. The second student is struggling with a weight problem but consistently exerts extraordinary effort and displays exceptional sportsmanship and cooperation. Nevertheless, this student is unable to perform at the same level as the athlete. Few teachers would consider it fair to use solely product goals related to performance in determining the grades of these two students (Guskey & Bailey, 2001).

Teachers also emphasize that if only product goals are considered, low-ability students and those who are disadvantaged—students who must work hardest—have the least incentive to do so (Guskey & Jung, 2006; Jung & Guskey, 2007). These students find the relationship between high effort and low grades unacceptable and, as a result, often express their displeasure with indifference, deception, or disruption (Tomlinson, 1992).

Meaningful Solutions to the Conflicts

A practical solution to the problems associated with these different learning goals, and one used by increasing numbers of teachers and schools as they develop standards-based report cards, is to report *separate* grades or marks on each set of goals. In other words, after establishing explicit indicators of product, process, and progress learning goals, teachers assign a separate grade or mark to each. In this way, the grades or marks assigned to demonstrations of study skills, work habits, effort, or learning progress are kept distinct from those representing assessments of achievement and performance (Guskey, 2002b, 2006c; Stiggins, 2008b). The intent is to provide a more accurate and more comprehensive picture of what students accomplish in school.

While teachers and schools in the United States are just beginning to catch on to the idea of separate grades for product, process, and progress goals, many Canadian educators have used the practice for years (Bailey & McTighe, 1996). Each marking period, they assign an "achievement" grade to students based on their performance on projects, assessments, compositions, and other demonstrations of learning. This achievement grade represents the teacher's judgment of students' levels of performance or accomplishment relative to explicit product goals or standards established for the subject area or course. Decisions about promotion, as well as calculations of grade point averages and class ranks at the high school level, are based solely on these achievement or product grades.

In addition, teachers assign separate grades or marks for homework, class participation, punctuality of assignments, effort, learning progress, and the like. Because these factors usually relate to specific student behaviors, most teachers record a numerical mark for each (e.g., 4 = Consistently; 3 = Usually; 2 = Sometimes; and 1 = Rarely). To clarify a mark's meaning further, teachers typically identify specific behavioral indicators for these factors and for the levels of performance in each. For example, the indicators for a "Homework" mark might include the following:

4—All homework assignments completed and turned in on time

3—One or two missing or incomplete homework assignments

2—Three to five missing or incomplete homework assignments

1—Numerous missing or incomplete homework assignments

When first learning of this multiple grade system, teachers sometimes assume that reporting four or five grades for each subject or course will increase their grading and reporting workload. But those who use the procedure claim that it actually makes grading easier and less work. Teachers gather the same evidence on student learning as they did before, but they no longer worry about how to weight or combine that evidence in calculating an overall grade. As a result, they avoid irresolvable arguments about the appropriateness or fairness of various weighting strategies.

Some schools develop report cards in which these behavioral aspects are recorded only one time, usually in the latter part of the report card. Elementary-level report cards often use this strategy and label the section "Study Skills" or, sometimes, "Citizenship." The vast majority of schools with which we have worked, however, choose to report these behaviors separately for each subject area or class. Teachers tell us that students' behavior and work habits, as well as their learning progress, often vary greatly from one subject to another at the elementary level and from class to class at the secondary level. Therefore, these teachers prefer to give separate marks for process and progress goals in each subject area or class. Several examples of these types of report cards are shown in Chapter 8.

Although standard-based report cards from preschool through the secondary level typically include both product and process goals, progress goals are much more prevalent on primary and elementary levels report cards. Progress reporting requires a clearly specified sequence or continuum of learning goals and appropriate measurement procedures to document improvements along that continuum. This type of progression of learning goals tends to be more common in curriculum development efforts at the elementary level than at the middle grade or secondary levels. So while we consider it appropriate to use progress indicators at any level, we also recognize the development and measurement challenges of doing so in the upper grades.

Reporting separate grades or marks for product, process, and progress goals also makes grading and reporting more meaningful. It removes nonachievement elements from the product grade or mark, making it a much more accurate indicator of what students have learned and are able to do. Teachers also report that when behavioral aspects, such as homework and class participation, are marked separately, students take them more seriously. When assessments of these behaviors are no longer disguised as some arbitrary portion of an overall hodgepodge grade, they cannot be ignored. Furthermore, if a parent questions the teacher about an achievement grade related to a specific product goal or standard, the teacher can simply point to the various process indicators and suggest, "If your child completed homework assignments and participated more frequently in class, I am confident that the achievement grade would be higher." We find that parents, too, generally favor this practice because it provides them with a more detailed and comprehensive profile of their child's performance in school.

For high school students, employers and college admission persons also like seeing separate grades or marks for product, process, and progress goals because they offer more detailed information about students' accomplishments. When all grades are reported on the transcript, a college admissions officer can distinguish between the student who earned high achievement grades with relatively little effort and the one who earned equally high grades through diligence and hard work. The transcript thus becomes a more robust document that presents a better and more discerning portrait of students' high school experiences (Adelman, 1999).

Schools still have the information needed to compute grade point averages and class ranking, if such computations are important. Now, however, those averages and ranks can be based solely on product goals related to academic accomplishments, rather than being tainted by undefined aspects of process and progress. As such, they represent a more accurate and more valid measure of achievement and performance. Pulling out the nonacademic factors from grades based on product goals also will likely improve the relationship between grades and the scores students attain on large-scale assessments (Conley, 2000; D'Agostino & Welsh, 2007; Welsh & D'Agostino, 2009; Willingham, Pollack, & Lewis, 2002).

The key to success in reporting multiple grades, however, rests in the clear specification of indicators related to product, process, and progress goals. Teachers must be able to describe how they plan to assess students' achievement, attitude, effort, behavior, and progress. Then they must clearly communicate these criteria to students, parents, and others. Clear criteria are important not only to ensure accuracy and fairness but also to provide direction to students in their efforts to make improvements.

Several examples of report cards that include separate grades or marks for product, process, and progress goals and reporting standards are illustrated in Chapters 7 and 8. Making clear the distinction among these different types of learning goals, then reporting students' performance on each separately, is a vital step in developing an effective standards-based report card.

Summary

Identifying specific *reporting* standards is essential to the development of a successful standards-based report card. The best reporting standards are clear, concise, and readily interpretable. They offer enough information of sufficient detail to communicate how well students are performing in relation to explicit learning goals, but they do not overwhelm parents with unnecessary detail that they cannot understand and do not know how to use. The best reporting standards are also limited in number, typically involving four to six performance or achievement standards in each subject area.

Reporting standards can relate to product, process, or progress learning goals. While product or "achievement" goals tend to be the primary focus in most schools, standards related to process (work habits and study skills) and progress (improvement over time) are important learning outcomes as well. Successful standards-based report cards typically include reporting standards specific to product, process, and progress learning goals and then report students' performance on each *separately.* This requires no additional work or record keeping for teachers since most keep separate records on each of these three types of learning goals already. Reporting on product, process, and progress goals separately actually makes grading and reporting easier for teachers by eliminating the need to weight and combine these diverse aspects of learning to determine a single, overall grade. Most teachers also find that students take process and progress goals more seriously when they are reported separately. Parents generally favor such distinctions as well because the report card provides them with a more meaningful profile of the different aspects of their children's performance in school.

5

Essential Steps in Development: Part I

In this chapter, we turn to the specific developmental steps involved in creating a standards-based report card. In particular, we will describe essential issues that need to be considered and crucial questions that must be addressed at each step. Some of these steps relate directly to the ideas presented in previous chapters. Others move us ahead in the development process by identifying additional aspects that are vital to success. We will continue this discussion of essential developmental steps in the next chapter as well, where we consider the practical aspects of report card format and design along with issues related to initial implementation.

Crucial Questions in the Development Process

Recall that in Chapter 1 we stressed that "no report card is perfect." That is certainly true. The effectiveness of any report card as a communication tool depends on the educators involved, the students they teach, the parents with whom they work, and the unique characteristics of their school and community. Adaptations to these contextual differences are vital to success.

Nevertheless, a common set of crucial questions must be addressed in any successful development effort. All of these questions relate to explicit decisions that need to be made by those involved in the development process. But equally important, these questions must be addressed *in specific order,* because how each question is answered has important implications for all of the questions that follow. Ignoring or leaving unresolved any of these questions will seriously jeopardize the success of further development work.

In this chapter and the next, we describe these crucial questions and offer recommendations for answering each one. The seven questions addressed here are listed in the box below. A second set of eight crucial questions will be addressed in Chapter 6.

SEVEN CRUCIAL QUESTIONS TO ADDRESS IN DEVELOPING STANDARDS-BASED REPORT CARDS

1. What is the purpose of the report card?

2. How often will report cards be completed and sent home?

3. Will a specific report card be developed for each grade level, or will a more general report card be used across several grade levels?

4. How many reporting standards will be included for each subject area or course?

5. What specific reporting standards will be included at each grade level or in each course?

6. Will standards be set for the grade level or for each marking period?

7. What specific process and progress standards will be reported?

Please remember, however, that even though the recommendations we offer for addressing these questions stem from our many experiences helping educators develop standards-based report cards, lots of exceptions exist. No single pathway will work for everyone, every time, or everywhere. One group of educators in a particular setting might make a series of decisions that is readily accepted and easily implemented. Another group of educators in a different setting might make exactly the same decisions and be met with vigorous criticism and staunch resistance. If unexpected difficulties arise at any step along the way, earlier questions may need to be revisited, answers and decisions reconsidered, and development procedures begun again. Flexibility and openness to alternative pathways are vital to success at every step in the development process.

1. What is the purpose of the report card?

As we described in Chapter 3, the first issue that must be addressed in developing a standards-based report card is deciding its purpose. Specifically, developers need to decide what information to communicate, who is the primary audience for that information, and how they would like that information to be used. No matter what purpose is chosen, however, we strongly recommend that it be clearly and boldly stated on the report card. One way to do this is to print the purpose in a special box on the front of the report card for readers to view before they consider any other information. Several examples are illustrated in Chapter 3.

Printing the purpose on the report card ensures that everyone understands its meaning and intent. It also helps clarify the reasons behind the reporting process and how the information included in the report card can and should be used. While we know of no research evidence that demonstrates any one purpose to be better, more important, or more acceptable across various contexts than any other, our experience shows that reaching consensus on the report card's purpose is an especially vital first step in any development effort.

2. How often will report cards be completed and sent home?

After deciding the report card's purpose, the next crucial question to address is how often report cards will be completed and sent home. The frequency of report cards can affect both their format and structure. As we mentioned earlier, teachers generally favor *less* frequent report cards, knowing the amount of work involved in report card preparation and distribution. Parents, on the other hand, consistently favor *more* frequent report cards. They want to know, on a regular basis, precisely how their children are doing in school and what steps need to be taken if problems arise.

In most cases, four options are considered when determining the frequency of report cards. These are listed in the box below. Each of these options has clear advantages as well as distinct shortcomings.

FREQUENCY OPTIONS FOR DISTRIBUTING STANDARDS-BASED REPORT CARDS

1. Every 6 weeks

2. Every 9 weeks or quarterly

3. Every 12 weeks or each trimester

4. Every 18 weeks or each semester

Every Six Weeks. This is the option preferred by most parents, especially those with children enrolled in the primary or elementary grades. Parents of young children recognize that small learning difficulties can quickly become major learning problems if not addressed promptly and effectively. Most parents also understand the vital importance of developing early literacy and numeration skills. As a result, they want to ensure that their children do not fall behind in mastering these fundamental proficiencies. Receiving specific feedback from the teacher about their child's learning progress every other month seems both reasonable and necessary to parents. Teachers, however, often feel pressed to provide such formal appraisals every six weeks. Many also find it difficult to offer a grade or mark when they may have had relatively few opportunities to assess students' learning formally. For these reasons, most teachers prefer to wait a bit longer so that they can be more certain of their assessments of students' performance before providing specific feedback to parents in a report card.

Every Nine Weeks or Quarterly. This is currently the most prevalent report card distribution time frame, at least in elementary and secondary schools throughout the United States and Canada. It represents a compromise between the desire of parents for more frequent information and the appeals of teachers for a reasonable reporting workload. Some schools supplement nine-week report cards with *interim reports* sent home after four-and-a-half or five weeks, either to assure parents that things are going well or to inform them of particular problems or difficulties that may be evident. Occasionally teachers send these reports only to parents whose children are doing substandard work and are at risk of receiving a low mark or failing grade. While teachers do this in hopes of increasing parents' involvement, it sometimes causes parents to regard interim reports as a source of "bad news only." It also communicates the message to parents that "no news is good news," and, therefore, may make parents wary of any contact or feedback from teachers. So even though it requires a bit more work, we recommend that if interim reports are used, that they be sent to every home, sharing good news as well as cautions, to keep the avenues of school-home communication open and constructive.

Every 12 Weeks or Each Trimester. This option is preferred by most teachers, especially those at the elementary level. Completing and sending report cards home every 12 weeks certainly reduces the reporting workload of teachers. It also gives teachers more opportunities to get to observe their students, gather evidence on learning, and document students' specific accomplishments and achievements. The major drawback is that many parents find it unacceptable to receive information about their children's learning only once every three months. To address this concern, most schools that use trimester reporting also offer some type of *interim report* after six weeks. These interim reports often take the form of "progress reports." They may be less detailed than the report card, and they usually offer a general prognosis of each child's learning progress. Other schools make use of regular *parent-teacher conferences or student-led conferences* (Bailey & Guskey, 2001) as interim reports, both to keep parents abreast of how their children are doing academically and to inform parents about classroom and school events.

Every 18 Weeks or Each Semester. The most common reporting frequency in colleges and universities, this is rarely used in elementary or secondary schools. Parents and teachers alike generally want reports on students' learning more often than once a semester. Even colleges and universities organized on the semester system are increasingly issuing midterm grade reports to encourage intervention strategies when academic problems are evident. Similarly, although secondary schools implementing semester-type, block-scheduling models sometimes make use of semester report cards, because students take a new set of courses each half of the school year, they typically distribute report cards after nine weeks or at midsemester as well to inform both parents and students about the adequacy of learning progress.

Based on our experience, we recommend completing and distributing report cards *every nine weeks or quarterly.* We further recommend considering the use of brief interim reports after four-and-a-half weeks when possible. Sending report cards home every nine weeks offers a meaningful compromise between the requests of parents and the concerns of teachers. It generally satisfies parents' need for regular information on their children's learning progress in school, without burdening teachers with unreasonable reporting responsibilities.

Another important factor to consider when deciding how often the report card will be completed and sent home is consistency across levels. Therefore, we recommend that educators at the elementary, middle school, and secondary levels within a school district come together and reach consensus about the frequency of report card distribution. Districts that allow different reporting schedules for elementary schools and middle or high schools inevitably encounter difficulties. Such inconsistency is especially troublesome to parents who have multiple children enrolled at different grade levels or in different schools within the district and must keep track of these varied report card schedules. Consistency in the report card distribution schedule adds greatly to its utility and effectiveness as a communication tool and, therefore, how well the report card is received.

3. Will a specific report card be developed for each grade level, or will a more general report card be used across several grade levels?

After deciding how often report cards will be completed and sent home, we must decide the format of the report card. In other words, what information will the report card include, and how will that information be presented?

Standards-based report cards at the secondary level typically are organized according to the courses in which students enroll. Because the reporting standards for each course are different and students' course schedules are different, each student's report card will be unique. In other words, while the general structure of the report card will be the same for all students, the specific content will reflect each student's particular program of courses. Examples of several high school reporting forms are shown in Chapter 8.

At the elementary level, however, all students at a grade level are usually engaged in the same curriculum with the same standards. Standards-based report cards at this level generally follow one of two basic formats.

1. Highly specific reporting standards that are unique to each grade level result in a different report card for each grade level.

2. More general reporting standards that are common across grade levels means that the same report card can be used for multiple grade levels, typically Grades 1–5.

Deciding which of these two basic formats to use is vitally important because it affects the direction of nearly all other development tasks.

Specific Standards Unique to Each Grade Level. With these standards, each grade level's report card will look different. In other words, the second-grade report card will include only second-grade standards, the third-grade report card will include only third-grade standards, and so forth. While some overlap may exist, each grade level's report card will include different content and have a distinctive appearance. Figures 5.1 and 5.2 (pages 63–65) include examples of report cards from a district that has developed different report cards for each grade level.

Figure 5.1   Example of a Standards-Based Report Card for Grade 2

EAST ELEMENTARY SCHOOL	MAYFIELD SCHOOL DISTRICT

GRADE 2 REPORT CARD	*The purpose of this report card is to describe students' learning progress to their parents and others. Standards listed below are end-of-year expectations for each second-grade student.*

Student Name:	Beverly Longo	ATTENDANCE			
Teacher Name & Phone:	Eva Smouse, 555-1234, ext. 24	1	2	3	4
Principal Name & Phone:	Bob Cloyd, 555-1234, ext. 20				

KEY TO MARKS: 4 = Exceptional   2 = Progressing
              3 = Proficient   1 = Beginning

	REPORTING PERIOD			
	1	2	3	4
READING				
Reads multisyllable words				
Recognizes and uses prefixes and suffixes				
Reads fluently (based on words correct per minute)				
Understands and can retell main ideas from reading				
Recognizes cause-and-effect relationships				
Identifies and uses nouns and verbs				
WRITING				
Writes topic sentences				
Revises drafts to include more detail				
Writes friendly letters and expository paragraphs				
Capitalizes proper nouns				
Uses punctuation (end marks and commas in a series) correctly				
Writes legibly				

(Continued)

Figure 5.1   (Continued)

KEY TO MARKS: 4 = Exceptional 2 = Progressing 3 = Proficient 1 = Beginning	REPORTING PERIOD			
	1	2	3	4
MATHEMATICS				
Counts and writes whole numbers up to 1,000				
Knows addition and subtraction facts 0–50				
Recognizes, names, and compares fractions				
Measures objects in inches and centimeters				
Describes and classifies geometric shapes				
Knows multiplication facts to 10 for 2s, 5s, 10s				

Figure 5.2   Example of a Standards-Based Report Card for Grade 4

EAST ELEMENTARY SCHOOL	MAYFIELD SCHOOL DISTRICT				
GRADE 4 REPORT CARD	*The purpose of this report card is to describe students' learning progress to their parents and others. Standards listed below are end-of-year expectations for each fourth-grade student.*				
Student Name:	Donald Moose	ATTENDANCE			
Teacher Name & Phone:	Jane Hunt, 555-1234, ext. 19	1	2	3	4
Principal Name & Phone:	Bob Cloyd, 555-1234, ext. 20				

KEY TO MARKS: 4 = Exceptional 3 = Proficient 2 = Progressing 1 = Beginning	REPORTING PERIOD			
	1	**2**	**3**	**4**
READING				
Applies vocabulary learned in daily work				
Uses context clues to figure out unfamiliar words				
Reads fluently (based on words correct per minute)				
Distinguishes fact from opinion				
Uses the concepts of compare and contrast to gain meaning				
Uses nonfiction text to gain information (e.g., textbooks, magazines, Web pages, encyclopedia, etc.)				
WRITING				
Uses a variety of sentence structures				
Writes multiple-paragraph compositions for a variety of purposes				
Applies a variety of prewriting strategies (e.g., story map, outline, etc.)				
Edits and proofreads own writing and the writing of others				
Uses proper grammar, punctuation, and other writing conventions				
Writes legibly in cursive				
MATHEMATICS				
Adds and subtracts multiple digits				
Knows multiplication facts 0–12				
Multiplies 3-digit numbers by 1- and 2-digit numbers				
Divides 3-digit by 1-digit numbers				
Describes and compares simple fractions				
Understands geometry concepts				

General Standards Used Across Grade Levels. With these standards, a common report card can be developed for use across multiple grade levels. This format requires two major development tasks. First, the curriculum standards for each subject area must be carefully analyzed to identify appropriately broad but meaningful reporting standards that are applicable across the various grade levels. As we described in Chapter 4, these broader categories already might be described as strands, domains, or areas of study within the curriculum framework. Since these categories typically extend over all grade levels, they may offer an excellent starting point when identifying the reporting standards to include in the report card.

The second development task involves creating a *supplementary document* to accompany the report card that describes more specifically what each standard involves at each level. Suppose, for example, that one of the broader reporting standards developed for mathematics is "Skills in Measurement and Geometry." This particular reporting standard might be included on the report cards for the first through the fifth or sixth grades. Then the supplementary document that accompanies the report card would inform parents what specific "Skills in Measurement and Geometry" students are expected to acquire at the first-grade level, the second-grade level, and so forth. Or it may explain that the same skills are involved at several grade levels but are considered in greater depth or at higher levels of complexity in each succeeding grade. Figure 5.3 shows an example of a report card that includes broader reporting standards applicable across several grade levels. Figures 5.4 and 5.5 (pages 69–78) show the supplementary documents that describe how each standard is somewhat different at each of the two grade levels.

Figure 5.3 Sample Report Card with the Same Standards Across Grades 1–5

	WEST ELEMENTARY SCHOOL	MAYFIELD SCHOOL DISTRICT				
	REPORT CARD	*The purpose of this report card is to describe students' learning progress to their parents and others, based on our school's end-of-year learning expectations for each grade level.*				
	Student Name & Grade:	Cora Tyson, Grade 2	**ATTENDANCE**			
	Teacher Name & Phone:	Linda Sahn, 555-7777, ext. 24	1	2	3	4
	Principal Name & Phone:	Jack Lyons, 555-7777, ext. 20				

KEY TO MARKS:	4 = Exceptional 3 = Proficient	2 = Progressing 1 = Beginning	REPORTING PERIOD			
			1	2	3	4

READING				
Uses a variety of skills to decode (sound out) unknown words				
Comprehends what is read and can accurately retell the story				
Reads fluently and with expression				
Recognizes different types of literature and understands basic literary elements				
Reads independently during assigned times				
WRITING				
Writes clearly and effectively				
Understands and uses the steps of the writing process				
Writes for a variety of purposes and audiences				
Uses proper grammar and conventions (i.e., capitalization, punctuation, etc.)				
Uses correct spelling				
Writes legibly				
MATHEMATICS				
Knows basic math facts and performs computations proficiently				
Measures accurately				
Makes mental calculations and reasonable estimates				
Uses geometry correctly to solve problems				
Collects, organizes, analyzes, and presents data				
Uses appropriate strategies to solve problems				
SCIENCE				
Uses steps in the scientific method				
Understands basic concepts in grade-level science units				
Correctly uses various scientific instruments and measurement tools				
Reads or listens for information in science				
SOCIAL STUDIES				
Demonstrates knowledge of local, state, or U.S. history				
Understands geography and its effect on society				

(Continued)

Figure 5.3 (Continued)

	1	2	3	4
Recognizes basic civic responsibilities and values in a democracy				
Understands the function of economic systems				
Demonstrates knowledge of current events				
Uses maps effectively				
Reads or listens for information in social studies				

KEY TO MARKS: 4 = Exceptional 2 = Progressing 3 = Proficient 1 = Beginning	REPORTING PERIOD			
	1	2	3	4
ART				
Participates in art activities				
Demonstrates responsibility				
Applies skills effectively				
MUSIC				
Participates in music activities				
Exhibits appropriate vocal development				
Exhibits appropriate instrumental development				
PHYSICAL EDUCATION				
Exhibits good participation				
Exhibits good sportsmanship				
Develops physical skill				

KEY TO MARKS: 4 = Consistently 2 = Sometimes 3 = Usually 1 = Not Yet	REPORTING PERIOD			
	1	2	3	4
STUDENT WORK HABITS				
Shows respect for self and others				
Follows directions				
Contributes appropriately as a group member				
Completes work thoughtfully and on time (class work and homework)				
Works independently at appropriate times				
Takes care of school and personal property				

COMMENTS 1ST REPORTING PERIOD:				
COMMENTS 2nd REPORTING PERIOD:				
COMMENTS 3rd REPORTING PERIOD:				
COMMENTS 4th REPORTING PERIOD:				
PARENT SIGNATURE 1ST RP: **PARENT SIGNATURE 3RD RP:**				
PARENT SIGNATURE 2ND RP: **PRINCIPAL SIGNATURE (End of Year):**				

Figure 5.4	Sample of Supplementary Document to Accompany Report Card in Figure 5.3

WEST ELEMENTARY SCHOOL   **MAYFIELD SCHOOL DISTRICT**

REPORT CARD SUPPLEMENT: GRADE 2 STANDARDS & EXPECTATIONS

EXPLANATION OF MARKS:

4 = Exceptional (Exceeds expectations)
Student demonstrates the skill or understands concepts at a level exceeding expectations for the reporting period.

3 = Proficient (Developing appropriately)
Student demonstrates the skill or understands concepts at the level expected for the reporting period.

2 = Progressing (Developing slowly)
Student is moving toward being able to demonstrate the skill or understand concepts and meets most expectations for the reporting period.

1 = Beginning (Developing too slowly and needs to improve)
Student is only beginning to develop the skill or understand concepts and needs to improve progress in order to meet expectations for the reporting period.

(Continued)

Figure 5.4   (Continued)

READING (Report card categories are listed below in bold.)

Uses a variety of skills to decode (sound out) unknown words

- Recognizes and sounds out new words (Skills: letter/sound, whole word chunks, word families, long and short vowels, digraphs like wh, irregular vowels ei, ie, ea, ue)
- Uses basic sight words correctly (teacher can supply list of basic sight words)
- Uses pictures, clues, prefixes, and suffixes to identify unknown words
- Creates mental pictures & questions

Comprehends what is read and can accurately retell the story

- Makes personal connections to reading
- Retells the main ideas of fiction and nonfiction
- Questions, predicts, makes inferences, rereads when meaning is unclear
- Constructs mental images representing ideas in text
- Compares and contrasts characters, events, and main ideas

Reads fluently & with expression

- Reads aloud using expression
- Uses punctuation (periods and question marks) effectively

Recognizes different types of literature & understands basic literary elements

- Identifies and describes poetry, fiction, and nonfiction
- Identifies and describes characters, time and place, problem/solution, sequence of events in a story
- Uses and understands boldface type, graphs, maps, diagrams

Reads independently during assigned times

- Chooses and reads silently at appropriate level for a sustained amount of time

WRITING

Writes clearly and effectively

- Writes stories with a beginning, middle, and end
- Writes simple, complete sentences
- Uses nouns and verbs correctly

Understands and uses the steps of the writing process

- Develops a plan for writing
- Responds orally to the writing of others
- Attempts to proofread and revise own writing

Writes for a variety of purposes and audiences

- Considers audience and purpose for writing
- Writes letter, directions, and personal narratives
- Writes poems based on reading a wide variety of poetry

Uses proper grammar and conventions (i.e., capitalization, punctuation, etc.)

- Uses contractions, capitalization, and correct end punctuation
- Uses commas in a series

MATHEMATICS

Knows basic math facts and performs computations proficiently

- Reads, writes, and compares numbers to 1,000 using the phrases same as, more than, greater than, fewer than; uses < and > symbols
- Counts by 1s, 2s, 5s, 10s and 100s, starting from any number
- Counts by 3s and 4s starting with 0
- Identifies first, second, etc. up to tenth
- Classifies numbers as odd or even
- Expresses numbers up to 1,000 using hundreds, tens, and ones (21 = 2 tens + 1 one)
- Uses a number line to add and subtract
- Adds and subtracts basic facts (less than 20) with quick recall
- Adds and subtracts two numbers up to two digits with and without regrouping
- Adds and subtracts two numbers with 3 digits with no regrouping
- Finds missing values in number sentences (42 + ___ = 57)
- Recognizes multiplication as the result of counting the total number of objects in equal groups
- Understands division as another way of expressing multiplication (e.g. $2 \times 3 = 6$ can be written as $6 \div 3 = 2$)
- Develops strategies for multiplying numbers up to 5×5

Measures accurately

- Estimates and measures length in meters, centimeters, inches, feet and years
- Draws and measures the perimeter of rectangles, squares, and triangles
- Compares lengths
- Finds the area of a rectangle using a grid
- Tells and writes time from analog and digital clocks to the hour, half-hour and five minutes
- Identifies the value of a penny, nickel, dime, quarter, half dollar, dollar, and five dollar bill
- Counts coin amounts up to a dollar
- Reads and writes values of money using decimals
- Reads temperature using the scale on a Fahrenheit thermometer
- Recognizes, names, and writes basic fractions ($\frac{1}{2}, \frac{1}{3}, \frac{2}{3}, \frac{1}{4}, \frac{2}{4}, \frac{3}{4}$)
- Compares fractions from $\frac{1}{12}$ to $\frac{1}{2}$

Makes mental calculations and reasonable estimates

Uses geometry correctly to solve problems

- Names, describes, and compares basic 2 and 3-dimensional shapes (e.g., square, circle, semicircle, rectangle, triangle, sphere, and rectangular prism)
- Describes position of objects, using words such as above, below, behind, in front of

Collects, organizes, analyzes, and presents data

- Reads and uses simple bar, pie, and other graphs appropriately
- Predicts the probability of simple events

Uses appropriate strategies to solve problems

- Writes or draws and solves addition and subtraction word problems
- Solves word problems involving length and money

(Continued)

Figure 5.4 (Continued)

SCIENCE

Uses steps in the scientific method
- Steps: observe, form hypothesis, perform experiment, collect data, summarize results

Understands basic concepts in grade level science units
- Animals and Habitats
- Electricity and Magnets
- Sound and Light
- Ecology

Correctly uses various scientific instruments and measurement tools
- Scales, glassware, rulers, etc.

Reads or listens for information in science
- Picks out main ideas and facts needed from reading or listening
- Understands, uses basic science vocabulary

SOCIAL STUDIES

Demonstrates knowledge of local, state, or United States history
- Distinguishes among past, present, and future
- Identifies who, what, and where in stories about the past
- Reads and understands a timeline

Understands geography and its effect on society

Recognizes basic civic responsibilities and values in a democracy
- Understands and explains core democratic values of truth, common good, and equality

Understands the function of economic systems
Distinguishes between wants and needs and goods and services

Demonstrates knowledge of current events

Reads or listens for information in social studies

Uses maps effectively
- Recognizes the difference between land and water on a map
- Points out directions (N, S, E, W)
- Uses the key and understands basic symbols
- Finds the title
- Identifies boundaries, continents, and oceans

ART

Participates in art activities
- Listens to teacher and classmates
- Follows directions
- Stays on task
- Completes projects

Demonstrates responsibility

- Uses tools and materials in a safe and proper way
- Cares for and cleans up materials
- Takes time to complete quality work

Applies skills effectively

- Creates lines, shapes, color, texture, form
- Describes and discusses various works of art and artists
- Concepts introduced: drawing, painting, paper construction, printing, clay, jewelry, sculpture and fiber
- Evaluates and makes good judgments about personal creations

MUSIC

Participates in music activities

- Follows directions
- Participates by singing, moving, playing instruments, creating, listening
- Stays on task during class

Exhibits appropriate vocal development

- Sings high/low, up/down, loud/soft
- Sings alone or with a group
- Sings the steps to the musical ladder (do, re, mi, fa, sol, la)
- Sings in more than one part
- Understands verse and refrain (chorus)

Exhibits appropriate instrumental development

- Reads patterns to play instruments
- Performs high/low, up/down, fast/slow, loud/soft
- Accompanies songs on instruments in parts
- Creates short pieces of music to create a beat
- Body percussion: stomp, pat, clap, snap, etc.

PHYSICAL EDUCATION

Exhibits good participation

- Wears appropriate shoes
- Participates with good effort
- Stays on task during class

Exhibits good sportsmanship

- Treats other respectfully
- Follows rules
- Demonstrates self-control

Develops skill

- Demonstrates correct technique for motor skills (walk, vertical jump, hop, run, gallop, slide, skip, horizontal jump)
- Demonstrates correct technique for object control skills (instep kick, foot dribble, underhand throw, catch rolling ball, hand dribble, underhand strike, catch fly ball, overhand throw, bat a ball, jump rope
- Demonstrates lift and carry posture
- Transfers skill practice to proper usage
- Achieves age appropriate fitness levels (aerobic, hi/low back flexibility)

Figure 5.5   Sample of Supplementary Document to Accompany Card in Figure 5.3

WEST ELEMENTARY SCHOOL	MAYFIELD SCHOOL DISTRICT

REPORT CARD SUPPLEMENT: GRADE 4 STANDARDS & EXPECTATIONS

EXPLANATION OF MARKS:

4 = Exceptional (Exceeds expectations)
Student demonstrates the skill or understands concepts at a level exceeding expectations for reporting period.

3 = Meets Standard (Developing appropriately)
Student usually demonstrates the skill or understands concepts and meets expectations for reporting period.

2 = Approaching Standard (Beginning to develop)
Student sometimes demonstrates the skill or understands concepts and meets some expectations for reporting period.

1 = Below Standard (Needs to develop)
Student seldom demonstrates the skill or understands concepts and is not meeting expectations for this reporting period.

READING (Report card categories are listed below in bold.)

Uses a variety of skills to decode (sound out) unknown words
- Uses context clues and prediction to understand the meanings of words
- Uses various cues to automatically sound out unknown words and decide meaning (e.g. base words, prefix/suffix, syllabication)

Comprehends what is read and can accurately retell the story
- Connects personal knowledge and experience to reading
- Summarizes narrative and informational text
- Determines the meaning of words and phrases in context
- Explains relationships among themes, ideas, and characters across texts
- Uses a variety of strategies to check for understanding while reading

Reads fluently and with expression
- Reads grade-level text fluently

Recognizes different types of literature and understands basic literary elements
- Identifies and describes a variety of poetry, mystery, biography, and tall tales
- Analyzes characters' thoughts and motivation and conflict and its resolution
- Explains how authors use foreshadowing, flashback, metaphor, and simile to depict time, setting, conflicts, and resolutions
- Identifies and explains the defining characteristics of autobiography, biography, personal narrative
- Given text, compares and contrasts ideas, identifies a position and supporting ideas
- Explains how authors use headings, subheadings, keys and legends, figures, glossaries, and indexes to enhance understanding

Reads independently during assigned times
- Chooses and reads silently at appropriate level for a sustained amount of time

WRITING

Writes clearly and effectively

- Writes with increasing elaboration
- Uses a variety of sentence patterns (complex, compound, simple)
- Groups sentences containing related information into paragraphs
- Establishes time, place, and situation in a passage
- Uses dialog correctly

Understands and uses the steps of the writing process

- Applies a variety of drafting strategies such as story maps, webs, Venn diagrams, to structure ideas
- Writes a multiparagraph, coherent essay
- Edits and proofreads own writing using dictionary, grammar check, and thesaurus, paying attention to "focused correction areas"
- Develops individual style and voice in writing

Writes for a variety of purposes and audiences

- Writes for a purpose and considers the audience in choosing words
- Uses tone appropriate to the audience
- Writes a personal narrative
- Writes poetry (limericks and cinquains)
- Writes on a theme, comparing two pieces of text

Uses proper grammar and conventions (i.e., capitalization, punctuation, etc.)

- Uses simple and compound sentences, adjectives, common and proper nouns, pronouns, regular and irregular verbs
- Uses hyphens between syllables, apostrophes in contractions, and commas in salutations and to set off words and phrases

Uses correct spelling

- Spells frequently encountered words correctly. For less frequently encountered words, uses other sources (word list, dictionary, etc.)

Writes legibly

- Writes fluently with both manuscript and cursive

MATHEMATICS

Knows basic math facts and performs computations proficiently

- Reads, writes, compares, and orders numbers to 1,000,000
- Finds all factors of a whole number up to 50
- Identifies prime numbers
- Solves problems about factors and multiples
- Adds and subtracts whole numbers fluently
- Recalls multiplication and related division facts through 12
- Multiplies one digit times any number of digits
- Multiplies 3 digits times 2 digits
- Multiplies two-digit numbers by 2, 3, 4, and 5
- Divides numbers up to four digits by one-digit numbers and by 10
- Finds unknowns in simple equations (e.g. $2 + n = 5$)

(Continued)

Figure 5.5   (Continued)

- Learns to check results of multiplication and division problems
- Locates tenths on a number line
- Reads, writes, interprets, and compares decimals up to hundredths
- Writes tenths and hundredths in decimal and fraction forms, and knows the decimal equivalents for halves and fourths
- Understands fractions as parts of a set of objects
- Locates and compares proper, improper, and mixed number fractions
- Adds and subtracts fractions less than 1 with like denominators to 12
- Compares and orders up to 3 fractions (proper, improper, or mixed numbers)
- Solves problems involving sums and differences for fractions, including word problems
- Adds and subtracts decimals up to two decimal places

Measures accurately

- Measures using common tools and selects proper units of measure
- Measures and compares temperatures in degrees (C and F)
- Measures surface area of cubes and rectangular prisms
- Carries out the following conversions from one unit of measure to a larger or smaller unit of measure: meters to centimeters, kilograms to grams, liters to milliliters, hours to minutes, minutes to seconds, years to months, weeks to days, feet to inches, ounces to pounds
- Knows and uses the formulas to calculate perimeter and area of a square and a rectangle
- Finds one dimension of a rectangle given the other dimension and its perimeter or area
- Finds the side of a square

Makes mental calculations and reasonable estimates

- Estimates the answers to calculations involving addition, subtraction, or multiplication
- Knows when approximation is appropriate and uses it to check the reasonableness of answers

Uses geometry correctly to solve problems

- Identifies and counts the faces, edges, and vertices of cubes, rectangular prisms, and pyramids
- Recognizes flips, slides, and turns of 2-dimensional objects
- Recognizes symmetry of plane figures
- Recognizes and draws right, obtuse, and acute angles
- Identifies angles as larger or smaller than right angles
- Recognizes and draws perpendicular, parallel, and intersecting lines using a straight edge
- Identifies the basic properties of quadrilaterals and triangles (isosceles, equilateral, and right) and uses these to solve problems

Collects, organizes, analyzes, and presents data

- Reads, creates, interprets, and compares pie, bar, and line graphs
- Constructs tables and graphs using given information
- Locates and places an ordered pair
- Orders a given set of data and finds mean and median

Uses appropriate strategies to solve problems

SCIENCE

Uses steps in the scientific method

- Steps: observe, form hypothesis, perform experiment, collect data, summarize results

Understands basic concepts in grade level science units

- Plants and Animals
- Electricity
- Matter

Correctly uses various scientific instruments and measurement tools

Reads or listens for information in science

- Picks out main ideas and facts needed from reading or listening
- Understands, uses basic science vocabulary

SOCIAL STUDIES

Demonstrates knowledge of local, state, or United States history

Understands geography and its effect on society

Recognizes basic civic responsibilities and values in a democracy

- Understands and explains core democratic values of life, liberty, and the pursuit of happiness

Understands the function of economic systems

- Understands and explains opportunity cost, scarcity, and barter

Demonstrates knowledge of current events

Reads or listens for information in social studies

Uses maps effectively

ART

Participates in art activities

- Listens to teacher and classmates
- Follows directions
- Stays on task
- Completes projects

Demonstrates responsibility

- Uses tools and materials in a safe and proper way
- Cares for and cleans up materials
- Takes time to complete quality work

Applies skills effectively

- Creates lines, shapes, color, texture, form, value, and space
- Observes, discusses, and describes the works of artists from various cultures
- Becomes aware of art in the natural and constructed environment

(Continued)

Figure 5.5 (Continued)

- Evaluates and makes judgments about personal creations
- Concepts introduced: drawing, painting, paper construction, printing, clay, jewelry, sculpture and fiber

MUSIC

Participates in music activities

- Follows directions
- Participates by singing, moving, playing instruments, creating, listening
- Stays on task during class

Exhibits appropriate vocal development

- Reads and sings the steps to the musical ladder (do, re, mi, fa, sol, la, ti, do)
- Sings partner songs and canons
- Vocalizes loud and soft using dynamic symbols
- Uses proper breathing and posture when singing

Exhibits appropriate instrumental development

- Plays basics on recorder
- Identifies music symbols through playing instruments
- Creates own music in several forms
- Reads note names and applies to all instruments

PHYSICAL EDUCATION

Exhibits good participation

- Wears appropriate shoes
- Participates with good effort
- Stays on task during class

Exhibits good sportsmanship

- Treats other respectfully
- Follows rules
- Demonstrates self-control

Develops skills

- Demonstrates correct technique for motor skills (leap, vertical jump, hop, run, horizontal jump)
- Demonstrates correct technique for object control skills (instep kick, foot dribble, underhand throw, catch rolling ball, forehand strike, hand dribble, underhand strike, catch fly ball, overhand throw, bat a ball, jump rope)
- Transfers skill practice to proper usage
- Achieves age appropriate fitness levels (aerobic, hi/low back flexibility, abdominal/low back strength, arm/shoulder strength)
- Participates in the President's Challenge physical fitness test

In another school district where we worked, the development team created a common report card for Grades 1–4 but then offered parents what they called "Curriculum Highlight Maps" (see www.wilmette39 .org/curriculum/curriculumhighlights.htm). These maps show parents the learning standards for each individual grade level along with those for the entire K–8 curriculum. The grade-level standards are organized in a calendar-based format so that parents can see what standards will be emphasized during the fall, winter, and spring. In describing their maps, however, the team emphasizes to parents and others that the actual timing and sequence of each unit of study is determined by individual teachers based on the needs of the students in their particular classes. They stress that teachers may address some goals separately and may integrate others into broader, thematic units of study. They also point out that curriculum topics may be covered in a different sequence than described, again depending on the judgment of individual teachers. Figures 5.6 and 5.7 (pages 80–89) show their report card for Grade 4 and the Curriculum Highlight Map for reading at Grade 4.

Some school districts develop supplementary documents that further specify the particular concepts and skills addressed during *each marking period* within the grade level or course (see Question #6 later in this chapter). These documents outline explicit learning goals for the first quarter (i.e., the first nine weeks), the second quarter, and so forth. This practice is evident in the Curriculum Highlight Map illustrated in Figure 5.7. While some elementary schools identify quarterly goals, the practice is much more prevalent at the secondary level.

The advantage of specifying quarterly goals is that doing so allows teachers to assign the highest mark available each marking period to students who do well rather than a mark that shows progress to an end-of-year goal. Parents who urge their children to strive for the highest grades or marks possible every marking period also favor this approach. The drawback is that it requires the articulation of explicit marking period expectations so that parents know the specific learning goals set for that portion of the school year. In addition, developers must consider how they will communicate the progress of students who were unable to meet a particular expectation or learning goal in the first quarter but successfully achieved that goal in the second or third quarter. After all, a standards-based grade or mark should always reflect students' current level of proficiency, based on the most current evidence available. Figure 5.8 (pages 90–91) shows another example of the detailed description necessary when learning expectations are defined for each marking period.

Figure 5.6   Sample Grade 4 Report Card

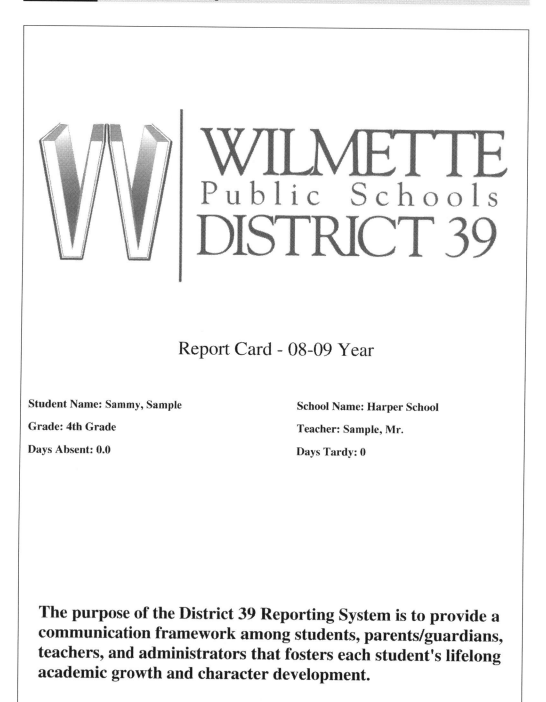

Report Card - 08-09 Year

Student Name: Sammy, Sample

Grade: 4th Grade

Days Absent: 0.0

School Name: Harper School

Teacher: Sample, Mr.

Days Tardy: 0

The purpose of the District 39 Reporting System is to provide a communication framework among students, parents/guardians, teachers, and administrators that fosters each student's lifelong academic growth and character development.

Harper School Report Card				
Sample, Sammy Teacher: Sample, Mr. - Grade: 4				November 17, 2008

Process Descriptors		
3- Consistently	**2-Sometimes**	**1- Seldom**

Characteristics of Successful Learners		**Term 1**	**Term 2**	Comments
Thinking Skills	Transfers knowledge to new situations			**Term 1:**
	Thinks flexibly			
	Is a self-directed learner			
	Thinks reflectively			
Work Skills	Listens actively			
	Demonstrates perseverance			
	Strives for personal best			**Term 2:**
	Takes responsible risks			
	Acts responsibly			
	Responds effectively			
	Maintains focus			
Inter-personal Skills	Thinks interdependently			
	Self-advocates			

Product Descriptors			
M - Meets Standards	**W - Working Toward Standards**	**E - Experiencing Difficulty**	**N/A - Not Assessed**

Reading	**Term 1**	**Term 2**	Term 1:
Uses decoding skills			
Reads fluently			
Broadens reading vocabulary			Term 2:
Applies comprehension strategies			
Responds thoughtfully to text			

Writing	**Term 1**	**Term 2**	Term 1:
Communicates ideas in writing			
Uses prewriting strategies			
Edits for punctuation, grammar, and spelling			Term 2:
Revises content into successive drafts (grades 2-4)			

Mathematics	**Term 1**	**Term 2**	Term 1:
Computes accurately			
Applies mathematical concepts			Term 2:
Uses problem solving strategies			
Communicates mathematical thinking			

(Continued)

Figure 5.6   (Continued)

Sample, Sammy - Grade: 4   November 17, 2008

Science	Term 1	Term 2	Term 1:
Uses subject area vocabulary			
Understands key concepts			
Draws meaningful conclusions			Term 2:
Engages in inquiry using scientific processes			

Social Studies	Term 1	Term 2	Term 1:
Uses subject area vocabulary			
Uses and interprets maps			Term 2:
Understands key concepts			
Draws meaningful conclusions			

Spanish	Sample, Mrs.	Term 1	Term 2	Term 1:
Process	Participates appropriately			
Product	Communicates using Spanish			Term 2:
	Identifies and comprehends vocabulary			

Art	Vandalay, Art	Term 1	Term 2	Term 1:
Process	Acts responsibly			
	Thinks interdependently			
Product	Demonstrates knowledge of skills			Term 2:
	Applies art concepts			
	Meets project criteria (Craftsmanship)			

Music	Kazoo, Karen	Term 1	Term 2	Term 1:
Process	Listens actively			
	Responds effectively			
Product	Demonstrates singing skills			Term 2:
	Demonstrates rhythmic skills			
	Demonstrates instrumental skills			

Physical Education	Mr. Skip	Term 1	Term 2	Term 1:
Process	Maintains focus			
	Acts responsibly			
	Demonstrates perseverance			Term 2:
	Thinks interdependently			
Product	Demonstrates skill development			

Figure 5.7

Curriculum Highlight Map for Reading in Grade 4: Quarterly Goals

Wilmette Public Schools, District 39

Created 2006-2007

Grade 4 Reading/Literature (*Master*)

Essential Questions	Content	Skills
Fall		
Comprehension & Fluency How does an organized story structure help in understanding other story elements? How do readers understand the broad range of reading materials and genres? How do readers apply reading strategies to improve understanding and fluency? **Decoding and Vocabulary** How do readers apply word structure and vocabulary skills to comprehend selections? **Reading Behaviors** How do students become active and engaged readers?	**Comprehension** A. Listening Comprehension Strategies B. Reading Comprehension Strategies -story structure -predictions -connections **Fluency** C. Phrasing -rate -automaticity **Vocabulary** D. Context Clues E. Word Analysis (morphology/meaning)	A. **Ask and respond** to questions based on read alouds, books on tape, shared reading A. Orally **summarize** the author's message **Narrative selections** B. **Use** word meaning to comprehend stories B. **Analyze** author's word choice to convey meaning B. **Set** purpose for reading B. **Analyze** story structure to enhance story comprehension -character -setting -problem/conflict -plot B. **Use** story structure to compare and contrast stories B. **Identify and analyze** elements of the author's craft -purpose -point of view B. **Predict** outcomes and **confirm or revise** as needed B. **Draw** conclusions B **Make** connections to personal experiences B. **Orally demonstrate** understanding of text using "think aloud" C. **Adjust** reading rate/pace according to the demands of the text C. Automatically **recognize and read** high frequency words -sight words -core lists -content area words C. **Reads** with expression C. **Interprets** punctuation in order to properly pace reading D. **Use** new words orally in a variety of contexts D. **Use** language for different purposes D. **Use** context clues to gain meaning of new words D. **Incorporate** new words in oral and written expression D. **Relate** new topics to known words and word meanings E. **Use** knowledge of roots, prefixes and suffixes to identify the meaning of words in context E. **Relate** dictionary definitions to prior experience and content E. **Use** glossaries, dictionaries, thesauruses to clarify word meaning

www.curriculummapper.com

1 of 7

(Continued)

Figure 5.7 (Continued)

| Master | Grade 4 Reading/Literature *(Master)* | Wilmette School District Administration |

Essential Questions	Content	Skills

	Decoding
	F. Word Structure Analysis
		E. **Adjust** definitions of words according to usage
		F. **Use** integrated strategies to pronounce unfamiliar words in context
		F. **Apply** with independence structural analysis generalizations
		  -rhyming words
		  -words with same start
		  -words with same end
		  -blends & digraphs
		  -compound words
		  -contractions
		F. **Break** words into syllables/identifiable parts
		F. **Apply** word analysis strategies to acquire reading independence

	Reading Behaviors G. Reading Attitudes	G. **Share** information about books G. **Choose** books of personal interest G. **Use** free time to browse and read independently G. **Share** personal responses to books with other students in a variety of ways G. **Read** aloud for others G. **Read** trade books on topics in content area classes G. **Use** the library as a valuable resource for gathering information for all content areas
	Literature Genres H. Exposure to literature strands -Classics I. Realistic Fiction	H. **Explore** literature I. **Recognize** details of daily life as they actually are or were I. **Identify** realistic portrayal of characters, setting, and conflicts

Comprehension & Fluency
How does an organized story structure help in understanding other story elements?
 	
How do readers understand the broad range of reading materials and genres?
 	
How do readers apply reading strategies to improve understanding and fluency?
 	
Decoding and Vocabulary
How do readers apply word structure
	Comprehension
	A. Listening Comprehension Strategies
	
	B. Reading Comprehension Strategies
	  -inferences
	
	Fluency
	C. Phrasing
	  -rate
	  -automaticity
	
	Vocabulary
		Skills taught in previous month should be reinforced as needed.
		A. -- Please see previous months for skills to be reinforced
		
		Narrative
		B. **Make** inferences from prior knowledge and text
		
		C. --Please see previous months for skills to be reinforced
		
		D. **Analyze** context clues to gain meaning of new words
		
		E. --Please see previous months for skills to be reinforced

Essential Questions	Content	Skills
and vocabulary skills to comprehend selections?	D. Context Clues	F. **Describe** language patterns and dialect
	E. Word Analysis (morphology/meaning)	G. **Demonstrate** self-confidence in his/her ability to learn to read
Reading Behaviors How do students become active and engaged readers?	**Decoding** F. Word Structure Analysis	H. **Explore** literature
		I. --Please see previous month for skills to be reinforced
	Reading Behaviors G. Reading Attitudes	
	Literature Genres H. Exposure to literature strands -Classics -Science Fiction/Time & Space/Fantasy	
	I. Realistic Fiction	
Comprehension & Fluency How does an organized story structure help in understanding other story elements?	**Comprehension** A. Listening Comprehension Strategies	Skills taught in previous months should be reinforced as needed. A. -- Please see previous months for skills to be reinforced
How do readers understand the broad range of reading materials and genres?	B. Reading Comprehension Strategies -text structure -main idea and supporting details	*Expository* B. **Use** background knowledge to understand informational text B. **Read** a variety of materials for different points of view B. **Evaluate** text structure, features, and content to prioritize reading and study
How do readers apply reading strategies to improve understanding and fluency?		B. **Identify** facts that support the main topic B. **Identify** the main idea
Decoding and Vocabulary How do readers apply word structure and vocabulary skills to comprehend selections?	**Fluency** C. Phrasing -rate -automaticity	B. **Differentiate** main ideas from supporting details B. **Relate** each detail to the main idea it supports B. **Refer** to text to answer questions or confirm comprehension B. **Generate** cross-curricular connections
	Vocabulary D. Context Clues	C. --Please see previous months for skills to be reinforced D.--Please see previous month for skills to be reinforced
	E. Word Analysis (morphology/meaning)	E. -- Please see previous month for skills to be reinforced
Reading Behaviors How do students become active and engaged readers?	**Decoding** F. Word Structure Analysis	F. **Apply** with independence structural analysis generalizations -possessives
	Reading Behaviors G. Reading Attitudes	G. **Read** a variety of materials for different viewpoints and topics G. **Read** to expand knowledge and appreciation of other cultures
	Literature Genres I. Exposure to literature strands	I. **Explore** literature

(Continued)

85

Figure 5.7 (Continued)

Master	Grade 4 Reading/Literature (*Master*)	Wilmette School District Administration
Essential Questions	**Content**	**Skills**
Winter	-Classics -Fantasy	
Comprehension & Fluency How does an organized story structure help in understanding other story elements? How do readers understand the broad range of reading materials and genres? How do readers apply reading strategies to improve understanding and fluency? **Decoding and Vocabulary** How do readers apply word structure and vocabulary skills to comprehend selections? **Reading Behaviors** How do students become active and engaged readers?	**Comprehension** A. Listening Comprehension Strategies B. Reading Comprehension Strategies -fact and opinion -relevant and irrelevant information **Fluency** C. Phrasing -rate -automaticity **Vocabulary** D. Context Clue E. Word Analysis (morphology/meaning) **Decoding** F. Word Structure Analysis **Reading Behaviors** G. Reading Attitudes **Literature Genres** I. Exposure to literature strands -Periodicals/Newspapers -Content Area Texts	**Skills taught in previous months should be reinforced as needed.** A. --Please see previous months for skills to be reinforced **Expository** B. **Distinguish** between facts and opinions B. **Compare and contrast** information from various expository texts B. **Relate** valid theories and predictions to relevant facts B. **Differentiate** between relevant and irrelevant information in a text B. **Summarize** information gathered from text B. **Select** appropriate texts and reference materials for a task C. --Please see previous months for skills to be reinforced. D. --Please see previous months for skills to be reinforced E. --Please see previous month for skills to be reinforced F. **Apply** with independence structural analysis generalizations -roots -prefixes -suffixes G. **Recognize** historical perspectives found in given literary works I. **Explore** literature
Comprehension & Fluency How does an organized story structure help in understanding other story elements? How do readers understand the broad range of reading materials and genres? How do readers apply reading strategies to improve understanding and fluency? **Decoding and Vocabulary**	**Comprehension** A. Listening Comprehension Strategies B. Reading Comprehension Strategies -fact and opinion -relevant and irrelevant information **Fluency** C. Phrasing - rate -automaticity **Vocabulary**	**Skills taught in previous months should be reinforced as needed.** A. --Please see previous months for skills to be reinforced **Expository** B. **Recognize** cause and effect relationships B. **Draw** conclusions C. --Please see previous months for skills to be reinforced D. --Please see previous month for skills to be reinforced E. --Please see previous month for skills to be reinforced F. **Describe** language patterns and dialect

	Essential Questions	Content	Skills
Master			G. Share personal responses to books with other students in a variety of ways
			G. Read aloud for others
	Reading Behaviors	D. Context Clues	
	How do students become active and engaged readers?	-word meaning	
		-acquisition of new words	
		E. Word Analysis (morphology/meaning)	
		Decoding	
		F. Word Structure Analysis	
			H. Explore literature
		Reading Behaviors	
		G. Reading Attitudes	
		Literature Genres	
		H. Exposure to literature strands	
		-Fantasy/Science Fiction/Time and Space	
		-Folktales	
		-Periodicals/newspapers	
	Comprehension & Fluency	Comprehension	**Skills taught in previous months should be reinforced as needed.**
	How does an organized story structure help in understanding other story elements?	A. Listening Comprehension Strategies	A. --Please see previous months for skills to be reinforced
		B. Reading Comprehension Strategies	
		-main idea and supporting details	**Expository**
	How do readers understand the broad range of reading materials and genres?	-summarizing	B. Identify facts that support the main topic
			B. Identify the main idea
		Fluency	B. Differentiate main ideas from supporting details
	How do readers apply reading strategies to improve understanding and fluency?	C. Phrasing	B. Relate each detail to the main idea it supports
		-rate	
		-expression	C. -- Please see previous months for skills to be reinforced
	Decoding and Vocabulary	Vocabulary	D. --Please see previous months for skills to be reinforced
	How do readers apply word structure and vocabulary skills to comprehend selections?	D. Context Clues	E. --Please see previous months for skills to be reinforced
		E. Word Analysis (morphology/meaning)	F. --Please see previous months for skills to be reinforced
		Decoding	G. Please see previous months for skills to be reinforced
		F. Word Structure Analysis	
		Reading Behaviors	
	Reading Behaviors	G. Reading Attitudes	H. Locate references to real people or events
	How do students become active and engaged readers?		H. Identify heroes and heroines with superhuman characteristics
		Literature Genres	H. Identify gods and goddesses who interact with humans
		H. Mythology	H. Recall how myths explain the natural world and human nature
			H. Locate references to mythical creatures
		I. Exposure to literature strands	
		-Folktales	I. Explore literature
Spring			**Skills taught in previous months should be reinforced as needed.**
	Comprehension & Fluency	Comprehension	A. --Please see previous months for skills to be reinforced
	How does an organized story structure help in understanding other story	A. Listening Comprehension Strategies	

(Continued)

Figure 5.7 (Continued)

Master   Grade 4 Reading/Literature (*Master*)   Wilmette School District Administration

Essential Questions	Content	Skills
elements? How do readers understand the broad range of reading materials and genres? How do readers apply reading strategies to improve understanding and fluency? **Decoding and Vocabulary** How do readers apply word structure and vocabulary skills to comprehend selections? **Reading Behaviors** How do students become active and engaged readers?	B. Reading Comprehension Strategies -Story structure -elements -Inference **Fluency** C. Phrasing -rate -expression **Vocabulary** D. Context Clues E. Word Analysis (morphology/meaning) **Decoding** F. Word Structure Analysis **Reading Behaviors** G. Reading Attitudes **Literature Genres** H. Exposure to literature strands -Science Fiction/Time & space -Free Verse Poetry -Structured Verse Poetry	**Narrative** B. **Analyze** story structure to enhance story comprehension -resolution -point of view B. **Identify and analyze** elements of the author's craft -style -foreshadowing -flashback B. **Make** inferences from prior knowledge and text B. **Identify** multiple goals and problems in stories during discussion B. **Detect** evidence indicating whether a story is fiction or non-fiction B. **Recognize** elements that distinguish poetry from prose B. **Compare and contrast** a variety of literary works based on their elements C. --Please see previous months for skills to be reinforce D. --Please see previous months for skills to be reinforced E. --Please see previous months for skills to be reinforced F. --Please see previous months for skills to be reinforced G. **Read** trade books on topics in content area classes G. **Read** a variety of materials for different viewpoints and topics G. **Use** the library as a valuable resource for gathering information for all content areas H. **Explore** literature
Comprehension & Fluency How does an organized story structure help in understanding other story elements? How do readers understand the broad range of reading materials and genres? How do readers apply reading strategies to improve understanding and fluency? **Decoding and Vocabulary**	**Comprehension** A. Listening Comprehension Strategies B. Reading Comprehension Strategies -Elements of Poetry **Fluency** C. Phrasing	**Skills taught in previous months should be reinforced as needed.** A. --Please see previous months for skills to be reinforced **Poetry** B. **Identify** elements of poetry -rhyme -alliteration -humor -rhythm -meter -simile -personification

Essential Questions	Content	Skills
How do readers apply word structure and vocabulary skills to comprehend selections? **Reading Behaviors** How do students become active and engaged readers?	-rate -expression **Vocabulary** D. Context Clues E. Word Analysis (morphology/meaning) **Decoding** F. Word Structure Analysis **Reading Behaviors** G. Reading Attitudes **Literature Genres** H. Exposure to literature strands -Science Fiction/Time & space -Free Verse Poetry -Structured Verse Poetry -Periodicals/Newspapers	-onomatopoeia -couplets/triplets C. --Please see previous months for skills to be reinforced D. --Please see previous months for skills to be reinforced E. --Please see previous months for skills to be reinforced F. **Apply** with independence structural analysis generalizations -rhyming words G. --Please see previous months for skills to be reinforced H. **Explore** literature
Comprehension & Fluency How does an organized story structure help in understanding other story elements? How do readers understand the broad range of reading materials and genres? How do readers apply reading strategies to improve understanding and fluency? **Decoding and Vocabulary** How do readers apply word structure and vocabulary skills to comprehend selections? **Reading Behaviors** How do students become active and engaged readers?	**Comprehension** A. Listening Comprehension Strategies B. Reading Comprehension Strategies -Inference -Story structure -Elements -Summarizing **Fluency** C. Phrasing **Vocabulary** D. Context Clues E. Word Analysis (morphology/meaning) **Decoding** F. Word Structure Analysis **Reading Behaviors** G. Reading Attitudes **Literature Genres** H. Exposure to literature strands -Science Fiction/Time & space -Classics	**Skills taught in previous months should be reinforced as needed.** A. --Please see previous months for skills to be reinforced **Narrative** B. --Please see September, October, and March for skills to be reinforced C. --Please see previous months for skills to be reinforced D. --Please see previous months for skills to be reinforced E. **Relate** dictionary definitions to prior experience and content F. **Apply** with independence structural analysis generalizations -possessives -plurals -roots -prefixes -suffixes G. **Read** a variety of materials for different viewpoints and topics G. **Use** the library as a valuable resource for gathering information for all content areas H. **Explore** literature

Figure 5.8 Learning Standards for Each of Three Marking Periods

WEST ELEMENTARY SCHOOL	**MAYFIELD SCHOOL DISTRICT**	

REPORT CARD GRADE 4

The purpose of this report card is to describe students' learning progress to their parents and others, based on our school's end-of-year learning expectations for each grade level.

Student Name & Grade:	Cora Tyson, Grade 2	**ATTENDANCE**		
Teacher Name & Phone:	Linda Sahn, 6666-7777, ext. 19	**1**	**2**	**3**
Principal Name & Phone:	Jack Lyons, 666-7777, ext. 20			

MATHEMATICS 1ST REPORTING PERIOD	1	MATHEMATICS 2ND REPORTING PERIOD	2	MATHEMATICS 3RD REPORTING PERIOD	3
Understand the concepts of multiple and factor.		Determine if a whole number is a multiple or a factor of a given one-digit whole number.		Solve problems about factors and multiples, e.g., since 100 = 4 x 25 and 200 = 2 x 100, then 200 = 2 x 4 x 25 = 8 x 25.	
Multiply fluently any one-digit whole number by another one-digit whole number.		Multiply fluently any one-digit whole number by a two-digit whole number.		Multiply fluently any whole number by a one-digit number and a three-digit number by a two-digit number.	
Read and interpret decimals up to two decimal places; relate to money and place value decomposition.		Write tenths and hundredths in decimal and fraction forms and know the decimal equivalents for halves and fourths.		Locate and compare common fractions and decimals up to two places on the number line.	
Construct tables and bar graphs from given data.		Order a given set of data, find the median, and specify the range of values.		Solve problems/ compare data represented in two bar graphs and read bar graphs showing two data sets (double bar graphs).	

MATHEMATICS 1ST REPORTING PERIOD	1	MATHEMATICS 2ND REPORTING PERIOD	2	MATHEMATICS 3RD REPORTING PERIOD	3
Convert one unit of measure to a larger or smaller unit of measure: meters to centimeters and feet to inches.		Convert one unit of measure to a larger or smaller unit of: kilograms to grams, liters to milliliters, ounces to pounds.		Convert one unit of measure to a larger or smaller unit of measure: hours to minutes, minutes to seconds, years to months, weeks to days.	

When educators first began constructing standards-based report cards, the majority based their work on the district, state, or provincial curriculum frameworks that identified detailed curriculum standards for each grade level or course of study. Because these standards were specific to a grade level or course, most educators developed unique report cards for each grade. This meant that an elementary school with kindergarten through fifth-grade classes, for example, would have six different report cards, one for each grade level.

While a number of school districts today continue to have success with this approach, many others find it cumbersome to manage and confusing to parents. Some parents have trouble interpreting report cards that change every year their child is in school. In addition, parents with multiple children at the same school sometimes struggle to make sense of the report card when each child's is different.

To avoid these difficulties, most of the schools and school districts with which we work today use report cards that include more general reporting standards that are common across grade levels. They then develop a series of supplementary documents to accompany the report card that explain differences in the meaning of the standards from one grade level to the next. In addition to having hard copies of these supplementary documents available, schools and school districts typically post them on their Web sites so that parents can read the descriptions and download copies if they choose. Teachers frequently refer to these documents when discussing students' progress with parents, especially during parent-teacher conferences. In this way, teachers can offer parents highly prescriptive information and more specific guidance in helping their children.

Educators in schools and school districts that use common report cards across multiple grade levels find that the consistency not only facilitates communication with parents, it also simplifies the development process. In addition, it eases the transition from more traditional reporting forms, which tend to look much the same across multiple grades, to a standards-based report card.

Sometimes educators question how creating a single report card for multiple grade levels can make the process of developing a standards-based report card any easier. After all, it involves preparing not only a new report card but also the supplementary documents that must accompany the report card at each grade level. We find, however, that developing a single report card with the supplementary documents is, indeed, easier in almost every case. Most district, state, or provincial curriculum frameworks provide nearly all the detail necessary for preparing the supplementary documents, although rewording in more parent-friendly language is usually required. With the supplementary documents posted at school or district Web sites, parents have easy access at any time to the curriculum and learning goals for each grade level or marking period. In addition, unlike report cards, which have limited space available for descriptions of the standards, supplementary documents can be many pages in length, allowing educators to offer as much detail as needed to clarify the reporting standards meaning.

The one exception to this general trend of using common reporting forms across grade levels is a standards-based report card for the kindergarten level. Even schools and school districts that use a common report card in Grades 1 through 5 or 6 typically have a kindergarten report card that looks different. In most cases, the different approach to the kindergarten report card is due to a kindergarten curriculum that includes academic, social, and behavioral standards that are quite different from those of other grade levels. So regardless of whether development efforts focus on a different report card for each grade level or a common report card to be used across multiple grade levels, the kindergarten report card usually remains distinctive. Three examples of kindergarten standards-based report cards are illustrated in Figures 5.9, 5.10, and 5.11 (pages 93–101).

Figure 5.9   Example of Kindergarten Standards-Based Report Card

Public Schools of Petoskey
Kindergarten Progress Report
2008 – 2009

page 1 of 2

Student Name: _____
Date of Birth: _____
Days Absent: ___Oct ___Dec ___Mar ___June
Days Tardy: ___Oct ___Dec ___Mar ___June

Teacher Name: _____
Building: _____
Principal: _____
Special Services Teacher: _____

Social Development

(KEY:

1 = Consistently   2 = Sometimes   3 = Not Yet   X = Not Assessed At This Time)

I use materials carefully.

I stay on task.

I try my best.

I work and play cooperatively.

I show appropriate feelings.

Nov	March	June	Nov	March	June	Nov	March	June	Nov	March	June	Nov	March	June

(Continued)

Figure 5.9 (Continued)

I am a good listener during group instruction.

I participate in group activities.

I take care of my belongings.

I respect others, my school, and myself.

I make appropriate choices.

Nov	March	June	Nov	March	June	Nov	March	June	Nov	March	June	Nov	March	June

Comments:
October:
December:
March:
June:

KEY: 1 = Meets Standards   2 = Approaching Standards   3 = Below Standards   N = Not Assessed At This Time

Language Arts	Nov	Mar	June
Word Study Skills			
Recognize rhyme			
Produce rhyme			
Concepts of print			
Letter identification			
Sound identification			
Onset of words			
Blending of words			
Segmenting of words			
Count Syllables in words			
Recognize word wall words			
Pre-Reading Skills			
Retelling			
Comprehension			
Reading at grade level			

Mathematics	Nov	Mar	June
Number Skills			
Recognizes Numbers 1-10 11-20 21-30			
Demonstrates one-to-one correspondence to 30			
Counts to **101 by 1s**			
Counts to **100 by 10s**			
Counts to **30 by 5s**			
Counts to **10 by 2s**			
Writes numbers to **30** Nov writes to: Feb writes to: June writes to:			
Demonstrates: Simple addition Simple subtraction			

(Continued)

Figure 5.9 (Continued)

Language Arts	Nov	Mar	June
Writing Skills			
Print first name			
Print last name			

I am involved in creative writing. I am at the following stage:

☐ **Picture only**
☐ **Using random letters**
☐ **Using some beginning consonants**
☐ **Using multiple consonant sounds in word**
☐ **Write complete sentence**

	Nov	Mar	June
Kindergarten Skills			
Coloring			
Cutting			
Recognizes basic colors			
Holds pencil correctly			

Mathematics	Nov	Mar	June
Patterning Skills			
Recognizes and creates patterns: AB AABB ABC			
Geometry Skills			
Recognizes shapes (checked)			
Graphing Skills			
Makes and reads simple graphs			
Measurement Skills			
Tells time to the hour			
Measures length, area, and weight			

Essentials Classes:

Music			
Art			
Physical Education			

Figure 5.10   Example 2 of a Kindergarten Standards-Based Report Card

REPORT TO FAMILIES – KINDERGARTEN

Bellingham
Public Schools
...where *every* student learns

Student: (place label here)

MARKING KEY	
Exceeds Grade Level Standards	4
Meets Grade Level Standards	3
Is Making Adequate Progress Toward Grade Level Standards	2
Is Not Making Adequate Progress Toward Grade Level	1
Does Not Apply at this time	NA
Please see Supplementary Comments	SC

ATTENDANCE Y (Yes) N (No) IMP (Improving) SC (See Comments)	1st Semester	2nd Semester
Attendance/tardiness is affecting progress		
Days Present		
Days Absent		
Days Tardy		

READING EXPECTATIONS: *Students read from a variety of types of materials.*	1st Semester	2nd Semester
Skills and Strategies • Phonemic awareness – hears sounds in language. • Phonics – uses letter recognition, sound/symbol relationships. • Reading Strategies – matches spoken and written word.		
Meaning • Print awareness. • Recounts and/or retells information.		
Engagement in Reading		

DISTRICT READING STANDARD:	1st Semester	2nd Semester
Your child's level on Developmental Reading Assessment (DRA)	See progress report	
District standard level for Kindergarten	Level	2

WRITING EXPECTATIONS: *Students write in a variety of forms and for different audiences and purposes.*	1st Semester	2nd Semester
Uses steps of the writing process to organize own writing – plans, drafts, publishes.		
Print Awareness • Writes own name and familiar words. • Copies print from the environment. • Writes left/right, top/bottom.		
Traits of Writing		
Ideas and Content: Draws and/or writes to convey meaning.		
Conventions: Attempts phonetic spelling, writes upper/lower case letters, begins to use punctuation.		
Engagement in Writing		

MATHEMATICS EXPECTATIONS: *Students understand the basic concepts and procedures of mathematics.*	1st Semester	2nd Semester
Math Strands		
Number Sense		Y/N
Names numerals to 20.	See progress report	
Counts objects to 31.		
Matches numerals to sets of objects to 20.		
Explores addition/subtraction stories with up to 10 objects.		
Applies concepts of more than, less than; equal, not equal using objects.		
Recalls number combinations to 4.		
Patterns and Relationships		
Copies patterns using sounds, objects, symbols.		
Creates patterns (e.g., red, red, blue, orange) by June.		
Geometry		
Names geometric figures: circle, triangle, square, rectangle.		
Identifies three-dimensional objects as ball-shaped, box-shaped, can-shaped.		
Describes and compares geometric figures: corners, curves, position.		
Measurement		
Explores measurement with non-standard units.		
Uses comparative language (longer-shorter, heavier-lighter).		
Probability		
Collects and sorts data to answer questions.		
Predicts results.		

Figure 5.10 (Continued)

REPORT TO FAMILIES – KINDERGARTEN

SOCIAL STUDIES	1st Semester	2nd Semester
Participates		
Focus of Study:		

SCIENCE/HEALTH	1st Semester	2nd Semester
Participates		
Focus of Study:		

Y (Yes) N (No) IMP (Improving) SC (See Comments)	1st Semester	2nd Semester
ART		
Participates		
MUSIC		
Participates		
PHYSICAL EDUCATION		
Participates		

SKILLS AND BEHAVIORS THAT SUPPORT LEARNING		
Y (Yes) N (Needs more experience) SC (See Comments)	1st Semester	2nd Semester
SELF MONITORING		
Follows school/class rules.		
Accepts new situations.		
Is responsible for own things.		
Stays on task without supervision.		
Functions independently.		
Completes tasks in reasonable time.		
Works carefully.		
Shows positive attitude.		
Demonstrates self-confidence.		
Uses materials appropriately.		
Respects authority.		
LISTENING AND SPEAKING		
Is attentive to speaker and discussions.		
Responds appropriately to oral directions.		
Makes relevant contributions to discussions.		
Listens without interrupting others.		
Seeks help when needed.		
Shares ideas willingly.		
PURPOSEFUL PLAY		
Communicates with others during play.		
Verbalizes feelings rather than acting out.		
Resolves own conflicts.		
Problem solves with respect to others' needs.		
Works and plays cooperatively with others.		
Respects property of others.		
Transitions to and from play situations.		
Makes appropriate play choices.		
Follows playground rules.		
Engages with materials and sustains play.		
Shares in clean-up.		

1st Semester

_____
Teacher Signature

_____
Date

2nd Semester

_____
Teacher Signature

_____
Date

STUDENT IS ASSIGNED TO THE _____ GRADE NEXT YEAR.

Figure 5.11 Example 3 of a Kindergarten Standards-Based Report Card

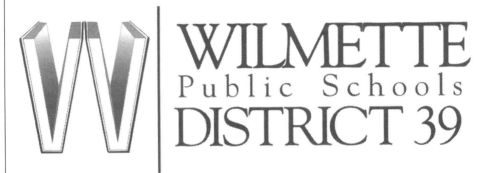

Report Card - 08-09 Year

Student Name: SAMPLE

Grade: Kindergarten

Days Absent:

School Name: My School

Teacher: SAMPLE

**Days Tardy: (For morning kindergarteners): 0;
(For afternoon kindergarteners): 0**

The purpose of the District 39 Reporting System is to provide a communication framework among students, parents/guardians, teachers, and administrators that fosters each student's lifelong academic growth and character development.

(Continued)

Figure 5.11 (Continued)

MY School Report Card

SAMPLE
Teacher: SAMPLE

April 3, 2009

Process Descriptors		
3 - Consistently	**2 - Sometimes**	**1 - Seldom**

Characteristics of Successful Learners		Spring	Comments
Inter-personal Skills	Works cooperatively in groups		Spring:
	Demonstrates self-confidence		
	Manages impulsivity		
	Self-advocates		
	Demonstrates flexible attitude		
	Respects and organizes materials		
Work Skills	Listens actively		
	Follows directions		
	Is a self-directed learner		
	Demonstrates persistence		
	Strives for personal best		

Skill Descriptors		
S - Secure	**D - Developing**	**B - Beginning**
+ A "plus" symbol on a continuum indicates competency in the indicated skill area		

Motor Skills		Spring	Comments
Large Motor	Uses playground equipment appropriately		Spring:
	Respects personal space		
Small Motor	Uses proper scissor grip		
	Uses proper pencil grip		
	Demonstrates self-care skills		
	Uses learning manipulatives appropriately		

Mathematics		Spring	Comments
Number Sense	Counts objects using one-to-one correspondence		Spring:
	Recognizes numbers		
	Counts in number sequence		
	"Skip counts" by 10		
	Identifies greater and lesser values of numbers		
Patterns and Geometry	Recognizes patterns		
	Completes patterns with missing elements		
	Generates patterns		
	Identifies basic geometric shapes		
Computation	Manipulates objects to show addition		
	Manipulates objects to show subtraction		
	Recognizes mathematical symbols for addition and subtraction		

Harper School Report Card

SAMPLE

Teacher: SAMPLE

April 3, 2009

Reading

Fluency Continuum

Skills	Looks at books independently	Reads using illustrations and/or memory	Understands that written words have meaning	Tracks print from left-to-right, top-to-bottom, front-to-back	Recognizes beginning sight words	Decodes simple words (c-a-t)	Reads simple texts independently
Spring							

Comprehension Continuum

Skills	Listens and enjoys stories read aloud	Connects stories read aloud to personal experiences	Discusses characters and events in stories	Identifies the main ideas of stories	Retells simple stories
Spring					

Letter Recognition

	Spring	Spring:
Recognizes upper case letters		
Recognizes lower case letters		
Associates corresponding letters with their sounds		

Skills	Uses pictures to convey meaning	Uses random "letter strings" to represent words	Uses the initial sounds of words to represent whole words	Uses initial and final consonant sounds of words to represent whole words	Writes words phonetically	Writes simple words conventionally
Spring						

Spring:

4. How many reporting standards will be included for each subject area or course?

The next major decision that must be addressed is how many standards will be reported in each subject area. This is a particularly crucial decision because it clarifies what is expected of students and what educators most value. It also influences many structural aspects of the report card and has important implications for teachers' record keeping.

In developing standards-based report cards, educators typically include far too many standards described in too much detail. Some do this because they base their report card on state or provincial standards. But as we described in the preceding chapter, state and provincial standards are designed to help educators plan instruction and design appropriate assessments, not to report student achievement or progress. They are typically too many in number and not expressed in parent-friendly language. Other educators are overreacting to traditional report cards, which require teachers to combine a wide variety of diverse elements of learning into a single grade. In an effort to offer more meaningful information, they construct a highly detailed reporting form that requires a separate grade or mark for an exceptionally large number of highly specific standards. This upsets teachers, who then must maintain comprehensive records for every student on each of those minute standards. It also frustrates parents, who struggle to make sense of so much detail.

Deciding how many standards to report in each subject area is best accomplished through a three-step process.

1. *The standards must be categorized as reflecting product, process, or progress goals.* Since nearly all content and performance standards included in district, state, or provincial curriculum frameworks fall into the product category, this rarely presents a problem. Distinguishing the specific process and progress goals to report can prove a bit more challenging, and we will deal with that later in the chapter.

2. *The exact reporting standards in each subject area that will be included on the report card must be identified.* As we described in Chapter 4, for product goals, educators typically must translate the highly detailed content and performance standards outlined in curriculum frameworks to broader and more general reporting standards.

3. *The reporting standards must be worded in clear, precise, and parent-friendly language.*

STEPS IN DECIDING HOW MANY STANDARDS TO REPORT

1. Categorize standards as reflecting product, process, or progress goals.

2. Identify specific reporting standards for each subject area.

3. Word the standards in clear, precise, and parent-friendly language.

As we emphasized earlier, an important balance must be struck when considering what reporting standards to include in each subject area. Specifically, the reporting standards must offer enough information to be meaningful but not so much that they confuse or overwhelm. In our experience, listing four to six reporting standards related to product goals in each subject area tends to be ideal. Fewer than four requires blending multiple elements, often confounding their meaning. More than six, however, tends to make the information too complicated and much more difficult to remember. As we described in Chapter 4, most people can keep track of four to six elements. Seven tests the upper limit of recall, and nine is simply too many.

We recognize, of course, that limiting standards-based report cards to only four to six reporting standards in each subject area represents a departure from nearly all standards-related documents. The National Council of Teachers of Mathematics's *Principles and Standards for School Mathematics* (2000), for example, includes ten areas of standards. The first five describe goals in mathematics content related to number and operations, algebra, geometry, measurement, and data analysis and probability. The second five describe the mathematics processes of problem solving, reasoning and proof, connections, communication, and representation (see http://standards .nctm.org/document/chapter3/index.htm). For reporting purposes, these content divisions seem ideal.

The *processes* then might then be included under each of the content areas, depending on their appropriateness at each grade level or in particular courses. Regardless of the strategy used in deciding what reporting standards to include, however, our experience indicates that keeping to four to six standards in each subject area works best when reporting to parents.

IMPORTANT NOTE

An effective standards-based report card lists four to six reporting standards related to product (achievement) goals for each subject area.

So in developing a standards-based report card, how many math, science, or social studies reporting standards should be listed on the report card? Answer: Four to six in each subject area.

In addition to adhering to a manageable number of reporting standards, it is important that developers agree on reporting standards that best represent the major concepts and skills students need to master for each subject area in the curriculum. Figure 5.12 shows examples of several possible reporting standards for math, science, and social studies. This list was compiled after reviewing dozens of standards-based report cards from across the United States and Canada. While these lists represent many more standards than we advocate using for reporting purposes, we include them here just to show the variation in reporting standards that exists.

Figure 5.12   Possible Reporting Standards for Math, Science, and Social Studies

Mathematics	Science	Social Studies

• Recognizes and writes numerals correctly
• Counts 1 to ___
• Knows basic math facts and performs operations proficiently for
   Addition
   Subtraction
   Multiplication
   Division
• Recognizes patterns and relationships among numbers
• Makes mental calculations and reasonable estimates
• Uses appropriate strategies to solve problems
• Chooses the correct operation (+, −, etc.) to solve problems
• Collects, organizes, and analyzes data
• Knows basic geometric shapes
• Uses geometry correctly to solve problems
• Measures accurately
• Creates accurate graphs
• Interprets graphs correctly
• Uses a calculator effectively
• Can predict the probability of events
• Can solve simple algebraic equations
	• Uses steps in the scientific method:
	   • Forms questions or hypotheses to explain events
	   • Performs experiments to solve problems
	   • Carefully observes and records data
	   • Summarizes and explains results
	• Understands basic concepts and ideas in (*name or topic of science unit*)
	• Correctly uses various scientific instruments and measurement tools
	• Reads or listens for information in science text
	• Questions results in experiments
	• Writes complete lab reports
	• Completes required sketches accurately
	• Learns and understands vocabulary specific to science
		• Demonstrates knowledge of local, state, U.S., or world history
		• Understands geography and its effect on society
		• Uses maps and globes effectively
		• Recognizes and understands basic civic responsibilities and values in a democracy
		• Understands the function of basic economic systems
		• Demonstrates understanding of current events
		• Reads or listens for information in social studies text
		• Learns and comprehends vocabulary specific to social studies
		• Sequences events chronologically
		• Participates in discussions about current events or social studies concepts

Language arts offers the one exception. Many school districts, states, and provinces divide their language arts standards into individual strands or subcategories related to reading, writing, speaking, and listening/viewing. In such cases, it would be appropriate to include on the report card four to six reporting standards in each of these subcategories. An example of these subcategories is illustrated in Figure 5.13.

One drawback to this approach is that it gives language arts the lion's share of space on the report card: limiting all other subject areas to four to six reporting standards but allowing language arts to include a comparable number in each of four subcategories could make the language arts section of the report card four times larger than any other section. Parents and others might interpret this to mean that educators consider language arts to be four times more important than any other subject (these format issues are discussed in more detail in Chapter 6). Yet because of the strong emphasis on language arts skills, especially in the primary and early elementary grades, and the foundational value of language arts to learning in other subjects, most educators find such an emphasis to be fitting.

Figure 5.13   Sample Reporting Standards for Language Arts Subcategories

Reading	Writing	Speaking	Listening/Viewing
• Uses a variety of word attack ("sounding out") skills • Reads fluently • Comprehends grade-level text, fiction, and nonfiction • Retells story with beginning, middle, and end • Reads different types of literature • Understands basic literary and story elements	• Writes legibly for a variety of purposes • Uses the steps in the writing process effectively • Uses proper grammar and mechanics (punctuation, capitalization, etc.) • Uses correct spelling • Organizes information effectively • Communicates own unique "voice" in personal writing	• Communicates ideas clearly and effectively in oral presentations • Speaks appropriately to different audiences • Asks pertinent questions • Speaks clearly with proper volume • Contributes ideas or information in group interactions	• Listens for and understands information from various sources • Follows oral directions (simple or multistep) • Listens actively without interrupting • Demonstrates good eye contact • Views pictures or videos and comprehends main ideas

Reporting standards related to process and progress goals are typically limited to about four to six as well. Some standards-based report cards list process and progress standards just once in a special section on the report card. Figures 5.3, 5.6, and 5.10 show examples of this format. Many of the educators with whom we have worked, however, consider it important to offer separate marks for these standards in each subject or course. Especially at the secondary level, teachers note that students often display drastically different study skills and work habits in different subject areas and courses. Therefore, they prefer to list standards related to process and progress goals with *each* subject area or course of study, even if these standards are exactly the same. Chapter 8 includes several examples of report cards that use this format.

5. What specific reporting standards will be reported at each grade level or in each course?

After deciding the number of reporting standards to include on the report card in each subject area, we next must determine what those standards will be. Reporting standards should always be clear, simple, and succinct. As we have described, they should be precise enough to communicate the knowledge and skills students are expected to acquire but not so detailed that they lose their meaning and usefulness when shared with parents and students.

Many of the examples of the reporting standards shown earlier in this chapter, as well as those included in later chapters, were derived from the strands or domains used to categorize standards in various district, state, or provincial curriculum frameworks. If suitable and relatively few in number, these often work well. Reporting standards drawn directly from these well-known curriculum documents ease teachers' transition to standards-based reporting. They also serve to facilitate the alignment of instruction, assessment, and reporting in teachers' classrooms.

In some cases, however, curriculum framework categories need to be revised and reworded. When making these revisions, foremost in mind should be the goal of effective communication. Developers at all levels must seek that crucial balance between providing enough detail to give a concise picture of students' performance in relation to specific learning goals but not so much that it overwhelms or confuses parents and students.

How Question 3 was answered will provide additional guidance. Recall that Question 3 asked, "Will a specific report card be developed for each grade level, or will a more general report card be used across several grade levels?" Deciding on a report card that includes highly specific reporting standards unique to each grade level will take developers in one direction. Choosing more general reporting standards common across several grade levels will take them in quite another. Chapter 7 includes examples of both of these approaches. The key to success is to keep in mind this caution to those seeking to explain complex phenomena, widely attributed to Albert Einstein: "Things should be made as simple as possible, but not any simpler."

6. Will standards be set for the grade level or each marking period?

On the surface, this seems a simple question with a straightforward answer. Nearly all content and performance standards are based on what we want students to know and be able to do as a result of their learning experiences at a specific grade level, over an academic semester or year, or in a particular course of study. Reporting standards, therefore, should reflect that same orientation. But this issue is a bit more complicated than most educators anticipate.

In constructing a standards-based report card, educators typically rely on learning goals or standards specific to a grade level or course of study. To interpret a reporting form based on grade-level standards accurately, however, parents must make one of two assumptions. Either

(a) each standard has one level of difficulty or complexity set for that grade level, and students are expected to meet the standard at that level before the end of the academic year; or
(b) each standard increases in its difficulty or complexity each marking period during the academic year, and students are expected to meet a new, more complex level each time.

Unfortunately, most educators *develop* standards-based report cards in reference to assumption (a), but most parents *interpret* those reporting forms on the basis of assumption (b). For example, if the standard states, "Students will write clearly and effectively," many parents believe their child should be doing this each marking period, not simply moving toward being able to do it by the end of the academic year. This is especially true of parents who encourage their children to attain the highest grade or mark possible in all courses or subject areas every marking period (see Guskey, 2002b).

To the educators using such forms, students who receive a mark of 1 or 2 for performance on a four-point grading scale during the first or second marking period of the school year are doing just fine. They are making appropriate progress and are on track for their grade level. But to many parents, a report card filled with 1s and 2s, when the highest mark is a 4, is cause for great concern. They believe that their child is failing. While including a statement on the reporting form such as "Marks indicate progress toward end-of-the-year learning standards," is helpful, it may not be enough to alleviate parents' concerns.

This dilemma is compounded if report cards list the same standards for multiple grade levels, a possibility we outlined under Question #3. In such cases, the standards listed on the reporting form for first grade are the same as those listed for second grade, and so on. While this eliminates the need for a different report card with different learning goals or reporting standards for every grade level, it requires parents to make different assumptions about the standards within a grade level than they make across grade levels. Interpretations within a grade level are to be based on assumption (a). But since exactly the same standards are listed on the reporting form for multiple levels, interpretations across grade levels are to be based on assumption (b). In other words, each standard maintains the same level of complexity across marking periods within a grade level, but it increases in complexity from one grade level to the next. Helping parents to understand this difference can prove exceptionally challenging for teachers and school leaders.

The problem for report card developers thus becomes how to facilitate appropriate interpretation. The typical response of parents when they first view a standards-based report card filled with various marks and numbers is to turn to the teacher and say, "This is great! But tell me, how is my child doing?" or, "What 'grade' would this be?" or, "How is my child doing compared to the other children in the class?" The reason they ask these questions is that they are uncertain how to interpret the information the report card contains and their only reference for comparison is what they experienced when they were in school.

Few parents have had any personal experience in standards-based learning environments. The educational experiences of most parents were in classes that used comparative, norm-based reporting systems instead of criteria- or standards-based systems. Their learning success was judged not in terms of specific learning goals but rather in terms of how they compared to their classmates. As a result, parents tend to be much more familiar with reports that compare each student to the other students in the class. They know and understand far less about reports that compare each student's progress to established learning standards and performance criteria.

The bottom line is that parents want to be able to make sense of the information provided in the report card. Their greatest fear is that their child will reach the end of the school year and will not have made sufficient progress to be promoted to the next grade. To ensure this does not happen, parents want accurate information that they can use to judge the adequacy of their child's progress. They also want that information as early as possible and regularly thereafter.

To prevent parental confusion and ensure accurate interpretations, developers can take one of two paths. The first is to establish quarterly goals, as we discussed earlier in this chapter. In that way, grades or marks on the report card represent students' achievement of the goals or standards set for that marking period. This works well so long as the use of "quarterly goals" or "marking period goals" is made clear in the stated purpose of the report card (see Chapter 3).

The second path, chosen by many developers, is to use a *two-part marking system* (Guskey, 2001a). With this system, each student receives two marks for each standard every marking period.

1. The first mark indicates the student's level of proficiency *with regard to the standard*. In this case, that mark might be a 1, 2, 3, or 4, indicating "Beginning," "Progressing," "Proficient," or "Exceptional."

2. The second mark relates that level of proficiency to established expectations for students' performance *at this time in the school year*. For example, a ++ might indicate "Advanced for grade-level expectations," a + might indicate "On target" or "Meeting grade-level expectations," and a – might indicate "Below grade-level expectations" or "In need of improvement."

An example of such a reporting form, adapted from one used in the Bellevue School District in Bellevue, Washington, is illustrated in Figure 5.14.

The advantage of this two-part marking system is that it helps parents make sense of the information included in the report card each marking period. It also helps alleviate their concerns about what

Figure 5.14	Example of a Standards-Based Double-Mark Reporting Form

Elementary Progress Report					
Student: **T. Nedutsa**			Grade: **1**		
Teacher: **Ms. Rotnem**	School: **Bloom Elementary**		Year:		

This report is based on grade-level standards established for each subject area. The ratings indicate your student's progress in relation to the year-end standard.

Evaluation Marks	Level Expectation Marks	Work Habits & Effort Marks
4 = Exceptional	++ = Advanced	E = Exceptional
3 = Meets Standard	+ = On Level	S = Satisfactory
2 = Approaches Standard	– = Below Level	U = Unsatisfactory
1 = Beginning Standard		
N = Not Assessed		

Reading	1st	2nd	3rd	4th
Understands and uses different skills and strategies to read	1+	2++		
Understands the meaning of what is read	1++	2+		
Reads different materials for a variety of purposes	1+	2–		
Reading Level	1++	2++		
Work Habits	S	S		
Writing	1st	2nd	3rd	4th
Writes clearly and effectively	1++	2++		
Understands and uses the steps in the writing process	1++	2++		
Writes in a variety of forms for different audiences and purposes	1+	2–		
Analyzes and evaluates the effectiveness of written work	N	1+		
Understands and uses the conventions of writing: punctuation, capitalization, spelling, and legibility	1–	2–		
Work Habits	S	S		
Communication	1st	2nd	3rd	4th
Uses listening and observational skills to gain understanding	1+	2–		
Communicates ideas clearly and effectively (formal communication)	1–	2+		
Uses communication strategies and skills to work effectively with others (informal communication)	N	1+		
Work Habits	U	S		

SOURCE: Guskey, T. R., & Bailey, J. M. (2001). *Developing Grading Reporting Systems for Student Learning.* Thousand Oaks, CA: Corwin.

they might perceive as "low grades" and lets them know if their child is progressing at a rate considered appropriate for the grade level. In addition, it helps parents take a standards-based perspective in viewing their child's performance. Their question is no longer "Where is my child in comparison to his or her classmates?" but rather "Where is my child in relation to the learning goals and expectations set for this level?" It may be, for example, that all students in the class are doing exceptionally well and progressing at a rate considered "Advanced" in terms of grade-level expectations. This would not be possible, of course, in a norm-referenced system, where even those students who are "Advanced" in relation to their classmates might be doing poorly in relation to grade-level expectations. Schools and school districts that use the two-part marking system generally find that parents like the additional information and believe it adds to the communicative value of reporting forms.

An important challenge in implementing the two-part marking system is maintaining flexibility to accommodate individual differences in children's cognitive skill development. Because children in any class differ in chronological age and cognitive development, some might not meet the specified criteria during a particular marking period, even though they are likely do so before the end of the year. This is especially common in kindergarten and the early primary grades, where students tend to vary widely in their entry-level skills but can make very rapid learning progress (Shuster, Lynch, & Polson-Lorczak, 1996). Flexibility is also important when evaluating the performance of students with special learning needs (see Guskey & Jung, 2006, 2009; Jung & Guskey, 2007). Developmental differences must be taken into consideration by educators and thoroughly explained to parents to avert their concerns.

So while we recommend the use of a two-part marking system, we always emphasize sensitivity to cognitive developmental differences. Teachers at all levels must take these differences into account when assigning grades or marks to the performance of their students. By doing so, they ensure that grading and reporting remain informative and helpful and never become stifling or punitive.

7. What specific process and progress standards will be reported?

Earlier we discussed how important it is to consider the reporting standards' degree of specificity. The reporting standards listed on the report card identify what students should know and be able to do as a result of their learning experiences in school. Standards that are too specific create record-keeping nightmares for teachers and make reporting forms too complicated for most parents to understand. Standards that are too broad or general, on the other hand, make it difficult to identify students' particular strengths or areas of difficulty.

Developing appropriate reporting standards related to product goals is a fairly straightforward process that most educators can accomplish with modest effort. The highly detailed academic content or performance standards included in most curriculum frameworks must be integrated and synthesized into four to six clear and concise reporting standards. This requires finding an appropriate balance between providing sufficient detail to describe student learning adequately but not so much detail that it diminishes the report card's usefulness as a communication tool. Several modern volumes offer educators guidance on developing standards that meet this critical balance (e.g., Gronlund, 2000; Marzano & Kendall, 1995; Wiggins & McTighe, 2005).

Reporting Standards Related to Process Goals

Identifying the reporting standards related to process and progress goals usually proves more challenging. Across schools and school districts, the process standards included on report cards vary widely. Listed in the box below are some of those most commonly considered (see Cizek et al., 1996; Cross & Frary, 1996; McMillan, 2001; McMillan & Nash, 2000).

REPORTING STANDARDS RELATED TO PROCESS GOALS

- Daily Work in Class
- Notebook or Journal Completion
- Class Quizzes or Spot-Checks
- Work Habits
- Neatness of Work
- Homework (Completion and Quality)
- Punctuality of Assignments

- Class Participation
- Class Attendance
- Class Punctuality
- Cooperation With Classmates
- Class Behavior or Attitude
- Effort

The most challenging aspect of reporting on process goals is establishing clear performance criteria or assessment rubrics for their evaluation. As we described in Chapter 4, some process goals relate to student behaviors that can be easily observed. Ascribing different levels of performance to such behavioral standards poses little difficulty since performance levels typically relate to simple frequency. Indicators for a process goal standard related to "Punctuality of Assignments," for example, might include the following:

4—All assignments turned in on the day they are due

3—Only one or two assignments turned in late

2—Three to five assignments turned in late

1—Multiple assignments turned in late or not at all

Other process goal behaviors, however, are more difficult to observe directly and, therefore, require more careful attention. Differences related to quantity versus quality can be particularly troublesome. In evaluating "Class Participation," for example, teachers must distinguish between students who frequently offer their opinions in class discussions but rarely demonstrate careful reasoning or deep understanding and other students who may speak rarely in class but, when they do, show thoughtfulness and keen insight.

Similarly, judging students' "Effort" can challenge the most discerning teachers. To record an accurate mark for "Effort," teachers must correctly distinguish between students who sincerely try hard and those who may act involved but are simply compliant or "faking it." Establishing clear performance criteria for making these distinctions can be exceptionally difficult. But doing so is essential if marks associated with such process goals are to be reported. Figure 5.15 shows examples of reporting standards related to process goals.

Figure 5.15 Sample Reporting Standards for Selected Process Goals

Independence and Initiative	Work Completion and Work Habits	Cooperation and Participation	Goal Setting and Problem Solving
• Attends regularly and is punctual • Completes tasks and assignments on time and with care • Follows routines and instructions without supervision	• Follows directions and completes tasks in class • Completes homework on time and with care • Uses time efficiently • Attends to the task at hand • Seeks assistance when necessary	• Participates in and contributes to class and group activities • Accepts responsibilities within the class and group • Shows respect for the ideas of others in the class and group • Listens without interrupting others	• Applies logic in solving problems • Identifies strengths and areas for improvement in own work and sets goals • Identifies specific steps to reach goals or improve • Evaluates own success in reaching goals

(Continued)

| Figure 5.15 | (Continued) |

Independence and Initiative	Work Completion and Work Habits	Cooperation and Participation	Goal Setting and Problem Solving
• Accepts responsibility for own behavior • Adheres to established time lines • Investigates and obtains information independently	• Attends regularly and is punctual • Works well without supervision • Persists with tasks to achieve quality work • Organizes and manages work effectively	• Follows classroom and school rules • Helps others and shares • Respects the opinions and property of others • Works and plays cooperatively with others • Seeks positive solutions to conflicts	• Perseveres to achieve goals

Reporting Standards Related to Progress Goals

Reporting standards related to progress goals pose a different but comparably thorny challenge. To report on students' progress requires a clearly articulated sequence of learning tasks or objectives along with assessment procedures to document students' advancement accurately. With these, a trajectory of each student's development can be mapped and reported along with the teacher's judgment of the adequacy of that development. In the absence of such a learning sequence and well-aligned assessments, however, reporting on progress goals is generally handled through a written narrative in which teachers describe the particular improvements students have made and the significance of that level of progress.

Reporting progress requires significant specification of learning tasks or goals accompanied by assessment procedures to follow student achievement along that learning progression. Narrative reporting, as long as it provides sufficient detail to inform parents of the extent and adequacy of students' progress, can also serve this purpose well.

Summary

Developing an effective standards-based report card requires that a set of crucial questions be addressed in specific order. Following are the seven crucial questions discussed in this chapter:

1. What is the purpose of the report card?

2. How often will report cards be completed and sent home?

3. Will a specific report card be developed for each grade level, or will a more general report card be used across several grade levels?

4. How many reporting standards will be included for each subject area or course?

5. What specific reporting standards will be included at each grade level or in each course?

6. Will standards be set for the grade level or each marking period?

7. What specific process and progress standards will be reported?

Answering each of these questions with forethought, attention to detail, and careful consideration of the implications of the answers is essential to the success of development efforts and the achievement of the communication goals of standards-based reporting.

6

Essential Steps in Development: Part II

In Chapter 5, we began our discussion of the steps involved in developing a standards-based report card. We described essential issues that must be considered and crucial questions that need to be addressed at each step. In this chapter, we continue that discussion, building on those steps that we outlined earlier. Here, however, we extend our conversation to the practical and functional aspects of standards-based report card format and design. In addition, we explore several issues vital to successful implementation.

Additional Crucial Questions in the Development Process

Although efforts to develop standards-based report cards must always be adapted to fit the contextual characteristics of individual schools and school districts, certain crucial questions need to be addressed to achieve success. As we stressed in the last chapter, these crucial questions relate to *explicit decisions* that must be made by those involved in the development process. Furthermore, these questions must be addressed in *specific order,* since each has important implications for all of the questions that follow. Admittedly, some of these questions may seem trivial or insignificant. Our experience shows, however, that failing to address any of these questions can seriously threaten the success of further development work.

In this chapter, we carry forward our discussion from Chapter 5 by describing eight additional crucial questions and offering detailed recommendations for answering each. The crucial questions to be addressed are listed in the box below.

EIGHT ADDITIONAL CRUCIAL QUESTIONS TO ADDRESS IN DEVELOPING STANDARDS-BASED REPORT CARDS

8. How many levels of performance will be reported for each standard?

9. How will the levels be labeled?

10. Will teachers' comments be included and encouraged?

11. How will information be arranged on the report card?

12. What are parents expected to do with this information?

13. What are students expected to do with this information?

14. What policies need to accompany the new reporting procedures?

15. When should input of parents and/or students be sought?

We want to emphasize again that our recommendations for answering these questions come from our experiences working with educators involved in the challenging task of developing standards-based report cards. But please do not consider these recommendations to be absolute and unquestionable. Adaptations may be necessary, and lots of exceptions exist. As the popular line from the film *Pirates of the Caribbean* makes clear, "These are not really *rules* but more like *guidelines*!"

The decisions made by one group of educators in a particular context may suit their situation well and result in highly successful implementation. The same decisions made by another group of educators in a different context could lead to disaster. If unexpected difficulties arise at any point in the decision-making process, then earlier decisions may need to be revisited, different choices considered, and development procedures begun again. The key to success is *always to remain guided by your purpose.* No matter what difficulties you experience, work to maintain a clear focus on effective communication and an unyielding commitment to do what is in the best interests of students. There are numerous pathways to success in this process, and no one way serves all developers equally well. Openness to alternatives, as long as they are in line with your purpose and what works best for your students, will be essential to achieving your goals.

8. How many levels of performance will be reported for each standard?

After deciding what reporting standards to include for each subject area or course of study on the report card, and then determining what specific performance criteria students need to meet to demonstrate their proficiency with or mastery of those standards, the next step is to identify graduated levels of performance, or benchmarks, on the way to achieving each goal or standard. Sometimes labeled "learning progressions" (Heritage, 2007), these levels allow teachers to locate students' current status on the learning continuum along which they are expected to progress. This typically requires establishing three or four identifiable steps, or subgoals, in students' progress toward mastery of each standard.

No hard rules apply about the best number of levels or steps to report. In addition, to our knowledge, no strong research exists as to what number of levels is preferred or ideal. Studies have shown, however, that while teachers typically gather sufficient information to make dichotomous decisions—that is, mastery or nonmastery—about students' performance in relation to particular standards, they seldom have enough valid information to determine performance accurately across multiple classifications (Smith, 2003). The same is true when classifying students' performance on large-scale assessments (see Norman & Buckendahl, 2008).

For this reason, national assessment programs in many countries classify student performance in only two or three levels. In New Zealand, for example, student performance on each standard measured in the national assessment program is scored as "Not Pass," "Pass," or "Exemplary" (see Guskey, Smith, Smith, Crooks, & Flockton, 2006). Similarly, the National Assessment of Educational Progress (NAEP) uses just three levels of classification: "Basic," "Proficient," and "Advanced" (2008). Nevertheless, in states, provinces, and districts throughout North America, classifying students' performance in four or five different levels is much more common.

How these four or five levels are structured tends to follow a fairly consistent pattern. The first step is to establish clear criteria for proficient performance or mastery of the standard. In most cases, this is labeled "Level 3" performance. The next step is to develop criteria that represent two distinct lower levels of performance, labeled "Level 1" and "Level 2." Occasionally, three lower levels are defined. These levels describe specific steps in students' progress toward proficiency or mastery of the standard. Finally, criteria for a higher "Level 4" performance are specified to recognize those students who display truly exceptional accomplishment or skill with regard to the standard.

Most report cards also include an additional category to identify goals or standards *not addressed* or *not considered* during a particular marking period. A letter or other symbol is assigned in the legend to represent this category. Including such a category helps parents understand that the goal or standard is important but not measured or assessed at this time. Parents often interpret goals or standards left unmarked as something the teacher forgot or missed. This is true even when the report card clearly states that "standards left unmarked were not considered during the marking period." By including a category and special designation for those standards not addressed, every standard receives a mark every time the report card is completed. In this way, parents will know that nothing has been missed or neglected.

The most important part of this process, however, is describing the precise meaning of each level or category. Parents and students need to know exactly what is expected and where each student stands in relation to those expectations. A student whose performance is judged to be at Level 2 needs to know specifically what he or she must do to reach Level 3. Similarly, those at Level 3 should have a clear understanding of what would represent Level 4 performance. Sharing examples of students' work that exemplify each level in this progression not only helps clarify expectations, it also guides parents and students in planning improvements and charting progress.

9. How will the levels be labeled?

Along with identifying graduated levels of performance for each reporting standard, specific names or labels must be assigned to those levels. These names or labels should aptly describe students' learning status and level of progress to their parents, others, and to the students themselves. But selecting labels that clearly communicate the meaning of these levels can sometimes prove tricky.

To determine what labels educators currently use to convey different levels of students' learning progress, we recently collected labels from standards-based report cards drawn from a nonrandom sample of school districts throughout the United States and Canada (see Guskey, 2004). We also gathered the labels used to denote different levels of student performance in a number of state assessment programs and several well-known standardized assessment programs. Next we grouped these labels into general categories based on our judgments of their intended meaning. While most judgments were easy to make, the distinction between categories involving "understanding," "quality," "mastery," and "proficiency" proved particularly troublesome and remains open to discussion. The labels we gathered and their projected categories are displayed below.

INDICATORS OF STUDENT PERFORMANCE

1. **Levels of Understanding/Quality**

Modest	Beginning	Novice	Unsatisfactory
Intermediate	Progressing	Apprentice	Needs Improvement
Proficient	Adequate	Proficient	Satisfactory
Superior	Exemplary	Distinguished	Outstanding

2. **Levels of Mastery/Proficiency**

Below Basic	Below Standard	Pre-emergent	Incomplete
Basic	Approaching Standard	Emerging	Limited
Proficient	Meets Standard	Acquiring	Partial
Advanced	Exceeds Standard	Extending	Thorough

3. **Frequency of Display**

Rarely	Never
Occasionally	Seldom
Frequently	Usually
Consistently	Always

4. **Degree of Effectiveness**

Ineffective	Poor
Moderately Effective	Acceptable
Highly Effective	Excellent

5. **Evidence of Accomplishment**

   Little or No Evidence
   Partial Evidence
   Sufficient Evidence
   Extensive Evidence

Finally, we shared these labels with groups of parents of school-age children in structured focus groups, asking them to identify which labels made sense and which did not. Their responses were amazingly consistent, highly informative, and in some cases, quite surprising.

We found that parents generally interpreted the labels based on their personal experiences with grading and reporting. Since most parents' experiences with grades tend to be restricted to letter grades, most parents immediately translated each label to a letter grade. So, for example, "Advanced" meant A, "Proficient" meant B, and so on. Regardless of the labels used, parents infer meaning from what they understand, and most parents understand letter grades—or at least believe they do.

By and large, parents also interpreted the labels from a norm-referenced perspective. Again, probably as a result of their personal experiences in schools where grades were based on each student's relative standing among classmates, parents interpreted the labels similarly. So to many parents, "Basic" and "Intermediate" implied "average" or "in the middle of the class."

After explaining to parents that these labels were designed to communicate students' learning progress with regard to specific learning goals or standards, rather than to designate a student's standing among classmates, we asked parents to identify the labels that seemed clearer or more meaningful. Most of the labels received mixed responses from parents, with no particular set clearly preferred. Certain labels, however, were singled out by parents as confusing or meaningless.

Parents were especially baffled by the labels "Pre-emergent" and "Emerging." Several replied jokingly that "Emerging" conveyed images of "a slimy creature coming out of a swamp." When we indicated that "Emerging" generally implies "Beginning," they responded, "If you mean 'Beginning,' why not just use 'Beginning'?"

Another label parents found particularly puzzling was "Exceeds Standard." Labels such as "Advanced," "Exemplary," "Distinguished," and "Outstanding" all seemed to have clearer meaning. Parents understood how specific expectations or criteria for judging performance might be set for students at these levels. But to many parents, "Exceeds Standard" was especially vague and imprecise. Several interpreted it as meaning "something more than what's expected, but we're unsure just what that might be."

To improve the usefulness and communicative value of standards-based report cards, we need to ensure that parents and others understand the information included. As we stressed earlier, we also must acknowledge that if parents do not understand the information in the report card, it's not their fault. As communicators, it is our responsibility to make sure that our message is clear and comprehensible to those for whom it is intended. This is the communication challenge involved in developing a standards-based report card.

Guidelines for Choosing Clear Indicators of Student Performance

In describing different levels of students' performance with regard to learning goals or standards, therefore, we need to choose labels that are expressive, precise, and meaningful. The following four guidelines should help in that effort:

1. *Avoid comparative language.* Because parents so often interpret grades in terms of norm-referenced comparisons, where their child's performance is judged relative to classmates, adjusting to a standards-based, criterion-referenced system can be particularly difficult. The transition is made all the more challenging when educators use comparative labels such as "Below Average," "Average," or "Superior." Instead, the labels used should always relate to clearly stated performance indicators that communicate where students stand in reference to specific expectations for their learning. This helps parents change their perspective of grading from "How is my child doing compared to other students in the class?" to "How is my child doing with regard to the learning standards and expectations set for this level?"

2. *Provide examples based on student work.* One of the best ways to promote understanding and to facilitate parents' transition from norm-referenced comparisons to standards-based reporting is to provide clear examples of student work at the various performance levels. Such examples enhance parents' knowledge of teachers' expectations. They also allow parents to become more discerning judges of their child's performance and then better assist their child in making progress. Providing such examples requires that school leaders give teachers time to engage in conversations about what is meant by "Proficient" and what examples of student work are illustrative of a "Proficient" label.

3. *Distinguish between "Levels of Understanding" and "Frequency of Display."* Parents get confused when educators use indicators that confound *what* students know and are able to do with *how often* they do it. The first implies "quality" to parents, while the second appears to signify "quantity" or "rate of occurrence." While "Frequency of Display" labels, such as "Occasionally,"

"Frequently," and "Consistently," work well when describing students' work habits, study skills, or behaviors in school, they often fall short when trying to explain to parents what students have learned and are able to do.

4. *Be consistent.* One reason so many parents translate labels into letter grades is that the latter provide a common basis for understanding and interpretation. This is particularly true in schools where one set of labels is used on the elementary report card, another set on the secondary report card, another set for state assessment results, and still another set for standardized assessment reports. No wonder in such cases parents ask, "Are 'Adequate' and 'Satisfactory' the same as 'Proficient,' and are they all equivalent to a B?" Achieving consistency may prove difficult in schools bound to the use of labels already incorporated in their state's assessment system. Still, by lessening the number of labels with which parents must contend, educators can greatly facilitate parents' understanding and encourage greater parent involvement in their child's education.

GUIDELINES FOR CHOOSING LABELS TO DESCRIBE DIFFERENT LEVELS OF STUDENT PERFORMANCE

1. Avoid comparative language.

2. Provide examples based on student work.

3. Distinguish between "Levels of Understanding" and "Frequency of Display."

4. Be consistent.

Labels must convey honest, meaningful, and useful information to parents and others to facilitate their understanding of educators' expectations for student learning. When parents and others recognize the intent of a standards-based report card and can make sense of the information it includes, they are better able to work with educators as partners in the improvement process (see Guskey, 2002b).

10. Will teachers' comments be included and encouraged?

Teacher comments on a report card represent one of the oldest forms of grading and reporting, dating back to the days when report cards were little more than handwritten narratives prepared by the teacher to describe each student's progress in a one-room schoolhouse (see Guskey, 1994a, 1996b). The comments teachers offer can be very general or highly specific, depending on individual teachers' inclinations and the guidelines provided by the school. Although elementary report cards include teacher comments most often, increasing numbers of middle and high schools have begun to realize the advantage of including teacher comments on their report cards.

Report cards designed to include teacher comments typically provide a box or series of boxes where teachers record their descriptive evaluations of what students have accomplished and what areas need improvement. Some computerized grading programs allow teachers to access students' records and then enter the comments they want to have printed on the reporting form. An example is shown in Figure 6.1. As is evident in this example, programs such as these allow teachers to offer specific and highly detailed comments in a fairly efficient manner.

Figure 6.1 Teacher Comments on a Report Card

York School District Elementary Reporting Form		
Student: **T. Trebor**		Grade: **2**
Teacher: **Ms. Yelaib**	School: **Tyler Elementary**	Year:
Reading	**Writing**	
In reading our class has been working on perspective in works of fiction. Although Teresa contributes regularly to class discussions, her reading speed is slow and her comprehension skills need improvement. She could benefit from additional supervised reading time at home.	This marking period we concentrated on sentence structure in writing. Teresa can construct complex sentences that show deep understanding and creative expression. Her writing has shown significant improvement in recent weeks.	
Mathematics	**Science**	
This marking period we worked on basic addition and subtraction skills, along with problem solving. Teresa can solve double-digit addition and subtraction problems and does exceptionally well with verbal problems applying these skills.	In science we are currently investigating classification systems. Teresa works well with her classmates in cooperative assignments and did a great job on her independent class project.	

SOURCE: Guskey, T. R., & Bailey, J. M. (2001). *Developing Grading Reporting Systems for Student Learning.* Thousand Oaks, CA: Corwin.

Some programs permit teachers to enter two types of comments: class comments and individual comments. For class comments, teachers first enter one or two sentences that describe the major concepts addressed or the topics explored during a particular marking period. These sentences are then printed on the report card of every student in that class. Next, teachers access individual student records and add a sentence or two about each student's accomplishments or learning progress. These two-part comments reduce the work required of teachers in completing the report card while providing parents and others with detailed and useful information. Examples of reporting forms that include both class and individual comments are illustrated in Chapter 7.

Guidelines for Effective Teacher Comments

The most effective teacher comments focus on the specific standards or learning goals students are expected to attain, but they convey information that might not be explained completely by the mark on the report card. Teachers can use comments to clarify students' particular strengths and explain what was achieved during the marking period. When necessary, comments can pinpoint students' learning problems and offer suggestions as to how those problems might be remedied.

Always remember, however, that any comments included on the report card should be helpful and instructive. *Never* should they include negative statements about students' behavior or character. Some teachers mistakenly believe that referring to students as "lazy" or "uncooperative" provides an honest and accurate appraisal of their conduct in school. They also believe that parents need to know these things if inappropriate behaviors are to be corrected. But comments such as these demean students, create barriers between parents and teachers, and have no place in a reporting form. For the same reasons, teachers should avoid using words such as *unable, can't, won't, always,* and *never* (Shafer, 1997).

Researchers further suggest that teachers use the most tactful means possible when it becomes necessary to communicate information about inappropriate student behaviors to parents and others (see Miller, Linn, & Gronlund, 2009). The box below includes recommendations on how this can be accomplished. But while suggestions for improvement are always desirable, they should never outweigh sensitivity to students' well-being. Inversely, tact must not become an excuse for obscuring the intended message. In developing their comments, teachers must do their best to find an appropriate balance between accuracy and sensitivity.

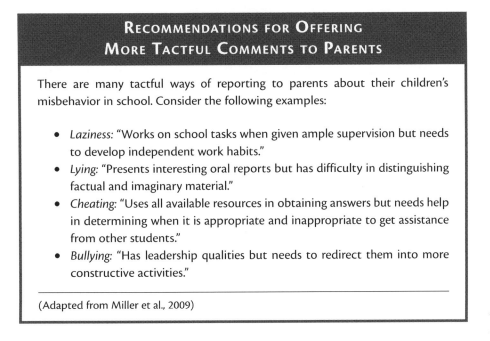

RECOMMENDATIONS FOR OFFERING MORE TACTFUL COMMENTS TO PARENTS

There are many tactful ways of reporting to parents about their children's misbehavior in school. Consider the following examples:

- *Laziness:* "Works on school tasks when given ample supervision but needs to develop independent work habits."
- *Lying:* "Presents interesting oral reports but has difficulty in distinguishing factual and imaginary material."
- *Cheating:* "Uses all available resources in obtaining answers but needs help in determining when it is appropriate and inappropriate to get assistance from other students."
- *Bullying:* "Has leadership qualities but needs to redirect them into more constructive activities."

(Adapted from Miller et al., 2009)

Recent research on formative feedback provides additional guidance on how to ensure that teachers' comments truly help students and facilitate communication with parents (see Brookhart, 2008; Hattie & Timperley, 2007; Shute, 2008). These guidelines include the following:

1. *Focus on the goals, not the learner.* Teachers' comments should address specific features of students' work in relation to the learning goals or standards, with suggestions on how to improve or what to do next. Goal-specific comments help students focus on effort, persistence, and work quality rather than on inalterable ability attributes. "Nicole has made excellent progress in mastering her math problem-solving skills," is far better than "Math is clearly Nicole's best subject."

2. *Provide detailed comments.* Comments should describe the what, how, and why of learning success or of a given problem. This kind of feedback is more effective than simply documenting good or poor results. "Carlos's prewriting outlines have made his writing clearer and more expressive," communicates much more than "Carlos's writing has improved."

3. *Offer small, manageable suggestions for improvement.* Directions for improvement should stress small steps to be taken. Presenting too much information or too many steps often overwhelms both

parents and students and, therefore, may be simply ignored or discarded. "Spending ten minutes every day with the math flash cards would help Elise improve her math skills," provides more useful guidance than "Elise needs to work harder in math."

4. *Relate comments to specific learning goals or standards.* The best comments are linked to specific learning goals or standards. Those that are explicit, direct, and free of jargon or complex technical language help both parents and students. Highly general or vague comments can impede learning and frustrate students. "A 20-minute walk every day would help James improve his endurance," is much more helpful than "James needs to get more exercise."

5. *Avoid comparisons with other students.* Comments should describe each student's work in relation to clear learning criteria, coupled with goal-specific suggestions for improvement. Never should a teacher's comments about one student relate to the performance of other students in the class. Positive comments such as "Natalie is the best math student in the class," and especially negative comments such as "Mary Ann is one of the poorest-performing students in social studies," or "Elroy's science test scores are always among the worst," prompt unhealthy comparisons that can be detrimental to learning progress.

GUIDELINES FOR INCLUDING TEACHER COMMENTS ON THE REPORT CARD

1. Focus on the goals, not the learner.

2. Provide detailed comments.

3. Offer small, manageable suggestions for improvement.

4. Relate comments to specific learning goals or standards.

5. Avoid comparisons with other students.

Standardized Comment Menus

To simplify the inclusion of teacher comments on report cards, many schools and school districts have adopted computerized grading programs that allow teachers to select comments from a standardized comment menu (Friedman & Frisbie, 1995). When using these programs, teachers simply scroll down a list of standard comments and click on the one or two they want to include; these are then printed on the report card.

Standardized comment menus typically include both positive and negative comments that cover a wide range of achievement and nonachievement aspects of students' performance (see the box below). While the number of comments available to teachers normally ranges from 50 to 100, teachers tend to use only 15 to 20 comments from the list. And while most programs allow teachers to offer a maximum of two comments per student for each subject area or cluster of standards, rarely do teachers select more than a single comment for each student (Friedman, Valde, & Obermeyer, 1998).

Studies of standardized comment menus indicate that teachers vary widely in the comments they select. Some offer only positive comments, while others assign mostly negative comments to their students every marking period. Negative comments tend to be used to inform parents what particular factors contributed to a low grade or marks. Ironically, the comments teachers select to explain poor grades usually relate to nonacademic factors, such as a student's level of effort, attitude, or classroom behavior, rather than specific aspects of academic performance (Friedman et al., 1998).

EXAMPLES OF STANDARDIZED COMPUTER COMMENTS

Type of Comment	Example
Positive Academic	"Asks appropriate questions."
Positive Behavioral	"Behaves appropriately in class."
Negative Academic	"Has difficulty understanding some concepts."
Negative Behavioral	"Disturbs other students."
General	"Fails to bring instruments/materials to class."

(Adapted from Friedman et al., 1998)

Despite the ease of use of computer menus, evidence gathered from teachers and parents shows that only a small portion of either group believes that computer menu-based comments are adequate. Parents in particular criticize the menu-based comments as too impersonal and imprecise. They want much more specific and more individualized comments that offer guidance on what can be done to bring about improvement (Friedman et al., 1998).

Results from our surveys and interviews with parents reveal much the same (see Guskey & Bailey, 2001). Few parents indicated that standardized, menu-based comments were helpful, and none found them prescriptive. Many of the parents with whom we spoke described such comments as "highly impersonal" and illustrated their point by citing how different teachers, teaching different subjects, often offered word-for-word identical comments about their child. Hence, while parents want more information than grades or marks alone provide and teachers want to provide it, one would be hard-pressed to suggest that either group finds standardized comment menus sufficient for this purpose.

Individually constructed comments, on the other hand, serve a valuable reporting purpose. They allow teachers to draw attention to students' particular learning strengths. They also provide teachers the means to point out unique learning difficulties and to recommend explicit improvement strategies. When used in conjunction with other standards-based grades or marks, comments bring added clarity and richness to the information included in the report card. Some research indicates that parents look forward to receiving teachers' comments for these very reasons. Many parents consider teacher comments more personal, less competitively oriented, and more capable of conveying explicit information about students' learning progress (Hall, 1990). Some parents even find comments more accurate and precise than grades or marks (Allison & Friedman, 1995).

So even though writing comments adds to the time teachers must spend completing report cards, we strongly encourage their inclusion in standards-based report cards. To ensure their positive benefits, however, we also recommend that schools and school districts provide teachers with professional development on how to compose appropriate and meaningful comments, paired with specific guidelines for preparing such comments. While teacher comments can be quite helpful, they also can be harmful, and offering no comment is better than including one that has damaging effects (see Hattie & Timperley, 2007). The tremendous variation researchers have noted in the detail and quality of teachers' comments on report cards is undoubtedly related to teachers' lack of explicit training on this important topic. Focused professional development will help teachers enrich the quality and clarity of their comments, enhance the communicative value of those comments, and, optimally, lead to improvements in student learning.

11. How will information be arranged on the report card?

Having decided what specific elements will be included in the standards-based report card, we now must consider how to organize and arrange those elements on the reporting form. Developers sometimes take the format of the report card for granted. They think that as long as they include all of the essential elements, the arrangement of those elements is unimportant. But those who organize their report card haphazardly, without careful planning and forethought, inevitably encounter problems with interpretation. Intentionally planning the report card's format is vital to success.

In our experiences working with schools and school districts, we find that parents often consider the report card's format an indication of what is most important to teachers and most vital to school success. In particular, parents seem to pay attention to two aspects of the report card's design: *order* and *space*. From parents' perspectives, the most important elements in the report card are those that are listed first and those that are allotted the most space. In other words, they view the subject area standards listed first on the report card to be more important than those listed later. In addition, the subject areas that take up the most space on the report card are interpreted as being more important than those given less space. Communication experts emphasize these same aspects of order and space in planning the layout of the front page of a newspaper when they describe what appears "above the fold."

PARENTS FREQUENTLY JUDGE WHAT IS IMPORTANT IN THE REPORT CARD BASED ON . . .

1. *Order:* What is most important appears first.

2. *Space:* What is most important is given more area.

For this reason, developers must intentionally design their standards-based report card keeping in mind the aspects of order and space. If language arts and mathematics are considered most fundamental to students' success in school, then the language arts and mathematics standards should be listed first. Similarly, listing standards related to product learning goals first on the report card will communicate to parents that these are the major focus of teachers and the school. Process and progress learning goals, while still vitally important, typically come after. Of course, listing process or progress standards with each subject area's product standards resolves this communication dilemma.

12. What are parents expected to do with this information?

The best standards-based report cards offer parents two important types of information.

1. They communicate the particular learning goals, standards, and expectations that have been set for students so that parents are able to collaborate better with educators to promote learning and development.

2. They identify students' learning successes, as well as areas of difficulty, so that in conjunction with teachers, parents can provide whatever encouragement and support may be needed.

While most parents are quite willing to offer assistance, many rely on teachers for guidance as to what particular types of encouragement or support will be most helpful.

To ensure that parents receive the report card and understand the information it contains, nearly all standards-based report cards include a section that requests parents' or guardians' signatures. Many early versions asked parents to sign and return the entire reporting form to the teacher or to the school. Most modern standards-based report cards, however, ask parents simply to sign the envelope in which the report was sent home and then return that alone. In this way, parents get to keep the report card, but educators still have evidence that it was received. Report card envelopes typically include boxes that parents or guardians can check if they wish a follow-up phone call or individual conference with the teacher.

Some recent versions of standards-based report cards incorporate a portion that parents are asked to sign, detach, and then return in an envelope. These returnable tabs include space where parents or guardians can offer comments, ask questions, or request a follow-up phone call or conference with the teacher if desired. And because they are returned in an envelope, parents' comments and requests are handled more discretely. An example is shown in Figure 6.2.

Figure 6.2 Example of a Returnable Portion of a Report Card

Please clip and return the bottom section of this page in the report card envelope. The remainder of the report card is yours to keep.

✂ -

Parent Comments

Parent	Teacher
Signature: _____	Signature: _____

Other standards-based report cards are designed to solicit much more detailed responses from parents or guardians. The detachable portion of these report cards may ask about specific parental concerns, individual student's learning goals, or even aspects of home support. Most also offer parents the option of a follow-up conference if they wish to discuss these or other issues with the teacher. Figure 6.3 shows an example of this kind of response form.

More detailed response forms can clarify for parents the particular problems or difficulties the teacher may have noted on the report card. They also can be used to offer specific guidance to parents in helping to resolve those problems. Equally important, they communicate to parents that teachers and other school personnel are open to discussing problems and ready to work with parents to resolve them. Such openness serves not only to increase parents' involvement, it also breaks down communication barriers between parents and teachers and ensures improvement efforts will be harmonious (see Guskey, 2002b).

Always remember that the most effective standards-based report cards communicate information that parents can easily interpret,

| Figure 6.3 | Example of a More Detailed Returnable Portion of a Report Card |

De Haven School Report Card Response Form
(To be Completed by Parents and Returned to the Teacher)

Student _____   Grade _____

Teacher _____   Date _____

Parent's/Guardian's Comments and/or Concerns Regarding Student Achievement,
Behavior in School, Learning Goals, and Home Support:

I received the report card and have no questions at this time.	I would like to discuss this report card. Please contact me.
_____ Parent's/Guardian's Signature	_____ Parent's/Guardian's Signature
_____ Student's Signature	_____ Daytime Telephone
	_____ Evening Telephone

NOTE: *For more information about grade level standards, visit the district website:* www.stps
.k12.pa.us.

readily understand, and then know how to use. Any guidance that educators can offer to parents and guardians on how best to use that information will be greatly appreciated and potentially could yield powerful benefits.

13. **What are students expected to do with this information?**

Most primary and early elementary grade educators emphasize that the main purpose of a standards-based report card is to communicate information about students' performance and learning progress in school to parents and others. In the upper elementary grades, and especially in middle school and high school, however, educators increasingly see students as another important recipient of the information in the report card. At all levels, of course, grading and reporting should always be honest and transparent. Information about how grades or marks are determined should never be secret, and students should never be surprised by the grade or mark that they receive. As they develop greater independence and become more self-directed in their learning efforts (see Guskey & Anderman, 2008), however, it is increasingly important for students receive the results of teachers' judgments of their performance directly and for them to have opportunities to react to that information.

To help students make appropriate use of the information included in standards-based report cards and encourage their active participation in the grading process, many educators design their report card to incorporate space for student comments or questions on their achievement and behavior in school, as in the reporting form shown in Figure 6.3. Occasionally, students are asked about their individual learning goals and the support they need from school or home to meet their goals. Such questions not only help promote greater student involvement, they also serve to increase students' personal responsibility for learning outcomes.

Some development teams go a step further and use the standards-based report card as the foundation for helping students construct individual "goal plans." Following report card distribution, teachers assist students in developing goal plans and then work with students to ensure steady progress in meeting their goals. The most effective plans include both short-term and long-term goals so that students need not wait until the end of the next reporting period to receive feedback on their success. An example of a form used to guide students in the development of goal plans is illustrated in Figure 6.4.

As part of the process of helping students develop goal plans, many teachers also offer students a rubric for evaluating their plans. This rubric gives students a better idea of the teacher's expectations along with the specific criteria by which their goal plans will be judged. In presenting the rubric, teachers go over examples of goals that are meaningful, appropriate, and attainable so that students recognize quality goals and gain a better understanding of what their plans

Figure 6.4   Example of a Goal Plan Form

GOAL PLAN

Name _____   **Date** _____

Goal/Aim

> (blank box)

Completion Date _____

Results, or How I Will I Know I've Reached My Goal

> (blank box)

Resources:

  People: _____

  Materials: _____

Obstacles: _____

Endurance Strategy: Overcoming the obstacles:

> Date:
>
> Step 1:
> Step 2:
> Step 3:
> Step 4:

Completion Date _____

SOURCE: From Guskey, T. R. *Implementing Mastery Learning*, 2nd edition. © 1997 Wadsworth, a part of Cengage Learning, Inc. Reproduced by permission. www.cengage.com/permissions

should include. The rubric then serves as a guide to students as they develop their individual plans. In many cases, students use self-assessment strategies or peer assessment in evaluating their plans. Figure 6.5 includes an example of a goal plan rubric.

Figure 6.5	Example of a Goal Plan Rubric

Goal Rubric			
Rating	*Goal Statement*	*Goal Plan*	*Evaluation*
Excellent Points: 3	▪ Reflects area needed ▪ Clear and understandable aim ▪ Achievable/realistic	▪ States steps and resources needed ▪ States timeline ▪ Includes a thorough evaluation plan	▪ Completed all steps of the goal plan ▪ Achieves goal
Acceptable Points: 2	▪ Area not a priority ▪ Not stated in specific terms ▪ Long term goals not broken down	▪ Some steps left out or resources limited ▪ Timeline unrealistic ▪ Evaluation plan unclear	▪ Followed most steps in the goal plan ▪ Showed improvement
Marginal Points: 1	▪ Reflects area where goal is not needed ▪ Goal unclear; goal underestimated ▪ Goal overestimated	▪ Inappropriate sequence of steps ▪ Only end date included ▪ Minimal/incomplete evaluation plan	▪ Followed few goal steps ▪ Little improvement
Unacceptable Points: 0	▪ No goal	▪ No steps ▪ No timeline ▪ No evaluation plan	▪ Did not follow steps ▪ Showed no improvement
Self			
Peer			
Teacher			
TOTAL			

SOURCE: From Guskey, T. R. *Implementing Mastery Learning*, 2nd edition. © 1997 Wadsworth, a part of Cengage Learning, Inc. Reproduced by permission. www.cengage.com/permissions

In addition to enhancing involvement, developing goal plans based on a standards-based report card helps students see reporting as an ongoing process in which change is not only possible but expected. It also helps focus and direct students' improvement efforts. But perhaps most important, sharing goal plans with parents encourages collaboration among students, parents, and teachers. It also helps ensure harmony in improvement efforts and undoubtedly will lead to higher levels of learning success.

14. What policies need to accompany the new reporting procedures?

Certain policy decisions have to be made when implementing any new report card or reporting procedure. Although sometimes taken for granted, these decisions can have an important influence on the success of implementation efforts. In the case of standards-based report cards, the policy questions that are particularly important include the following.

Will a cumulative record be included on the report card?

In addition to offering information about students' current level of performance, many standards-based report cards also include a record of students' past performance. In most instances, this cumulative record is simply a listing of the grades or marks students received in previous reporting periods during that particular school year. The list may be placed next to each reporting standard on the report card, with a special indicator showing the most current grade or mark. Many of the report cards shown in Chapter 7 use this format. In other report cards, the cumulative record is included as a special section at the end of the form or on the back.

Providing a cumulative record helps parents and guardians keep track of progress and improvements. It also communicates whether or not corrective efforts designed to remedy past difficulties have been successful and where additional assistance still may be needed. Most important, it helps illustrate the adequacy of students' progress toward meeting the course or grade level performance goals and standards. For these reasons, we strongly encourage the inclusion of a cumulative record in all standards-based report cards.

What grades or marks will be included on the permanent record or transcript?

In most elementary schools, students' grades or marks are recorded in a permanent record that follows students as they advance in grade levels. These records also can be transferred with students if they move to another school. At the secondary level, students' grades and marks become part of a transcript. Most colleges and universities require students to submit copies of their transcripts as part of the admissions process. In addition, some employers request that copies of students' transcripts be included in their job application portfolios.

Permanent records and transcripts rarely include *all* the grades or marks that students have earned. Instead, they include only overall or "summative" grades from a grade level or program of courses. Some permanent records and transcripts contain only the summative "achievement" grades from a standards-based report card, reflecting product goals. But increasingly, schools that use standards-based report cards also include students' grades or marks for process and progress goals, especially if these reflect study skills or work habits. Educators in these schools believe this information provides a truer picture of students' performance in school. In addition, it gives colleges and universities, as well as prospective employers, a better idea of students' distinctive strengths and capabilities.

The most vital issue in determining what should be recorded in the permanent record or on the transcript is ensuring that each grade or mark reflects a current and accurate depiction of students' performance. *Current* means that the record is up-to-date and reveals what students know and are able to do at that time, rather than presenting an "average" of past accomplishments (see Guskey, 2002a). *Accurate* means that the grade or mark for achievement reflects precisely that—achievement—and is not tainted by other aspects of students' behavior, such as homework completion, punctuality in turning in assignments, or class participation. Regardless of the structure or format of permanent records or transcripts, the information they contain will be meaningful only if it is both current and accurate.

How will the report card be distributed?

As part of their development tasks, leaders also need to establish formal procedures for distributing standards-based report cards. In other words, how will parents and guardians, and in some cases students, receive or gain access to the report card and the information it includes? While many developers simply continue the same report card distribution procedures that have been always been used, advances in technology allow a host of other possibilities to be explored. Some of the options for report card distribution include the following:

- *Distribute report cards to students in school and ask that they carry them home to their parents and guardians.* This option must be accompanied by other notification procedures that alert parents to precisely when they should expect their children to be bringing the report card home.

- *Mail report cards directly to parents and guardians.* Although this option is used in many schools, it requires accurate mailing addresses for all parents and guardians, and it incurs the additional expense of postage.
- *Have parents and guardians pick up report cards at school, with special provisions made for those who may not be able to get to the school during regular school hours.* While this option encourages parents to visit the school on a regular basis, it may be limiting to parents who do not have ready access to transportation.
- *Give report cards to parents and guardians as part of a scheduled parent-teacher conference.* This option also encourages parent visitations to school but again puts a transportation burden on parents.
- *Notify parents and guardians that report cards can be viewed online, with special provisions made for those who may not have access to such technology.* This option must also be accompanied by notification procedures that make parents aware of precisely when the report cards will be ready for them to access.

Whatever option is chosen, parents and guardians must be notified well in advance so that they know what to expect and when to expect it.

How will the report card, or some portion of it, be returned?

To ensure that parents and guardians have received and understood the report card, nearly all developers establish a policy to check on that. In many cases, confirmation of receipt is accomplished by including a line on the report card for parents or guardians to sign each marking period. After the report card is signed, the student typically returns it to the teacher or the school. An increasingly popular option, however, is to have some small, detachable portion of the report, similar to that shown in Figure 6.2, signed and returned. More detailed forms, like the one in Figure 6.3, are also increasing in popularity. These forms permit parents to keep a record of their children's performance in school while allowing teachers and school personnel to know that the information was received. An additional part of the policy must stipulate what will be done if the report card or signature receipt is not returned within a certain time. In most cases, follow-up involves a phone call to the home or other means of contacting the parents or guardians.

What other reporting elements will accompany the report card?

In many schools, additional reporting documents are included with the report card when it is sent home. These can include the following:

- *Curriculum documents* that describe the specific learning goals or standards in which students were engaged during that particular marking period. Sometimes this includes lists of established quarterly goals.
- *Individual student goal plans* that outline the goals students set for themselves for the marking period. As described earlier in the chapter, goal plans not only help students focus their efforts in school, they provide a mechanism for documenting gains and reflecting on improvements. Goal plans also offer parents and students the opportunity to review the goals, evaluate the progress that has been made, and then discuss next steps.
- *Progress reports* that might be related to Individual Educational Program (IEP) goals. These goals often are based on developmental skills that may be needed in students' daily routines and activities. They might also describe specific modifications that have been made in the standards for individual students (see Guskey & Jung, 2009; Jung, 2009).
- *Supplemental reports* that outline the advanced learning goals set for gifted and talented students along with descriptions of their progress related to those goals. Because a standards-based report card typically will not include information on the extended learning goals designed to challenge fast learners, supplemental reports that document the special learning activities in which these students have been engaged and the progress they have made are a necessary addition.

What is the process for questioning a grade or mark?

Another policy that needs to be considered in developing a standards-based report card describes the specific procedures parents, students, or others should follow if they have questions about a grade or mark. Often parents or guardians want clarification as to how the teacher arrived at a particular grade or mark. Because of the explicit and transparent nature of standards-based grading, parents rarely question the teacher's judgment. Most simply want to gain a better understanding of the reporting standards and grading process so that they can help their child make whatever improvements might be needed. Generally, these procedures begin by offering parents or guardians the opportunity to schedule a conference with the teacher. If questions persist, a follow-up meeting involving the school principal might be considered. Openness and transparency in all aspects of the reporting process should remain foremost in establishing these procedures.

What is the role of technology in the development of the new report card?

A final policy that will have to be addressed is the role of technology in the development and distribution of the new report card. Many schools and school districts today use computer grading programs and electronic grade books to record information on student learning and then to report results. These programs allow teachers to keep highly detailed records on students' performance. Some even permit daily access by parents to the information so that they can keep track of their children's learning progress. Unfortunately, many of these programs are based on antiquated reporting practices (e.g., averaging scores to attain a final grade), which make their adaptation to a standards-based format exceptionally difficult (Guskey, 2002a, 2007). In addition, most strictly dictate the reporting format and do not offer teachers the flexibility needed to assign grades or marks based on specific learning standards.

For this reason, we strongly recommend including school, district, or provincial technology experts on the development team. These individuals can familiarize other team members with the adequacy and flexibility of current programs. They also can lead efforts if it becomes necessary to find or develop an entirely new system. Many of the schools and school districts with which we have worked, upon discovering that no commercially available grading program adequately met their needs, created their own record-keeping and reporting programs with great success.

IMPORTANT POLICY DECISIONS THAT ACCOMPANY THE IMPLEMENTATION OF NEW REPORTING PROCEDURES

1. Will a cumulative record be included on the report card?

2. What grades or marks will be included on the permanent record or transcript?

3. How will the report card be distributed?

4. How will the report card, or some portion of it, be returned?

5. What other reporting elements will accompany the report card?

6. What is the process for questioning a grade or mark?

7. What is the role of technology in the development of the new report card?

---

15. When should input of parents and/or students be sought?

Parent Involvement

As we have stressed throughout this discussion, the success of any standards-based report card will *always* depend on how effectively it communicates valuable and useful information to parents and others. Gaining the trust and acceptance of parents in this process is essential. Yet because parents' perspectives on grading and reporting are fashioned primarily by their own experiences in school, the transition from a traditional report card to a standards-based report card can be difficult. Including parents in the development process and taking seriously their input can greatly ease this transition.

At the same time, parents can be involved too early in the process or in unproductive ways. For example, including two or three parents or guardians on the development team is particularly helpful, especially if they are involved in preliminary study sessions and initial training. This ensures that parents' perspectives are represented in early discussions about the advantages of standards-based report cards and the reasons for making the change. Involving large numbers of parents at this time, however, can be counterproductive. Like teachers, parents have had widely varied experiences with grading, many of which were negative (see Guskey, 2006b). Getting past these experiences and the irresolvable disagreements that they often instigate can often prove particularly challenging.

Nevertheless, parent involvement and input in the development process is vital at three crucial points.

1. When Forming the Development Team. As we already mentioned, the first is when forming the development team. Two or three parents or guardians should be invited to serve as equal members of the team. These parents should be open-minded and willing to work toward consensus on the myriad of decisions the development team will have to address. Equally important, they should not be shy but should be willing to express their points of view openly and honestly in development team meetings so that effective communication with other parents later in the process can be ensured.

2. When Reviewing Initial Versions of Newly Developed Standards-Based Report Cards. In many schools and school districts, this involves parent participation in focus groups organized by development team members. At these meetings, parents learn about the work that has been done to that point and the rationale behind that work. They are then shown the new form and asked to review it and to offer their candid feedback. Careful records are kept of reactions and recommendations for improvement so that these can be considered as the development team plans revisions.

3. During the Early Stages of Schoolwide or Districtwide Implementation. Probably the most crucial time parent involvement and input are important is during initial implementation. Right from the start, parents need to know why this change is being made, what it is intended to accomplish, and how a standards-based report card is *better* than the reporting forms used in the past. Often this information is communicated through presentations at open house meetings or parent association meetings, newsletters, or special announcements sent to every home. Without a dedicated effort to inform parents about the purpose of the new report card and what advantages it has over previous forms, confusion and misunderstanding will abound.

For this reason, we always recommend piloting the newly developed report card for a year prior to full-scale implementation and soliciting broad-based parent input during that time. This process is discussed in detail in Chapter 8. Inevitably, some parents will prefer traditional forms simply because these are what they know and believe they understand. Taking specific steps to gather input systematically from parents early in the implementation process, and then using that input to make purposeful revisions, helps parents see the transition to a standards-based report card as open and inclusive. It also helps avert opposition and gain broad-based support.

WHEN PARENT INVOLVEMENT AND INPUT ARE CRUCIAL IN DEVELOPING STANDARDS-BASED REPORT CARDS

1. When forming the development team

2. When reviewing initial versions of newly developed standards-based report cards

3. During the early stages of schoolwide or districtwide implementation

---

Student Involvement

At the secondary level, where standards-based report cards often are seen as a way to communicate information to students as well as parents, student involvement and input in the development process can be crucial as well. Only rarely have we seen instances where students are involved as full members of the development team. In many cases, however, focus groups with students are used to inform them of the reasons behind the change and to gain their perspectives. In addition, most schools and school districts seek input from students during initial implementation either through questionnaires or by tallying the comments students make on the report card.

Summary

As we emphasized in Chapter 5, developing an effective standards-based report card requires that a series of crucial questions be addressed in specific order. The eight crucial questions discussed in this chapter follow the seven presented in Chapter 5:

8. How many levels of performance will be reported for each standard?

9. How will the levels be labeled?

10. Will teachers' comments be included and encouraged?

11. How will information be arranged on the report card?

12. What are parents expected to do with this information?

13. What are students expected to do with this information?

14. What policies need to accompany the new reporting procedures?

15. When should input of parents and/or students be sought?

Addressing each of these questions openly and honestly, with thoughtfulness and careful attention to the implications of the answers, is indispensable in the development process and essential to success in achieving the communication goals of standards-based reporting.

7

Special Cases

Secondary Schools, Special Education, and Gifted Education

Thomas Guskey and Lee Ann Jung

N ow that we have considered the development steps involved in creating a standards-based report card, we need to explore a few special cases. Three cases in particular will be the focus of this chapter.

1. The particular aspects of developing a standards-based report card for middle schools and high schools

2. The adaptations necessary to provide fair and accurate grades or marks for students with special needs who are included in regular classrooms

3. The adaptations necessary to provide fair and accurate grades or marks for students considered to be especially gifted or talented

We will consider the challenges presented by each of these special cases and offer specific suggestions on how to address them. Attending to these special cases during the planning stage can greatly improve the chances of successful implementation.

Standards-Based Reporting in Secondary Schools

The accuracy and fairness of grading practices in middle school and high school classes have been questioned for decades (see Guskey, 1996b). In recent years, however, investigations showing the mismatch between students' grades and their scores on large-scale assessments have prompted increased scrutiny. Educators generally consider the assessments to be the source of this mismatch problem. They believe that state or provincial accountability assessments are inadequate and often invalid indicators of students' actual level of achievement (Brennan et al., 2001). Indeed, these limited, once-a-year assessments may not reveal the true scope or depth of students' knowledge and skills.

Policymakers and government officials, on the other hand, argue that teachers are the source of the problem. They think the mismatch between grades and accountability assessment results stems from bias and subjectivity in teachers' grading practices (Bennett, Gottesman, Rock, & Cerullo, 1993; Hills, 1991; Wiles, 1992). Ample evidence demonstrates, for example, that most teachers receive little training in effective grading and that unintentional bias often influences the grades or marks that teachers assign (Austin & McCann, 1992; Boothroyd & McMorris, 1992; Stiggins, 1989). A more likely explanation, however, lies in the nature of grading itself and in the challenges teachers face in assigning grades that fairly and accurately depict students' achievement and performance in school.

The Challenge of Grading in Secondary Schools

Middle school and high school teachers today draw from many different sources of evidence in determining students' grades. Studies show that teachers also differ in the procedures they use to combine or summarize that evidence (Ornstein, 1994). Some of the major sources of evidence that teachers use include the following:

- Major exams or compositions
- Class quizzes
- Reports or projects
- Student portfolios
- Exhibits of students' work
- Laboratory projects
- Work habits and neatness
- Effort
- Attendance
- Students' notebooks or journals
- Classroom observations
- Oral presentations
- Homework completion
- Homework quality
- Class participation
- Punctuality of assignments
- Class behavior or attitude
- Progress made

When asked *which* of these indicators they consider in determining students' grades, some teachers usually report using each. When asked *how many* of these sources of evidence they include, however, responses vary widely. Some teachers base grades on as few as two or three indicators, while others incorporate evidence from as many as 15 or 16—and this is true even among teachers who teach in the same school.

Two reasons appear to account for this variation. First is a lack of clarity about the purpose of grading. Deciding what evidence to use in determining students' grades is extremely difficult when the purpose of grading is unclear. Different sources of evidence vary in their appropriateness and validity depending on the identified purpose. That is why, as we described in Chapter 3, defining the purpose of grading is such a crucial first step.

A second reason comes from the format of grading itself. Most middle school and high school reporting forms allow only a single grade to be assigned to students for each course or subject area. This forces teachers to combine whatever diverse sources of evidence they use into a single symbol, resulting in the "hodgepodge grade" we discussed in Chapter 4, which includes elements of achievement, attitude, effort, and behavior (Brookhart, 1991; Cross & Frary, 1996). Even when teachers clarify the weighting strategies they use to combine these elements and employ computerized grading programs to ensure accuracy in their computations, the final grade remains a confusing amalgamation, which is impossible to interpret and rarely presents a true picture of students' proficiency (Conley, 2000; Guskey, 2002a).

To make middle school and high school grades more meaningful, we need to address both of these factors. First, we must clarify our purpose in grading at this level. Second, we must decide what evidence best reflects that purpose and how best to communicate a summary of that evidence to parents and others.

Clarifying Purposes and Criteria

When asked to identify the purpose of grading, most middle school and high school teachers indicate that grades should describe how well students have achieved the learning goals established for a course. In other words, grades should reflect students' performance based on specific learning criteria. Both teachers and students prefer this approach because they consider it fair and equitable (Kovas, 1993). But teachers use widely varying criteria in evaluating students' performance. In most cases, these different criteria or goals can be grouped into the three broad categories we described in Chapter 4: *product, process,* and *progress* criteria.

- *Product criteria* are favored by educators who believe the primary purpose of grading is to communicate a summative evaluation of student achievement and performance (Friedman, 1998; O'Connor, 2007, 2009). In other words, these criteria focus on what students know and are able to do at a particular point in time. Teachers who use product criteria typically base grades exclusively on final examination scores, final products (reports or projects), overall assessments, and other culminating demonstrations of learning.

- *Process criteria* are emphasized by educators who believe product criteria do not provide a complete picture of student learning. From their perspective, grades should reflect not only the final results but also *how* students got there. Teachers who consider effort or work habits when assigning grades are using process criteria. So are teachers who count regular classroom quizzes, homework, punctuality of assignments, class participation, or attendance.

- *Progress criteria* are used by educators who believe the most important aspect of grading is how much students gain from their learning experiences. Teachers who use progress criteria typically look at how much improvement students have made over a particular period, rather than just where they are. As a result, grading criteria may be highly individualized, and each student's grade may mean something different.

As we discussed in Chapter 4, few teachers use only product criteria in determining grades because of their concerns about student motivation, self-esteem, and the social consequences of grading. Instead, most routinely base their grading procedures on some combination of all three types of criteria (Brookhart, 1993; Cross & Frary, 1996; Friedman & Manley, 1992; Nava & Loyd, 1992). Many also vary their grading criteria from student to student, taking into account individual circumstances (Friedman & Troug, 1999; Natriello et al., 1994). Although teachers defend this practice on the basis of fairness, it seriously confounds the meaning of any grade. Interpreting grades thus becomes exceptionally challenging, not only for parents but also for administrators, community members, and even the students themselves (Friedman & Frisbie, 1995; Waltman & Frisbie, 1994; Willingham et al., 2002). A grade of A, for example, may mean the student knew what was intended before instruction began (product), did not learn as well as expected but tried very hard (process), or simply made significant improvement (progress).

A Practical Alternative

A practical solution to these problems, which is increasingly used by teachers in middle schools and high schools, is to report *separate* grades or marks for students on product, process, and progress learning criteria or goals. In this way, the grades or marks assigned to particular study skills, work habits, effort, or learning progress are kept distinct from those representing assessments of achievement and performance (Guskey, 2002a, 2006c; Stiggins, 2008a). The intent is to provide a more comprehensive and accurate picture of what students accomplish in school.

While middle school and high school teachers in the United States are just beginning to catch onto the idea of separate grades for product, process, and progress criteria, many Canadian educators have used the practice for years (Bailey & McTighe, 1996). An example of one such form is shown in Figure 7.1. This reporting form was adapted from one used in a Canadian school district. It also includes our idea of a Dream Team of teachers. It consists of a single sheet of paper, folded in the center. The front of the form includes a statement of purpose, information about the student, and information about the school. Inside are eight slots, four on each side of the page, corresponding to as many as eight different courses. Figure 7.1 depicts one side of the inside of the form, or four classes.

The slot for each class begins with a photograph of the teacher. These are included primarily to personalize the report card, since most middle school and high school report cards tend to be rather impersonal documents. It also helps parents become familiar with their child's teachers. Following the photograph is the teacher's name and the name of the class. In this district, the report card designers merged the reporting program with the scheduling

Figure 7.1   Example of a Secondary Reporting Form

Ms. Angelou	Ms. Angelou—Language Arts				
	Achievement A	Participation 4	Homework 2	Punctuality 3	Effort 3
	This quarter, we focused on poetry and different poetic forms. Students read both well-known and lesser-known poets and constructed their own poems. Chris actively participated in class discussions and wrote several excellent poems but needs to be more conscientious about completing homework assignments on time.				
Mr. Mori	Mr. Mori—Algebra II				
	Achievement B	Participation 3	Homework 1	Punctuality 3	Effort 3
	Our class worked on solving complex problems using higher order equations. We also explored problem applications in physics. Chris did fairly well on class quizzes and assessments, and I am sure Chris would do better if homework exercises were completed.				
Ms. Roosevelt	Ms. Roosevelt—Western Civilization				
	Achievement A	Participation 4	Homework 3	Punctuality 4	Effort 4
	We explored the influence of the Roman Empire on modern society, especially in language and government. Students also worked in teams to develop cooperative projects related to various aspects of Roman society. Chris was an active participant in all class activities, demonstrated a deep understanding of all issues, and was a valued contributor on the project.				
Mr. Einstein	Mr. Einstein—Physics				
	Achievement B	Participation 2	Homework 2	Punctuality 3	Effort 3
	This quarter, we concentrated on the physics of atomic and subatomic particles. Students solved problems related to relativity. Chris did well on most classroom quizzes and large assessments but needs to become a more active participant in class discussions.				

PHOTO CREDITS: Maya Angelou (Source: U.S. Federal Government, Executive Office of the President of the United States); Shigefumi Mori (Source: Wikimedia); Eleanor Roosevelt (Source: Wikimedia); Albert Einstein (Source: Library of Congress).

program so that students' report cards appear in the order of their class schedules.

Under the teacher's name is a row of grades. First comes the "Achievement" grade based on students' performance on projects, assessments, and other demonstrations of learning. Often expressed as a letter grade (A = Advanced, B = Proficient, C = Basic, D = Needs Improvement, F = Unsatisfactory) or percentage, this achievement grade represents the teacher's judgment of the student's level of performance or accomplishment relative to explicit learning goals established for the course. Decisions about promotion, as well as calculations of grade point averages and class ranks, are based solely on these achievement or product grades.

In addition, teachers assign separate grades or marks for class participation, homework, punctuality of assignments, and effort. Because these factors typically relate to specific student behaviors, teachers record numerical marks for each. So, for example, the class participation mark might relate to descriptors such as these:

4 = Consistently

3 = Usually

2 = Sometimes

1 = Rarely

The educators designing this form decided to focus only on the frequency of participation, rather than its quality. Some might argue that it would be helpful to distinguish between students who speak every day in class but say nothing of substance and those who rarely speak but when they do, offer comments reflecting clear insight and careful reasoning. While reporting on aspects of quality is certainly appropriate, gathering and accurately recording such evidence can be challenging for any teacher.

When necessary, teachers also clarify the mark's meaning by identifying more specific behavioral indicators for each level of performance. For example, the indicators for a "Homework" mark might include the following:

4—All homework assignments completed and turned in on time

3—Only one or two missing or incomplete homework assignments

2—Three to five missing or incomplete homework assignments

1—Numerous missing or incomplete homework assignments

As was true of the mark for "Participation," these indicators focus exclusively on homework completion and set aside issues related to correctness or quality. Developing accurate indicators of "Effort" can be comparably challenging.

Below the grades is a narrative composed of two distinctive parts. For the first part, each teacher types two or three sentences describing the focus of the class during that particular marking period. In Ms. Angelou's language arts class, for example, she states:

> *This quarter, we focused on poetry and different poetic forms. Students read both well-known and lesser-known poets and constructed their own poems.*

After typing these sentences, the teacher enters a class code, and the sentences are printed on the report card of every student enrolled in that class. In other words, the teacher needs to type these sentences only one time. The teacher then accesses each student's individual record and adds a sentence about the performance of that student. In the language arts class, for example, Ms. Angelou added:

> *Chris actively participated in class discussions and wrote several excellent poems, but he needs to be more conscientious about completing homework assignments on time.*

Looking over the report card, it seems clear this particular student has a problem with homework. Several teachers have noted the problem. A report card like this offers parents, students, and others a highly detailed and informative report about each student's performance during the marking period.

The Advantages of Multiple Grades or Marks

On first viewing this form, some educators express concern that it will require a great deal of extra work. But the teachers who use forms such as this claim that it actually requires *less work* than traditional reporting forms. They collect no additional information than what they gathered previously, and they eliminate the final step of deciding how those various forms of evidence will be combined. As a result, they avoid all of the arguments and debates about how best to weight and integrate the different sources of evidence to determine a single hodgepodge grade.

The teachers who use such multiple grade forms further maintain that students take process elements, such as class participation and homework, more seriously when they are marked separately. No longer can poor performance in these elements be disguised in an overall course grade. Teachers also say that it helps them provide more specific guidance to parents concerned with what steps might be taken to improve their child's achievement or product grade.

Occasionally teachers question the need for this level of specificity. Upon reflection, however, most discover that when they include homework assignments as part of an overall grade for students, they face this challenge anyway. In determining an overall grade, teachers must decide how much credit to give students for completing homework assignments or how much credit to take away for assignments that are missing or turned in late. The same is true when reporting a separate grade or mark for homework. In this case, however, teachers must ensure that students understand the various performance levels so that they know what their mark signifies and what can be done to make improvements.

Reporting separate grades for product, process, and progress criteria also makes grading more meaningful. If a parent questions the teacher about a product grade, for example, the teacher simply points to the various process indicators and suggests, "Perhaps if your child completed homework assignments and participated more in class, the achievement grade would be higher." Parents generally favor the practice because it provides a more comprehensive profile of their child's performance in school. Employers and college admissions decision makers also like it because it offers more detailed information on students' accomplishments. With all grades reported on the transcript, a college admissions officer can distinguish between the student who earned high achievement grades with relatively little effort and the one who earned equally high grades through diligence and hard work. The transcript thus becomes a more robust document, which presents a more discerning portrait of students' high school experiences (Adelman, 1999).

Schools still have the information needed to compute grade point averages and class ranking, if such computations are important. Now, however, those averages and ranks are untainted by undefined aspects of process and progress. As such, they represent a more valid and appropriate measure of achievement and performance. Furthermore, to the extent that classroom assessments and state accountability assessments are based on the same standards for learning, the relationship between product grades and accountability assessment results will likely be much higher.

The key to success in reporting multiple grades, however, rests in the clear specification of indicators related to product, process, and progress criteria. Teachers must be able to describe how they plan to evaluate students' achievement, attitude, effort, behavior, and progress. Then they must clearly communicate these criteria to students, parents, and others.

Using Multiple Grades or Marks

Education leaders often grow frustrated in their efforts to introduce standards-based grading in middle schools and high schools, citing teachers' resistance and a general reluctance to change. But middle school and high school teachers face very different challenges in implementing standards-based grading than do elementary teachers, due primarily to curriculum differentiation. In most instances, all students in the third grade are expected to achieve the same learning goals or standards established for each subject area at that grade level. That is not the case, however, of all students in their sophomore year of high school. Middle school and high school students typically take different courses and engage in highly diverse programs of study. To develop reporting standards for every course in every program at the middle school and high school level represents a huge task.

Providing separate grades or marks for product, process, and progress goals on a secondary report card offers an efficient and effective intermediate step. No school or district we know that uses this type of multiple-grade system has told teachers how to determine students' achievement or product grades or even what elements must be included in those grades. That decision is left to individual teachers. All the administration requires is that nonachievement factors related to behavior, work habits, study skills, and the like be pulled out from the achievement grade. *Achievement* should reflect just that: what students know and are able to do at the time of reporting.

When this is done, moreover, it always seems to result in wonderful and highly professional conversations among teachers. Those who teach the same or similar courses begin discussing what sources of evidence they use to determine students' achievement or product grades. They evaluate the quality of that evidence based on the established purpose of the grade. Many initiate the use of common assessments to bring greater consistency to their grading practices and often base those common assessments on carefully articulated goals or standards for the course. After separating product or achievement from process and progress elements, teachers begin to see common assessments as a reasonable and necessary next step.

Developing meaningful, honest, and equitable grading policies and practices will continue to challenge middle school and high school educators. The challenge remains all the more daunting, however, if we continue to use reporting forms that require teachers to combine many diverse sources of evidence into a single symbol. Distinguishing specific product criteria and reporting an achievement grade based on these criteria allow teachers to offer a more precise description of students' academic achievement and performance. To the extent that process criteria related to homework, class participation, attitude, effort, responsibility, behavior, and other nonacademic factors remain important, they too can be reported, but they must be kept separate. Doing so will clarify the meaning of grades and greatly enhance their communicative value.

Standards-Based Reporting for Students With Special Needs

Another serious challenge educators face in implementing a standards-based report card relates to communicating the achievement and performance of students with special needs who are included in general education classrooms (Jung & Guskey, 2007). Families of children with disabilities find the detailed information offered through standards-based reporting especially vital as they consider placement and intervention decisions. The Individuals with Disabilities Education Acts (IDEA) of 1997 and 2004 recognize this critical need and require that Individualized Education Program (IEP) teams plan and document how progress will be monitored and communicated for students with disabilities (20 U.S.C. §1414[d][1][A]). Yet, despite this legal provision and widespread agreement on its importance, evidence indicates there is less compliance with appropriate progress monitoring than with any other IEP requirement (Etscheidt, 2006).

Grading Challenges in Special Education

The number of students with disabilities included in general classes, as well as the amount of time they spend there, has increased dramatically in recent years (Handler, 2003). Although a wealth of research verifies the positive effects of including students with disabilities (Baker, Wang, & Walberg, 1995; Carlberg & Kavale, 1980; Hunt, Farron-Davis, Beckstead, Curtis, & Goetz, 1994; Waldron, 1998), doing so poses challenges for grading and reporting. For students whose education occurs primarily in special education class-rooms, the special education teacher typically assigns most grades. General education teachers determine grades only for the few subject areas in which students are included. For students with disabilities who are fully included in general education classrooms, however, the division of grading responsibilities is less clear (Bursuck et al., 1996; Polloway et al., 1994).

A common strategy for grading students who are included involves the general education teacher taking responsibility for assigning all grades on the report card and the special education teacher taking responsibility for a separate report on progress toward IEP goals. Although this division of labor seems logical, deciding the appropriate grade for a general education content area can be especially complicated if performance in that content area is affected by the disability.

Take, for example, a fifth-grade student who is unable to demonstrate proficiency on fifth-grade standards because of multiple, severe disabilities but has worked hard and progressed well toward IEP goals. To fail this student, who has shown tremendous effort and progress, clearly seems unfair. Nevertheless, giving passing marks to a student who has not yet met performance standards for that grade level also seems inappropriate. Complicating matters still further are the legal requirements of grading students with disabilities. Most notably, IEPs must "enable the child to achieve passing marks and advance from grade to grade" (*Board of Education v. Rowley*, 1982, p. 4). Therefore, a failing grade for a student receiving special education services is considered an indication that appropriate educational services were *not* provided.

Despite more students with disabilities being included in general education classrooms for greater portions of the school day, little guidance has come from the special education community to address the challenge of grading included students (Jung & Guskey, 2007). Lacking specific policies or recommendations, most general education teachers make informal, individual grading adaptations for such students (Bursuck, Munk, & Olson, 1999; Polloway et al., 1994). These adaptations generally fall into five broad categories: (a) considering progress on IEP goals, (b) measuring progress over time, (c) prioritizing assignments or content differently, (d) considering indicators of effort or behavior, and (e) modifying the weights or scales for grading (Silva, Munk, & Bursuck, 2005). While these adaptations theoretically provide encouragement and opportunities for success, evidence indicates that in most cases they lead students to see grades not as an indication of their performance but as a reflection of who they are. The result tends to be decreased motivation and a diminished sense of efficacy (Ring & Reetz, 2000). Furthermore, even with these adaptations, most students in special education continue to receive low passing grades, placing them at risk for low self-esteem and for dropping out of school (Donahue & Zigmond, 1990).

Setting a Solid Foundation

To assign fair and accurate standards-based grades to students in special education, schools must first develop a high-quality grading and reporting system for all students (Guskey & Bailey, 2001). The initial step in establishing a high-quality, standards-based grading system requires that teachers distinguish the three types of learning goals and related standards that we stressed earlier: *product, process,* and *progress* goals (Guskey, 1996b, 2004). While product goals hold greatest importance in most standards-based environments, progress goals often become a major focus in evaluating the performance of students with special needs.

Recall that progress goals consider how much students gain from their learning experiences. In other words, they focus on how far students have come and how much improvement has been made, rather than just where they are (Guskey, 1996b, 2006c; Guskey & Jung, 2006). As we showed in Chapter 4, most of the research evidence on progress criteria comes from studies of individualized instruction (Esty & Teppo, 1992) and special education programs (Gersten, Vaughn, & Brengelman, 1996).

High-quality grading and reporting systems establish clear standards for product, process, and progress goals and then report each separately (Guskey, 1994a, 2006c; Stiggins, 2008a; Wiggins, 1996). For parents of students in special education, a high-quality grading and reporting system means they receive not only specific feedback about their children's achievement on grade-level standards but also essential information on effort and progress that can be key to making appropriate intervention and placement decisions (Jung & Guskey, 2007).

An Inclusive Grading Model

To guide educators in the process of developing appropriate policies for grading students with disabilities, Jung (2009; Jung & Guskey,

2007) developed the Five-Step Inclusive Grading Model. This model, shown in Figure 7.2, is designed to fit any standards-based learning environment and meet the legal requirements for reporting on the progress of students who have IEPs. Following are the five steps in the model.

1. Establish clear standards for student learning that distinguish product, process, and progress goals. An essential first step in developing an effective standards-based reporting system is to establish clear learning standards related to product, process, and progress goals. Then, based on explicit indicators of these goals, teachers assign separate grades or marks to each. In this way, grades or marks for learning skills, work habits, effort, and learning progress are kept distinct from evaluations of achievement and performance of grade-level product goals. The intent is to provide a more accurate and much more comprehensive picture of students' performance in school (Guskey, 2006c).

The key to success in reporting multiple grades, however, rests in the clear specification of indicators related to the product, process, and progress learning goals. Teachers must be able to describe clearly how they plan to evaluate students' achievement, attitude, behavior, effort, and progress. Then they must clearly communicate these criteria to students, families, and others.

2. For each standard, determine if it needs to be adapted for the student. Every student who qualifies for special education must have an IEP that outlines a specific plan of individualized annual goals, along with instructional strategies and adaptations needed to reach these goals. The student's IEP team, composed of the parents or guardians, the special education teacher, the regular education teacher, and related administrators, meets at least once per year to discuss progress and to update the IEP.

Considering each grade-level standard individually, teams should first consider whether or not any adaptation is needed. Teams often decide that the student has the ability to achieve the standard as described for that grade level. In these cases, no change in the standard or in reporting is needed. At other times, however, teams may decide that the student will likely need adaptations to achieve this standard. When this is true, teams move to Step 3.

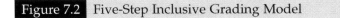

Figure 7.2 | Five-Step Inclusive Grading Model

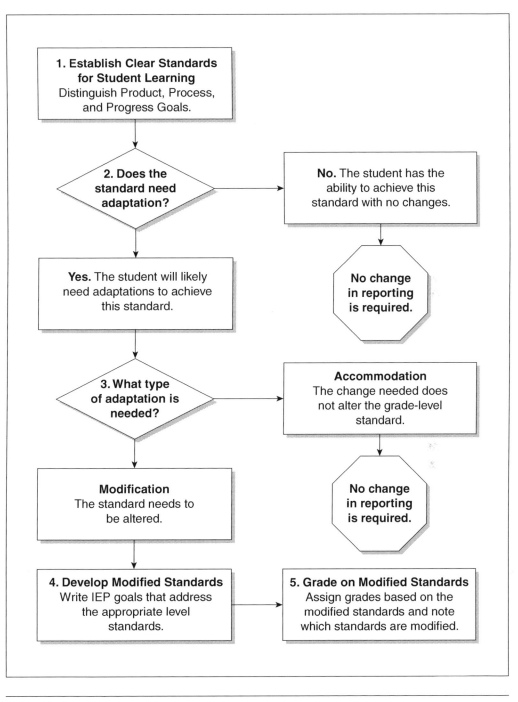

SOURCE: Adapted from Jung & Guskey, 2007.

3. If adaptation is needed, determine if that adaptation requires accommodation or modification. For standards that the team decides must be adapted for the student, the next step is to determine whether that adaptation will take the form of *accommodation* or *modification*. Adaptations that provide access to the general education curriculum but do not fundamentally alter the grade-level standard are considered *accommodations* (Freedman, 2005). For example, a fourth-grade student who has a learning disability in the area of reading may have audiotapes of social studies and science materials. This student also may take exams orally. Although the format for answering questions on exams is different in this case, the content of the questions and the substance of responses remain the same.

In subject areas where only accommodations are needed, students receiving special education should be assigned grades or marks according to the same criteria as all other students in the class, with no penalty for the accommodation. Similarly, a student with a learning disability who requires extra time to complete exams should be assigned a grade or mark based on the content of his or her responses. The grade should not be lowered because of the time extension, which simply provides access—it does not alter the standard. At the same time, the grade also should not be raised based on effort, progress, or any other factor that does not reflect learning or achievement.

In contrast, some students receiving special education need adaptations that are more substantial than accommodations. For these students, the IEP team may decide that some or all of the grade-level standards may not be achievable during the academic year and curricular *modifications* are required. A modification is an adaptation that fundamentally alters the grade-level expectation (Freedman, 2005). In other words, while accommodations serve primarily to level the playing field, modifications shorten the field or lower the goal. The IEP team may conclude, for instance, that in the current academic year, the fourth-grade student from the above example will not be able to achieve some of the fourth-grade language arts standards, such as the ability to recognize and use grade-level vocabulary in text. The team must then determine a more appropriate, lower-level standard for the IEP. This student will thus have both accommodations and curricular modifications.

The IEP team decides the need for accommodations or modifications for each standard. Some students may have only accommodations; others will have only modifications. Many students will require a combination of accommodations for some standards and modifications for others. Although IEPs typically include both types of adaptations, historically, IEP teams may not have recorded these differently. For grading and reporting purposes in a standards-based environment, however, this distinction is necessary.

4. If modification is required, develop an appropriate modified standard. For the fourth-grade student in the example above, communicating failure on a grade-level language arts standard provides no meaningful information about the student's current level of performance or achievement. The IEP team must, therefore, determine a modified standard that this student will be able to achieve with appropriate special education services. Modified standards should be clearly linked to the grade-level standard and recorded on the IEP as an annual goal. So instead of "recognize and use fourth-grade vocabulary words in text," a more appropriate standard might be to "recognize and use second-grade vocabulary words in text." The student should then be graded based on performance on this modified standard, not failure to meet the defined grade-level standard.

5. Assign a grade or mark based on the modified standard and note on the report card which standards have been modified. By providing information on students' specific achievements, separate from indicators of effort and progress, and then clearly communicating the meaning of each grade assigned, educators can offer families much better information about children's learning success (Guskey, 2002b). If some or all of the grades for achievement are based on modified standards, then the reporting system must include additional information to ensure that families understand their children's success is based on work appropriate for their development level, not their assigned grade level. To base grades or marks on modified standards without communicating what was truly assessed is no more meaningful or fair than giving failing grades based on grade-level standards. Schools might use a superscript letter or place an asterisk beside the report card grades or marks for those standards that are modified. The accompanying footnote might then state, "Based on modified standards," and direct the reader to the standards on which the grade was based.

Understanding that modifications were provided is important to anyone trying to interpret the grade or mark, including families, potential employers, and even postsecondary institutions. By law, however, the notation on the transcript must not in any way identify the student as receiving special education services or as receiving accommodations. Noting that modifications were provided is legal but only if modifications are available to any student who needs them, regardless of special education eligibility (Jung, 2009).

Furthermore, a footnote to the notation for a modified standard can use the word *modified* on the report card. However, phrases such as *special education goals* or *IEP goals* on the transcript would be considered a violation of Section 504 of the Rehabilitation Act of 1973 and Title II of the Americans With Disabilities Act of 1990. When *modified* is used, an accompanying report might then include the IEP goals or a narrative describing the details of the IEP.

Although federal legislation does not explicitly prohibit schools from making notations of special education status in a report card, provided that it is shared only with families, it discourages the practice for two reasons. First, the special education status of a student is not needed to interpret grades in a standards-based environment. And second, families of students who receive special education services already know their children have disabilities or developmental delays. Reminding them of this with each report card is unnecessary.

FIVE STEPS IN THE INCLUSIVE GRADING MODEL

1. Establish clear standards for student learning that distinguish product, process, and progress goals.

2. For each standard, determine if it needs to be adapted for the student.

3. If adaptation is needed, determine if that adaptation requires accommodation or modification.

4. If modification is required, develop an appropriate modified standard.

5. Assign a grade or mark based on the modified standard and note on the report card which standards have been modified (see Jung, 2009).

Determine the Need for Additional Goals

One additional factor needs to be considered when assigning grades to students with special needs in a standards-based environment. Some students receiving special education may have additional IEP goals that are pertinent to the student's development but extend beyond the general education curriculum. A student with Pervasive Developmental Delay, for example, may have IEP goals related to social-emotional development. A goal such as "initiate and maintain interaction with peers," may be particularly important for this student. Although such goals may not be included on the general report card, monitoring and reporting on these goals remain important. To do so, schools should continue to provide this information on a regular basis through a report card supplement. Doing so will allow families and others on the IEP team to make appropriate decisions based on all aspects the child's progress and achievement in school (National Center on Secondary Education and Transition, 2005).

Standards-Based Reporting for Students Who Are Gifted or Talented

A third major challenge that confronts educators implementing a standards-based report card is how to report accurately on the learning of students considered exceptionally gifted or talented. How do we appropriately communicate the achievement and performance of these students when, in many instances, they will go beyond whatever standards are established for their grade level or their courses? A grade of A may tell gifted students and their parents very little about the new knowledge or skills gained, since many gifted students master the learning standards for a particular grade level one to three years before entering that grade (Peckron, 1996).

In addition, as soon as educators indicate that a student has mastered the knowledge and skills outlined in the standards set for a grade level or course, parents immediately ask, "What more are you going to do for my child?" Although this puts educators on the spot, it is an honest and reasonable question. One of the greatest concerns shared by the parents of gifted or talented students with regard to standards-based approaches is that when their children demonstrate proficiency, which they may be able to do before instruction begins, they will simply be assigned busywork to keep them occupied while the other students catch up. Furthermore, because gifted or talented students typically are ahead of grade-level work, a standards-based report card focused on grade-level standards tells nothing about the true scope or level of their learning and achievement.

To provide adequately for the needs of these advanced learners, educators must be prepared to go beyond the curriculum expectations set for a grade level or course. Specifically, teachers need to be ready to expand or extend the learning opportunities they offer such students. These opportunities should go further in the subject or explore topics more deeply in order to challenge these students and enhance their learning. To report accurately on how well students have performed with regard to these expanded learning opportunities also requires broader reporting options.

Supplemental Reports

Regardless of its quality, a standards-based report card can rarely communicate the true achievement and performance of students considered gifted or talented. We also find that the parents of gifted or talented students seldom are satisfied simply knowing that their child has mastered grade-level standards. In many cases, they already know that. For these reasons, we recommend that a supplemental report be developed both to record the extended learning goals or standards on which these students are working and to report on their level of performance with regard to those standards.

This supplemental report should have four major parts: (1) a clear description of the extended learning goals or standards on which students are working, (2) an outline of the learning tasks or activities in which students have engaged as part of their learning experiences, (3) a list of the criteria used to judge or evaluate students' achievement or performance, and (4) a record of students' current level of progress or accomplishment. Let's consider each of these parts in greater detail.

1. A Clear Description of the Extended Learning Goals or Standards. To provide appropriate learning opportunities for students who are gifted or talented, educators must develop learning goals or standards that encourage them to go beyond established grade-level or course standards. These extended standards should tap the highest levels of cognitive skill (see Bloom, 1956) and may involve expressions of creativity and/or critical thinking. They also should be appropriate for students' development level. Most important, these extended standards should focus on topics or issues that are interesting and engaging to students. If they involve merely solving more and harder problems, then they are unlikely to be meaningful to students or provide them with valuable learning experiences. Depending on the age of the students, many teachers find it beneficial to involve students directly in the development of these extended learning standards.

2. An Outline of the Learning Tasks or Activities in Which Students Have Engaged. Parents want to know not only the learning goals on which their children are working but also the means by which those goals are to be accomplished. Sometimes these tasks involve self-selected learning experiences in which students engage individually. Developing a special project or preparing a report on a topic that holds keen interest for students would be examples. At other times, the tasks involve group activities where students work collaboratively to plan, develop, and carry out a project. To report on individual performance, each student may have a specific role and unique responsibilities in the project.

FOUR MAJOR PARTS OF A SUPPLEMENTAL REPORT FOR GIFTED OR TALENTED STUDENTS

1. A clear description of the extended learning goals or standards on which students are working

2. An outline of the learning tasks or activities in which students have engaged as part of their learning experiences

3. A list of the criteria used to judge or evaluate students' achievement or performance

4. A record of students' current level of progress or accomplishment

---

3. A List of the Criteria Used to Judge or Evaluate Students' Achievement or Performance. As we stressed in Chapter 2, students need to know the expectations for their performance and how it will be judged. For meaningful reporting, parents need to know these expectations, too. So accompanying the tasks or activities designed for students who are gifted or talented should be specific criteria for judging their achievement or performance. In many instances, educators articulate these criteria in *independent study agreements* or *learning contracts* developed collaboratively by the teacher and students (Peckron, 1996). Sometimes parents are involved as well so that they know what guidelines have been set and the timeline for completion. In some cases, mentors or specialists from the school district or community provide additional support for students' contract work. Reporting typically includes copies of the agreements or contracts, along with the completed reports, photographs, video, or digital records of the project.

4. A Record of Students' Current Level of Progress or Accomplishment. Most of the activities related to extended learning goals or standards in which gifted or talented students engage can be completed within the marking period. Their grades or marks are, therefore, based on a summative evaluation of their achievement of the goals, made in reference to the established criteria. Some activities require more time, however, and students may work on them over two or three marking periods. When this is true, teachers must be able to communicate to parents not only what students have done but also the quality of their performance to that point. Independent study agreements or learning contracts can be very helpful in making these assessments because they include timelines for completion. In most cases, the agreements or contracts also specify checkpoints or benchmarks that can be noted in students' progress toward successfully completing the project or task.

This description of the parts of a supplemental report may make it sound painfully detailed and extremely time consuming for teachers to develop. But rarely is that the case. In fact, most supplemental reports are simply narrative descriptions of the special activities in which gifted or talented students have been involved and how well they have performed. The box below shows one example.

TEACHER ASSESSMENT AND COMMENTS

Jessica's scientific investigation of population trends shows her ability to follow appropriate data collection techniques, use proper testing procedures, analyze information, report results, and draw logical conclusions. Her identification and evaluation of factors that may have affected her results required high-level thinking skills and deductive reasoning. Her project shows her skill in setting goals, determining priorities, and meeting deadlines. She demonstrated excellent time management and organizational skills. She also showed she has the courage to take risks and defend her interpretations of evidence. Jessica met all of the expectations set for her project and produced a truly excellent report.

Surveys of parents of gifted or talented students indicate that they value these types of written comments from teachers more than high grades or marks (Peckron, 1996). Such descriptions show parents much more clearly than traditional report card grades that teachers recognize the special talents and abilities of their children. They also assure parents that extra efforts are being made to meet their children's unique learning needs.

Summary

The three special cases presented in this chapter pose distinct challenges to educators in their efforts to develop and implement standards-based report cards. The first challenge relates to grading and reporting in middle schools and high schools. An essential step in transitioning to a standards-based system at these levels is to move away from reporting forms that require teachers to combine diverse sources of information into a single grade or mark. Reporting forms must distinguish specific achievement or product criteria from those representing process—such as homework, class participation, attitude, effort, responsibility, and behavior—and progress, which relates to specific improvement or gain. Making this distinction and reporting separate grades for each criterion type will greatly clarify the meaning of grades and significantly enhance their communicative value.

The second challenge involves the adaptations necessary to provide fair and accurate grades or marks for students with special needs who are included in regular classrooms. Reporting separately on product, process, and progress learning goals and situating product or achievement grades within the context of accommodations and modifications offer a promising alternative to adapted grading within a standards-based environment (Jung, 2009). The IEP can serve to document the curricular accommodations and modifications made for students who receive special education. If the IEP team decides that only accommodations are needed, then no change in reporting is necessary. However, if the IEP team decides to modify particular standards that they judge to be inappropriate for the student, then modifications should be noted on the report card, making no reference to "IEP" or "special education." Process and progress indicators remain an important part of grading and reporting, but they are kept separate from indicators of students' achievement of specific learning standards. As a result, students with disabilities and their families have honest information that they are able to interpret accurately and use effectively.

The third challenge concerns appropriate standards-based grading for students considered to be especially gifted and talented. Because of the advanced skills and abilities these students bring to classrooms, standards-based report cards rarely communicate their true achievement and performance. Furthermore, in many cases, they have already mastered the learning goals and standards set for their grade level. For these students, we recommend that a supplemental report be developed to record the extended learning goals or standards planned for them and report on their level of performance with regard to those standards.

Considering the distinct challenges presented by each of these special cases while developing a standards-based report card and planning its implementation will greatly improve the chances of success.

8

Additional Development Issues

Although we have already discussed the essential steps involved in the process of developing a standards-based report card, several additional issues deserve special attention. These issues can profoundly affect development procedures and the success of implementation. Attending to these issues early in the development process will ease the transition to a standards-based system and greatly enhance positive interactions among those involved in this significant change effort.

Always Return to the Purpose

As we stressed earlier, the adage from architecture that "form follows function" provides a lesson for educators involved in developing standards-based report cards: *method follows purpose*. In our work with schools and school districts throughout the United States and Canada, we have reviewed numerous report cards and learned about the reporting methods used at every grade level from preschool through college and university classes. This work, along with our own informal surveys and interviews with parents, students, and teachers, has shown us that the reporting methods perceived most positively are those designed to serve a particular purpose and intended for a particular audience. In other words, they are *context-specific*. A form or method of reporting that works well in one setting with a particular audience may not work equally well in a different setting with a different audience. In all contexts, a clearly defined purpose *must* precede the development of a reporting form and every other element in a comprehensive reporting system.

What do we mean by *clearly defined purpose?* Suppose, for example, that the initial purpose defined for one element in a district's reporting system is to provide information students can use for self-evaluation. Developers might then ask further probing questions that contribute to the development of appropriate reporting tools or forms that serve this purpose:

"How frequently do we want to provide students with information for self-evaluation?"

"How will we ensure that students use the information for self-evaluation?"

"Will that information also be shared with parents or others?"

"How will students demonstrate appropriate self-evaluation?"

"What evidence shows the effects of self-evaluation procedures?"

If the purpose is actually "to encourage student self-evaluation on a frequent and consistent basis," then portfolios or exhibits of student work would be excellent tools. If, however, the purpose is "to engage students in evaluating their own performance after being given summative information from teachers each marking period," then a more appropriate approach may be to add a special section to the report card for students to record evaluative comments, set goals, and determine what evidence would best reflect attainment of those goals.

Four Qualities of Effective Report Cards

No matter what purpose is chosen, all effective standards-based report cards share several common characteristics. In our review of dozens of report cards and reporting forms, we find that the most effective ones do several things well. Specifically, an effective standards-based report card

1. reports on product, process, and progress goals separately;

2. creates an accurate picture of academic strengths and challenges;

3. balances detail with practicality; and

4. is concise, understandable, and easy to interpret.

Following are some guidelines and real-life samples to illustrate each of these qualities.

Report on Product, Process, and Progress Goals Separately

We cannot overemphasize the importance of separating information about students' achievement, performance, and academic *products* from information about their work habits, study skills, life skills, workforce skills, interpersonal skills, and other noncognitive *process* skills (see Silva, 2009). Reporting forms that do this well provide parents with information about different aspects of students' achievement in each subject area (product) but also communicate information about students' consistency in demonstrating process elements, such as "Demonstrates Self-Control" and "Uses Time Well." Figure 8.1 shows

Figure 8.1	Elementary Reporting Form Illustrating Grades for Learning Behaviors (Process Skills)

Learning Behaviors	1st	2nd	3rd	4th
Works and plays cooperatively.				
Works well independently.				
Accepts responsibility for returning homework, books, and school-related materials on time.				
Uses time profitably.				
Demonstrates self-control.				
Demonstrates neatness and organizational skills.				
Respects rights, opinions, and property of others.				
Follows rules and displays appropriate behavior.				
Follows oral and written directions.				
Listens during instructional lessons.				
Seeks help when needed.				
Effectively solves social conflicts.				

Key to Process Skills Grades:

    4 = Consistently or Independently

    3 = Usually

    2 = Sometimes

    1 = Seldom

    NE = Not Evaluated

an example of a reporting form that focuses on process elements specifically related to learning behaviors. This form comes from an elementary school that serves students in kindergarten through Grade 5.

Multisection reporting forms that include grades or marks for both product and process elements give parents explicit information about students' academic performance, as well as important feedback about students' learning behaviors or work habits. This information allows parents to develop a clearer picture of their child as a learner. But perhaps more important, it helps parents better target improvement efforts when needed.

High school standards-based reporting forms often have sections devoted to process skills like the "Work Ethic Checklist" shown in Figure 8.2. Though displaying only 4 of the 37 total skills included in

Figure 8.2 Excerpt from a High School Work Ethic Checklist (Skills 1-4 of the 37 Skills Assessed)

WORK ETHIC CHECKLIST

Student: _____   Grade: _____

Advisor: _____

Reporting Period: ❑1   ❑2   ❑3   ❑4

Work Ethic Description	Evaluation		
	Still Developing	Satisfactory	Exemplary
1. Dresses and grooms in a manner that satisfies the school dress code.	❑	❑	❑
2. Comes to school on time each day, except for unavoidable personal emergencies and serious illness.	❑	❑	❑
3. Accepts criticism and suggestions in a positive manner.	❑	❑	❑
4. Is present and at work during all school hours.	❑	❑	❑
[Complete checklist includes 37 items]			

Notes:

Comments:

the Checklist, this figure offers a clear picture of the form's intent. Teachers developed this list of skills based on interviews with business leaders regarding the behaviors they want students to master before entering the workplace. The Checklist also helped these educators communicate emphatically their desire to have *all* students develop specific employability skills prior to graduation.

One team of secondary teachers with whom we worked is primarily responsible for entering ninth-grade students. This ninth-grade "school within a school" was established to monitor and prepare ninth-grade students better for the rigors of high school and to promote student success in the freshman year. These teachers decided they needed to stress the importance of process skills to encourage students to develop good study practices and classroom work habits. They coordinated their schedules to include a daily common planning period when they compared notes on students' achievement and planned essential corrective activities when needed. In addition, they worked closely with the counselor assigned to the ninth-grade students to unify efforts to help students with specific problems or needs.

To emphasize the importance of specific process skills, the team developed the form shown in Figure 8.3. This form is filled out by each subject area teacher and attached to the regular report card. In meetings with parents to gather information about their reactions to the form, the teachers were surprised to hear parents' overwhelmingly positive response. Parents said things such as,

> *Of course, I want my child to get good grades. But what I value most is that he is respectful to others, that he shows responsibility, and that he tries his hardest to get all of his work done. That's what he'll need when he goes to work!*

Many parents also commented that the form enabled them to see more clearly how their children behaved differently from class to class, explaining at least partially the differences in the achievement or product grades. These discrepancies in the process skills reports became the topic of many discussions at home and frequently resulted in additional face-to-face conversations or telephone conferences among parents, students, and teachers. Some parents further reported that they typically glanced at the grades but then turned immediately to the process skills reports to find out about behavior, homework completion, and other work habits.

Teachers found that these reports took little time to complete because they required teachers simply to circle the appropriate level on the report to describe each student's work habits. This form and various adaptations of it are being used successfully in several secondary schools today.

Figure 8.3 Process Skills Report for Secondary Students

Process Skills Report				
Skill	4—Exemplary	3—Good	2—Fair	1—Needs Improvement
Attendance	No absences.	Seldom absent, always excused.	Occasionally absent (excused).	Often absent, sometimes unexcused.
Punctuality	No tardies.	Tardy 1 or 2 times.	Tardy 3 to 5 times.	Tardy more than 5 times.
Preparedness	Consistently brings materials.	Usually brings materials.	Sometimes brings materials.	Rarely brings materials.
Learning Behavior	Consistently sustains good attention; self-engages in classroom tasks.	Usually sustains good attention; may need support to become engaged in classroom tasks.	Sometimes able to maintain attention; has difficulty staying engaged in classroom tasks.	Rarely maintains attention; disrupts other engaged learners.
Citizenship	Consistently respects the rights of others and follows classroom rules.	Usually respects the rights of others and follows classroom rules.	Sometimes respects the rights of others or needs teacher guidance to follow rules.	Rarely respects the rights of others, including teacher, or disregards classroom rules.
Cooperation or "Team Player"	Consistently participates and contributes well in group tasks and is open to working in a group.	Usually participates and contributes in group tasks but may be reluctant to work in a group.	Sometimes does not contribute or participate in group activities or has difficulty working in a group.	Rarely participates well in a group or disrupts others in group activity.
Work Completion (During Class)	Consistently completes class work or tests.	Usually completes class work or tests; makes up missing work promptly.	Sometimes completes class work or tests; makes up missing work infrequently.	Rarely completes class work; rarely makes up missing work.
Homework Completion	Consistently completes homework on time; no assignments missing.	Usually completes homework on time; one or two missing assignments.	Sometimes completes homework on time; several missing assignments.	Rarely completes homework on time; many missing assignments.
Homework Quality	Consistently produces quality work.	Usually produces quality work.	Sometimes produces quality work.	Rarely produces quality work.

Separate Grades or Marks for Product and Progress

To provide a clear picture of what students have accomplished, it is also best to separate information about students' achievement, performance, and academic products from information about how much learning *progress* they have made. As we described earlier, certain academically talented students might demonstrate a high level of achievement based on grade-level standards yet make relatively little learning progress. Conversely, other students might make significant progress and still not reach a proficient level with regard to the standards set for a grade level or course. Such differences are important to parents in evaluating the performance of their children.

The high school reporting forms in Figures 8.4 and 8.5 provide examples to show how progress might be communicated. These forms offer a detailed account of students' progress in compiling a portfolio of work required for graduation. The educators who developed this form identified ten academic standards directly related to skills needed in the workplace. Included are proficiencies such as career preparation, oral and written communication, and teamwork. The criteria for meeting each standard are clearly articulated for students, parents, and others, including employers.

As students advance through their four years in high school, they collect artifacts and other examples of their work to demonstrate their mastery of each standard. The reporting form illustrates their progress on all ten standards. Each marking period, the teachers record the number of artifacts assembled to date, the total number of artifacts required, and the percent completed. In addition, every student has a

Figure 8.4   Example of Portfolio Criteria for the Careers Learning Standard

---

Portfolio Standard 1: Careers

Students will prepare for careers of their own choosing.

While performing individual or group tasks, students will do the following:

1.01 Demonstrate awareness of a variety of career options.

1.02 Demonstrate awareness of the changing qualifications necessary for a variety of career options.

1.03 Maintain an accurate personal resume.

1.04 Demonstrate skills and knowledge necessary to complete a variety of application forms accurately for jobs, schools, colleges, and universities.

1.05 Demonstrate effective interviewing skills.

1.06 Demonstrate mastery of essential career skills, including those measured on the Comprehensive Test of Basic Skills (CTBS) and the Higher Council for Science and Technology (HCST).

Figure 8.5 Report Card Showing Progress in Meeting Portfolio Criteria

Portfolio Assessment Report

Student: Olivia Grad-Soon

Advisor: Mortimer Relba

Assessment Date: October 20 (First-Quarter Report)

Grade: 11

Standard	I Careers	II Communication	III Human Diversity	IV Human Relations	V Information	VI Math	VII Resources	VIII Systems	IX Technology	X Thinking
Total Artifacts Presented	14	30	20	25	12	12	12	31	2	13
Total Artifacts Required	15	42	24	27	15	42	12	31	31	15
Percent Completed	93%	71%	83%	93%	80%	29%	100%	100%	6%	87%

Advisor's Recommendations and Comments:
Olivia has been working hard this quarter and has made considerable progress since our last assessment. She has completed Core Portfolio requirements for Standards I, IV, VII, VIII, and X. Next she should concentrate on those standards below the 85% mark. In particular, Olivia should try to focus on mathematics and technology during the next quarter. Olivia's communication artifacts show excellent progress, and she should soon complete this area of study. Good work, Olivia!

Student's Recommendations and Comments:
I don't have too many items in mathematics or technology because I was in the Language Arts/Social Studies division this quarter. My goal is to complete either the mathematics or the technology standards before our next assessment. I really worked hard in my communications standards, and I'm not sure why I still don't have enough artifacts. I plan to do more of my work this time. (I know I said that last time, but this time I really mean it!)

"teacher advisor," who completes a brief narrative on the reporting form that describes both the level of achievement and amount of progress to date. Finally, students contribute to the form by writing recommendations and comments regarding their own work and progress.

The clarity and detail of the reporting form shown in Figure 8.5 provides parents with specific information each marking period about where students stand on completing important graduation requirements. Not only does it describe teachers' appraisals of the products and artifacts students have compiled, it also gives parents and others a clear picture of how much progress students have made.

Creates an Accurate Picture of Academic Strengths and Challenges

In our work helping educators design standards-based report cards, we have talked with numerous groups of teachers, students, and parents. We also have conducted informal surveys with these same groups. Among parents, we find they most frequently mention three needs:

1. Parents want clearer and more understandable information about teachers' expectations for their child's learning and behavior in school.

2. Parents want more specific and detailed information about their child's learning progress in school.

3. Parents want practical suggestions from teachers about how best to help their child when problems or difficulties arise.

Our experience indicates that most parents dearly love their children and sincerely want them to succeed in school (see Henderson & Berla, 1994). At the same time, they are uncertain of teachers' specific expectations and precisely what they can do at home to help (Hoover-Dempsey et al., 2005). This formative aspect of reporting is very important to parents, but it is frequently neglected or ignored by educators (Kreider & Lopez, 1999).

We have also learned in our work with parents that many prefer letter grades on reporting forms. It's not that they are convinced of the merits of letter grades in comparison to other reporting methods. Rather, it is because they experienced letter grades in their educational backgrounds and believe they understand what letter grades mean. To most parents, letter grades possess two highly desirable qualities: they communicate information clearly, and they are easy to interpret. As educators, however, we know that when a single letter grade is assigned to describe a student's performance in a subject area, a large quantity of information must be combined into that single symbol. One overall letter grade simply cannot provide information of sufficient detail to give parents a clear picture of how their child is doing or how best to help their child improve or succeed. This formative aspect of reporting is impossible to support with a simple letter grade.

So how is it possible to create a clear picture of student achievement in meeting learning standards, while also providing sufficient detail on student strengths and weaknesses to encourage parent participation in the learning process? Some districts have gone to a two-part marking system, different from the two-part system we described in Chapter 5, which combines what parents view as an easy-to-interpret letter grade with separate marks on the important, discrete standards or skills students need to learn to achieve mastery or proficiency in that subject area or course. Figure 8.6 shows an example of this two-part marking system.

The student in this example received an overall B grade in mathematics. However, the marks for each skill area show more detailed feedback aimed at helping parents and the student identify areas of strength and challenge. This particular student, for example, completes assignments and understands basic math concepts studied for the marking period. She also computes accurately and shows a good understanding of basic math facts. At the same time, she has difficulty with mental calculation and making reasonable estimates. In addition, the teacher made a special note that this student needs to work on analyzing data (see the skills circled by the teacher with the added note). With this detailed information, teachers can make specific suggestions to parents about what might be done at home to help their child improve specific math skills. At the same time, the overall grade of B conveys that this student is achieving at a rate of 80–89 percent mastery of mathematics standards for the marking period—a very acceptable level of mastery.

Ensuring Accuracy in Reporting Academic Strengths and Challenges

We need to note, however, that the type of reporting form discussed above presents a new and significant challenge to teachers who have not yet fully adopted a standards-based approach to grading and reporting. Specifically, these teachers will want to assign subject area grades based on the total number of points accumulated during the marking period or an overall average of scores. They might, for example, look at the report card in Figure 8.6 and presume that this student received 23 out of a possible 32 skills points (eight skills, each worth a maximum of 4 points). Therefore, the student achieved at a 72 percent level and deserves a grade of C. Or they might look at the same example a different way and deduce that this student "usually"

Figure 8.6	Elementary Reporting Form Illustrating an Overall Grade for Achievement in Subject Area With Separate Math Skill Marks

	1st	2nd	3rd	4th
MATHEMATICS OVERALL GRADE:	B			
MATHEMATICS SKILLS MARKS:				
Demonstrates understanding of concepts.	3			
Shows work to demonstrate sound mathematical thinking.	3			
Computes accurately.	3			
Makes mental calculations and reasonable estimations.	2			
Uses strategies to solve problems.	3			
Collects, organizes & analyzes data. ←Area of difficulty	2			
Demonstrates a knowledge of basic facts.	3			
Completes assignments to provide adequate skill practice.	4			

OK!

Key to Marks

Subject Area Grade:
A = Outstanding (90–100% Mastery of Subject Goals)
B = Very Good (80–89% Mastery)
C = Satisfactory (70–79% Mastery)
D = Experiencing Difficulty (Below 70%)

Skills Marks:
4 = Consistently or Independently
3 = Usually
2 = Sometimes
1 = Seldom
NE = Not Evaluated

or "consistently" demonstrated mastery on six out of the eight discrete skills—or achieved at an "average rate" of 75 percent. This, too, would result in a grade of C, according to the report card scale.

Teachers who assign grades according to students' progress toward meeting specific learning standards, however, would consider the assessments, quizzes, demonstrations, projects, or other work that has been gathered and then decide what evidence

- is most important;
- is most closely aligned to each standard; and
- provides the most comprehensive picture of student mastery or proficiency.

If students do well on the learning tasks that are the most important and most comprehensive indicators of subject area mastery, then the student's overall grade also should reflect a solid mastery of the subject.

Again, using the example in Figure 8.6, this student appears to be computing accurately, understanding basic concepts, using sound mathematical thinking, and using correct problem solving strategies most of the time. In other words, this student shows good, solid mastery of these required skills. The B grade assigned by the teacher provides a more accurate reflection of this student's achievement than the C that might have been given had the teacher considered simply a total number of points or an overall average to determine the grade.

In addition, in a standards-based environment, teachers must always consider the recency of evidence they use in assigning a grade or mark. When using an overall average to determine grades, teachers usually weight the assessments, quizzes, and other evidence gathered at the beginning of a marking period the same as those sources of evidence gathered in the latter part of the marking period. But if the purpose of the grade is to show students' *current* level of mastery, then the most recent evidence is clearly the most accurate and most valid. Thus, it must be considered primary in determining the grade assigned.

In summary, when teachers use reporting forms aimed at communicating a clear and accurate picture of students' academic strengths and challenges, they must attach greatest importance to the evidence that is most comprehensive and most closely aligned to the specific learning standards. Furthermore, they must always give priority to the most recent evidence of student achievement to ensure accuracy in the grades assigned. By focusing on the most appropriate evidence, teachers can effectively use a two-part marking system, such as the one described here, to provide a detailed picture of students' learning that will assist parents in their efforts to help at home.

Using Narratives to Highlight Academic Strengths and Challenges

Another way to report academic strengths and challenges is through the use of narratives. Teachers assign letter grades as before, but then provide specific comments about students' academic strengths and challenges in a space included on the report card. As shown in the example in Figure 8.5, this type of reporting gives parents much more information than a single-letter grade offers. Such a report card does, however, require significantly more time for teachers to complete. Teachers with large numbers of students (e.g. elementary teachers for art, music, and physical education, who may see several hundred students each week, or secondary teachers with several large classes) will be challenged to complete even short narrative reports on every one of their students.

In one school district with which we are familiar, educators created a special report card attachment that utilized short written narratives from teachers, parents, *and* students. They use this form during conferences to give students individualized feedback on their specific academic strengths and challenges from both the teacher's and parents' point of view. After viewing these comments, students engage in self-evaluation activities and then write about their perceptions of areas of strength and areas needing improvement. An example of this type of form is illustrated in Figure 8.7.

Balances Detail With Practicality

In choosing an appropriate reporting form based on purpose, educators must seek a balance between detail and practicality. A standards-based report card should present a comprehensive picture of students' academic strengths and challenges. It also might include space to record students' self evaluations, depending on the defined purpose. But regardless of the form, a standards-based

Figure 8.7   Conference Form for Recording Academic Strengths and Challenges

Conference Assessment Form: Strengths and Challenges

Student: _____ Date: _____

Student	Teacher/Parent
What I do well:	**Teacher**: What you do well:
	Parent: What you do well:
What I want to learn more about:	**Teacher**: How I can help you:
	Parent: How I can help you:
What I need to improve:	**Teacher**: What you need to improve:
	Parent: What you need to improve:
Steps I will take to improve:	**Teacher**: Steps I will take to help you improve:
	Parent: Steps I will take to help you improve:

_____   _____   _____
Student Signature   **Teacher Signature**   **Parent Signature**

report card should be compact and understandable and should not require inordinate time for teachers to prepare or for parents to interpret (Linn & Gronlund, 2000).

Through our work with groups developing standards-based report cards, we regularly encounter elementary teachers who want to include highly detailed checklists of numerous skills or standards in each subject area. They resist efforts to reduce these checklists because they believe all of these skills and standards are important to students' learning. In addition, they want to be able to pass this information along to other teachers so that future instruction can be better tailored to the needs of each student.

Along with detailed checklists of academic skills or standards, many teachers feel it is important to report information on specific process skills, along with attendance information (absences and tardies). Some also want to include narrative comments to personalize the report card and further clarify the meaning of the information it contains. Invariably, these same teachers tell us that the inordinate time they spend preparing report cards takes away from the time they have to prepare lessons and organize instructional activities. As we stressed in Chapter 4, report cards consisting of multiple pages with long lists of skills and multiple categories of information are not only terribly time consuming for teachers to complete, they typically overwhelm parents with information they do not know how to use. More often than not, such report cards simply confuse parents.

Furthermore, the secondary teachers with whom we have worked often point out that preparing lengthy checklists of skills or standards to report on the learning of the large numbers of students they see throughout the school day would be extremely burdensome, if not impossible. For the most part, they favor a single letter grade, perhaps with a menu of predetermined comments that can be selected and inserted electronically on each student's report card. In fact, many secondary educators use electronic grading programs designed to do just that. Others use programs that print on the report card only comment numbers and then refer parents to a numbered comment list. But as we described in Chapter 6, although such programs may be efficient and easy to use, both our surveys and those of others reveal that these reporting tools are the *least* favored by parents. Many parents indicate that such forms depersonalize the reporting process and they really do not like them.

Striking an appropriate balance between detail and practicality is essential for everyone involved in the reporting process—parents, students, and teachers. At all levels, the report card should offer information that is sufficiently detailed to provide parents and students with information that is meaningful and helpful in portraying students' current level of achievement and performance in school. At the same time, the information cannot be so detailed that it overwhelms parents and students with information they do not understand and cannot use appropriately. A clearly stated purpose will facilitate the tough decisions that need to be made regarding the amount of detail included on the report card. Parents and students— the primary recipients of the report card—can also be called on to provide valuable feedback about meaningfulness and practicality during the development process.

Is Concise, Understandable, and Easy to Interpret

As we stressed in Chapter 3, *developing a standards-based report card is primarily a challenge in effective communication.* While the purpose of a standards-based report card may vary from one setting to another, it always serves primarily as a communication tool. As such, recipients of the report card (i.e., parents, guardians, other adults, and/or students) must be able to understand and make sense of the information it includes. To this end, we know that report card developers must do the following:

- Avoid educational jargon or words that are simply unfamiliar to parents, such as *phonological awareness* or *emergent literacy.*
- Organize the report card so that the most important information is conveyed first.
- Aim for simplicity and brevity in both the number of standards and the number of categories reported.
- Provide a key to grades or marks that is easy to understand.

Perhaps the most important step report card developers can take to ensure these qualities in the forms they construct is to have groups of parents, students, and others review draft versions. By conducting simple focus groups, developers can receive excellent feedback and comments that are invaluable in making the report clear, concise, and easy to understand. One development team with whom we worked, for example, believed that literacy skills were vitally important for all students in the early elementary grades. As part of their development efforts, they put together a checklist of skills for reading similar to the one shown in Figure 8.8.

| Figure 8.8 | Checklist of Reading Skills for a Standards-Based Report Card |

Early Literacy Skills

- Has made the transition from emergent to "real" reading.
- Reads aloud with accuracy and comprehension any text that is appropriately designed for the first half of the year.
- Accurately decodes regular, one-syllable words and nonsense words (e.g., *sit*, *zot*) using print-sound mapping to sound out unknown words.
- Uses letter-sound correspondence knowledge to sound out unknown words when reading text.
- Monitors own reading and self-corrects when an incorrectly identified word does not fit with cues provided by the letters in the word or the context surrounding the word.
- Reads and comprehends both fiction and nonfiction that is appropriately designed for grade level.
- Creates own written text for others to read.
- Notices when difficulties are encountered in understanding text.
- Reads and understands simple written directions.
- Predicts and justifies what will happen next in stories.
- Exhibits prior knowledge of topics in expository test.

After careful review by a focus group consisting of parents, upper elementary and middle school teachers, a principal, and a few high school students, they revised the checklist to one more like that illustrated in Figure 8.9.

Without the insightful comments and suggestions from the focus group, the development team would have released a draft version of these important skills that certainly would have been met with questions, some confusion, and perhaps negativity. The revised version of the skills, however, was positively received by all groups. Having small groups of parents, students, and others review draft forms

| Figure 8.9 | Revised Checklist of Reading Skills |

Early Reading Skills

- Reads aloud with smoothness and accuracy.
- Accurately sounds out unknown words.
- Monitors own reading and self-corrects when the text does not make sense.
- Reads and understands both fiction and nonfiction.
- Recalls the beginning, middle, and end of a story.
- Reads and understands simple written directions.
- Predicts what will happen next in stories.
- Shows knowledge of most grade-level reading topics.

before implementation is a great way to find out quickly if the report card is concise, understandable, and easy to interpret.

In addition to ensuring clear wording of the reporting standards, report card development teams also must make sure the grades, marks, and labels chosen to represent the various levels of student achievement or performance are easy to understand (see Chapter 5 for more information on such labels). One standards-based report card development team with which we worked put together the "Key to Grades" shown in Figure 8.10. Because the decision was made not to use traditional letter grades (i.e., A, B, C, D, F), developers constructed this key to marks that included a description for each proficiency level, along with a simple comment to capture the level of achievement (e.g., "This is a "WOW!"). While some parents indicated they still would rather see traditional letter grades, most parents really appreciated the extra descriptors. In addition, the extra commentary gave parents a quick, "plain English" way to think about student achievement.

Figure 8.10   Key to Marks With Additional Proficiency Level Descriptors

Key to Grades	Description of Proficiency Level in Meeting Standards	Comments
ME Meets With Excellence	This student . . . Consistently demonstrates **excellent** achievement of the standards. Shows an in-depth understanding of the concepts and skills included in the standards. Makes insightful connections to other ideas and concepts. Grasps, applies, and extends the key concepts and skills beyond the grade level.	This is a "WOW!"
MP Meets Proficiency	This student . . . Demonstrates **solid, proficient** achievement of the standards. Shows a good understanding of the concepts and skills included in the standards. Uses appropriate strategies to solve problems and connects some concepts to previous learning. Grasps and applies the key concepts and skills for the grade level.	This is a "YES!"

Key to Grades	Description of Proficiency Level in Meeting Standards	Comments
MA Marginal Proficiency	This student . . . Demonstrates marginal achievement of the standards. Shows partial understanding of the concepts and skills included in the standards but has not achieved all of them yet. Is beginning to grasp and apply the key concepts and skills for the grade level.	This is an "ALMOST." Teacher and parents need to discuss options for extra help.
BP Below Proficiency	This student . . . Demonstrates unacceptable achievement of the standards. Needs additional learning opportunities to achieve even partial understanding of the standards. Has difficulty grasping key concepts and skills for the grade level.	This is a "NO, NOT YET." Teacher and parents need to discuss immediate interventions to help the student improve.
NE Not Evaluated at This Time	This standard has not been addressed at this time. However, a grade will be issued by the end of the school year.	This is "NO EVALUATION can be made at this time." The skills or concepts may not have been taught this marking period.
SC See Teacher Comments	May refer to an attachment, such as special teacher or counselor notes, or any other relevant documents that would explain the lack of a grade.	This means "SEE ATTACHMENT."

Additional Considerations in Creating Effective Report Cards

Combining Methods of Reporting

Feedback we have received from parents, students, and teachers tells us that the most effective reporting forms are those that use a combination of methods to provide clear and concise information. With deliberate planning and technological support, it is possible to design reporting forms that include all of the following components:

- Checklists that show students' progress toward subject area standards
- Narratives to clarify student strengths or areas of concern in each subject
- Ratings of students' work habits, class behaviors, and/or social development
- Records of attendance
- Sections for students to complete on self-assessment and goal setting
- Reports of progress on portfolio or service learning requirements
- Space for parent comments, questions, and signatures

When design efforts begin by establishing the purpose of the report card, decisions about what information to include are much easier to make. Teachers and school administrators usually find that gathering feedback from parents and, sometimes, students when developing draft forms helps greatly in the decision-making process. When teachers, administrators, parents, and other stakeholders work together to design the reporting form, the product is usually something that all find useful and informative.

Student Self-Assessment and Goal Setting

In many schools and school districts, the standards developed for all students stress the importance of self-evaluation and goal setting. These schools typically devote space on the report card or devise a special form to accompany the report card for recording reflections and comments in these two areas. One such form is included in Figure 8.11. This particular form is completed during a parent-teacher conference or student-led conference, and it provides a focal point for conversations among students, parents, and teachers.

Other schools use slightly different forms to accomplish the same purpose, like the one shown in Figure 8.12 (page 192). Students fill out this page during class with the help of their teacher. Students and teachers then discuss the outlined goals and complete an action plan together. Finally, the page is sent home to parents for their approval and signatures.

Forms like these have been used with very positive results at all grade levels. Teachers tell us that they find the goal-setting process particularly helpful at the start of the school year or when a new course of study is beginning. Such forms provide a quick, informal assessment of

Figure 8.11	Example of a Goal-Setting Conference Summary Report

Goal-Setting Conference Summary		
Student:		Grade:
Teacher:	School:	Date:
Step 1: Review Progress Report and All Evaluation Materials.		
Step 2: Parents' Goals:		
Step 3: Student's Goals:		
Step 4: Teacher's Goals:		
Step 5: Shared Discussion Items to Note:		
_____	_____	_____
Student's Signature	**Parent's Signature**	**Teacher's Signature**

each student's needs and encourage students to take increased responsibility for their own learning. Furthermore, both parents and students report that the self-evaluation and goal-setting information helps them to reflect on progress and to set high expectations.

Figure 8.12	Example of a Self-Assessment and Goal-Setting Conference Reporting Form

Self-Assessment and Goal Setting
(To be completed by the student in consultation with the teacher.)

Accomplishments:

Goals for Next Reporting Period:

Action Plan:

Parental Support

(Please discuss this evaluation with your child and respond below to his or her self-assessment and goal-setting statements. Then sign and return this page of the report to the teacher.)

Date: _____   **Parent/Guardian Signature:** _____

Narratives

It has been our experience in working with report card development teams that most teachers want to include narrative sections on a report card. Narratives provide an opportunity to highlight special strengths and to provide encouragement to the student. Teachers also use narratives to describe specific challenges and provide suggestions parents can use at home to help their child improve in specific skill areas. At the same time, narratives can be very time consuming for teachers to prepare. Furthermore, we have discovered that parents often compare notes with other parents and grow upset if they discover that their presumably unique children received exactly the same narrative comments. This leads many parents to conclude that the teacher must not know their child very well or simply did not want to spend the time needed to offer more specific, truly personalized comments.

Technology systems can greatly assist teachers in writing effective narratives. The copy/paste feature in most word processing software allows teachers to enter a short description of the class learning goals or standards for that marking period on every student's report card. Some software programs offer options that allow teachers to type in such a description just one time and then enter a class code to print those sentences on the report card of every student in the class. (Recall Figure 7.1, which showed an example of such a report card.) Teachers can then add other, more personalized comments about each student's particular performance.

When short narratives are combined with other ways of reporting student achievement and performance, such as a checklist of skills or letter grades, they can be very effective in communicating important information to parents, while still being manageable for teachers. In addition, they offer teachers the opportunity to clarify the information presented in other sections of the report card and, thus, truly individualize the report.

Special Comment Sections

When the stated purpose of a report card is to communicate information about students' learning to parents, it is vital that parents be able to read the form and understand the meaning of the information it includes. To obtain feedback from parents about their understanding of the report card, some schools ask parents to add their own written comments on the report card or on a special form that accompanies the report card. This not only guarantees that parents have received the report card, it also encourages their input to the reporting process.

Other schools stress the importance of having students clearly understand reported information. Therefore, these schools ask students to write comments in one section of the report card. Schools that define a purpose that includes the importance of student involvement in cocurricular activities may add sections to record student involvement in community service or extracurricular activities. The inclusion of such comments makes the reporting process more encompassing and interactive. Figure 8.13 shows an example of a form that can be attached to any report card to record these special comments.

Figure 8.13 Special Comments: Cocurricular Activities

SPECIAL COMMENTS SECTION	
Teacher Comments:	*Student Comments:*
Community Involvement and Extracurricular Activities:	*Parent Comments:*

In an effort to encourage increased parent involvement and better two-way communication between teachers and parents, some schools include a section on the report card or add a form for parents to use in describing students' learning activities at home. We have seen this approach most often in the early elementary grades, kindergarten through Grade 2, although it can be adapted to any grade level. Usually these sections or forms include a checklist that serves as a reminder to parents about the importance of reading to their child or providing extra support at home. Figure 8.14 illustrates an example of one such "Parent Report to School" form.

Special Comments: Parent Report to School

PARENT REPORT TO SCHOOL Potts Elementary School				
Student:	Grade:			
Teacher:	School Year:			
Please mark using the following key: *R* = Regularly (4–5 times per week) *S* = Sometimes (2–3 times per week) *O* = Once in awhile (1 time per week) *N* = Not necessary for my child				

This is what I do at home:	Marking Period			
	1st	2nd	3rd	4th
I ask about my child's school day.				
I read to my child daily.				
I check my child's backpack for notes and schoolwork.				
I help my child with homework.				
I encourage my child to do his or her best in school.				
I read school newsletters.				
I look over my child's graded papers and ask questions when needed.				
I call the teacher whenever I have questions or concerns.				
Parents or Guardians: Please check the box to the right if you wish to schedule an appointment to discuss your child's progress. Parent contact phone number: ——————				

Please sign and return this report to your child's teacher.
———————————————————————   ————————— **Parent's Signature**   **Date**

Still other schools have created a small section on the report card to record "Parent's Conference Attendance." This typically consists of an area for recording a check mark by the dates of scheduled parent-teacher conferences. Keeping a record of conference attendance on the report card reminds parents of the importance of these events.

Format, Organization, and Graphic Layout

A vital element in helping parents, guardians, students, and others accurately interpret the information included in a standards-based report card is a clear explanation of the grades, marks, or symbols used on the form. This explanation usually takes the form of a legend, or "key to marks," with accompanying definitions. If the purpose of the report card is to communicate students' mastery of specific learning goals or standards, then those who receive the form should be able to understand the information it includes and easily interpret it. The example of a "Key to Marks," shown in Figure 8.6 (page 181), shows one school's attempt to make the meaning of grades or marks clear to parents and students. A legend or key to marks certainly may provide less detail and still communicate the criteria and levels of performance clearly. Whatever key is used, however, developers must make sure that parents fully understand the precise meaning of every grade, mark, or symbol included in the form.

If the purpose of the reporting form is clearly stated and the marks or grades included are precisely explained, then the report card may be organized and laid out in many formats and still communicate effectively. In our review of report cards used at different grade levels, we found a multitude of organizational styles, formats, and graphic layouts. Some schools use very modest, one-page, black-and-white reporting forms. Others use graphic representations and two or three colors to emphasize different aspects of the report. Still others have developed glossy, multipage, detailed reports that include photographs of the student, teachers, and even the school building.

The graphic design and layout of the report card can enhance or detract from its intended message. If not carefully considered, the format can also distort or mislead. One kindergarten reporting form that we reviewed, for example, listed the letters of the alphabet in very large, bold type. Teachers would circle those letters that students recognized visually and phonetically. Because this section of the report stood out from all other sections, it gave parents the impression that the teachers placed more emphasis on letter recognition than on other skills. (Recall our discussion in Chapter 6 about the importance of order and space.)

When we questioned the building principal about this apparent emphasis, she told us that the kindergarten teachers did *not* stress letter recognition over other literacy skills. The report card developers had not noticed, however, that the layout of the report made this one skill appear much more prominent than any other literacy skill. After reviewing the form and realizing this and a few other inconsistencies between the report card's design and the message they wanted to communicate, staff members completely redesigned the form. Educators must always keep in mind that the graphical layout of a reporting form contributes greatly to the message communicated to readers.

Many schools and school districts use experienced graphic designers to gain advice and direction regarding format and layout options when developing their report cards. Font sizes and print style, graphics and photo options, paper quality, report length, and color all must be considered in designing the form. A person knowledgeable in graphic design can help ensure that design details enhance rather than detract from the report card's intended purpose and message.

Technology Considerations

Schools using electronic grade book programs or computerized grading systems often must use or modify one of a selection of prefabricated report cards provided by the software vendor. In such cases, it is vitally important to include a member of the district technology department on the report card development team. Technology staff members will have questions and concerns that other educators might not consider, such as the following:

- Can prefabricated reports be modified by district personnel at little or no expense, or would the district need to incur the additional expense of contracting with the vendor to make changes to the report card's design and format?
- How are grades transferred from the electronic grade book to the report card?
- What software was used to design prefabricated reports? Is the report designer software something district personnel already own, or would acquisition of the design software be an added expense?
- How are report cards archived in the system? How easy is it to access report cards from prior years?

- Can teachers have remote access to the electronic grade book, or must the work of issuing grades be done on-site in a classroom or office?
- How do reports print? Is there capacity for back-to-back printing to conserve paper? Do reports require color, or can they be done in black and white to lower costs, if necessary?
- Can district secretaries have access to teacher report cards for printing and filing?
- Can report cards be sent electronically to other school districts when a student moves out of the district?

Another valuable member of any report card team is a guidance counselor or school secretary. This person typically has the primary responsibility for maintaining student records for several years. The guidance counselor or secretary may raise additional questions for team consideration, such as these:

- Parents need copies of report cards, and student files must be kept up-to-date with current copies of report cards. How and when will report cards be filed (e.g. every marking period or end of year only)?
- Who will have primary responsibility for adding report cards to student files?
- Can the report card be designed with mailing considerations in mind? In other words, can the parents' names and addresses be printed on the report card so they appear in a window envelope when folded?
- Can the report be easily customized to include a building's logo or special graphics?
- Is the report so lengthy that it may require additional postage for mailing?
- Will parents have online access to report card information?

Technological, record keeping, and secretarial demands are important considerations for any report card development team. Including these staff members from the beginning of development efforts will likely prevent problems that other team members may not recognize until too late in the process.

Summary

Written report cards are just one piece of a school district's reporting system. Yet because they are frequently the most prominent piece, developers must take special care to establish a clear purpose for the report and then consider essential characteristics of effective report cards. Specifically, an effective report card does the following:

- Reports on product, process, and progress goals separately.
- Creates an accurate picture of academic strengths and challenges.
- Balances detail with practicality.
- Is concise, understandable, and easy to interpret.

We also know that a variety of methods, such as checklists, narratives, letter grades, and other special comments sections, may be used to report student achievement and performance in school. The most effective report cards combine methods to provide parents, guardians, students, and others with specific information on student performance in an easy-to-read, readily understandable format. Finally, developers should include technology experts, guidance counselors, and secretarial staff members on the development team to ensure that the report card will be something that works for everyone.

9

Beyond the
Report Card

Developing a Reporting System[1]

Throughout this book, we have emphasized that as the goals of schooling become more complex, the need for better quality and more detailed communication about student learning grows increasingly important. A carefully constructed standards-based report card helps address both of these issues. It not only offers better and more detailed information about student learning to parents, students, and others, it also brings focus to improvement efforts when needed. We also have stressed, however, that no single reporting device can adequately serve these ever-expanding communication needs. That is why reform efforts that consider report cards alone so often fail. Either they attempt to accomplish too much with a single reporting device, or they ignore important principles of effective communication.

What we need instead are comprehensive, multifaceted reporting systems that communicate multiple types of information to multiple audiences in multiple formats. A well-designed standards-based report card always provides the foundation for such systems. But these systems also include a wide variety of other communication tools, each with a specific purpose and designed for a particular audience. Reporting systems such as these are built on the premise that

---

[1]This chapter is based in large part on "Guidelines for Developing Effective Reporting Systems," Chapter 10 in *Developing Grading and Reporting Systems for Student Learning* (Guskey & Bailey, 2001).

successful reporting is more a challenge in effective communication than simply a process of documenting student achievement.

In this chapter, we turn our attention to the steps involved in building a comprehensive reporting system. We outline a set of guidelines for educators to follow to ensure their reporting system focuses on the qualities of effective communication. We then describe some of the reporting tools that might be included in such a system. Finally, we show how adhering to the principles of honesty, accuracy, and fairness helps ensure that grading and reporting systems truly enhance the teaching and learning process.

The Importance of Purpose

The most crucial issue to be addressed in selecting the tools included in a reporting system is what purpose or purposes we want to serve. In other words, why are we conveying this information, and what do we hope to accomplish? To determine the purpose or purposes, three aspects of communication must be considered: What information or message do we want to communicate? Who is the primary audience for that message? How do we want that information or message to be used? Once our purposes are clear, we can then select the tool or tools that best serve those purposes.

CRITICAL ISSUES IN DETERMINING A REPORT CARD'S PURPOSE

- What information or message do we want to communicate?
- Who is the primary audience for that message?
- How do we want that information or message to be used?

When developing their reporting systems, many educators make the mistake of choosing their reporting tools first, without giving careful attention to the purpose of each tool. As we described in Chapter 3, far too many schools and school districts charge headlong into developing their standards-based report cards without first addressing core questions about why they are doing so. Others incorporate student portfolios or implement student-led conferences simply because "they seem to be a good idea" and "other schools are doing it."

Such efforts almost always encounter unexpected resistance and rarely bring the foretold positive results. Parents and teachers often perceive new reporting tools as newfangled fads that require extra work and present no real advantage over more traditional reporting methods. As a result, many of these efforts end up being short-lived experiments that are abandoned after a few troubled years of implementation.

Efforts that begin by clarifying their purpose, on the other hand, make their intentions explicit from the start. A clear purpose not only helps mobilize everyone involved in the reporting process, it also keeps efforts on track. Furthermore, being clear about the purpose prevents distraction by peripheral issues that waste crucial time and divert energy (Guskey & Bailey, 2001). As we mentioned before, the famous adage that guides architecture also applies to reporting student learning: "Form follows function." In other words, *method follows purpose.* Purpose must always come first. Once the purpose or function is decided, questions regarding form and method become more relevant and much easier to address.

This is not to imply, however, that there is or ever should be a single purpose in reporting student learning. Most schools and school districts recognize multiple reporting purposes. That is why they require comprehensive reporting systems that include multiple reporting tools, each with a specific and clearly articulated purpose.

The Challenge of Communication

Most teachers and school administrators want to do a better job of communicating student learning, especially to parents. They recognize that such communication is essential to involving parents in students' learning efforts and to gaining parents' support for school programs. At the same time, many have no idea how to go about building a positive and effective communication system and, consequently, are fearful of trying (Epstein, 1995).

Teachers and school administrators are also aware of the formidable barriers to parent involvement. These include both parents working outside the home, single parents with heavy responsibilities, transportation difficulties, child care needs, cultural and language barriers, and some parents who are just too stressed or too depressed to care (Kirschenbaum, 1999). Still, strong evidence indicates that parents at all socioeconomic levels and of all educational backgrounds are willing to help their children succeed in school (Hoover-Dempsey et al., 2005). Many are dependent, however, on guidance from the school and, especially, their child's teacher as to how best to offer that support (Chrispeels, Fernandez, & Preston, 1991; Floyd, 1998).

Surveys of parents consistently show that most would like more information about their child's progress in school. They want to receive that information more regularly and in a form they understand and can use (Fan & Chen, 1999). As we described earlier, parents generally perceive the report card as the primary and, sometimes, only source of such information. Therefore, the majority of parents indicate they want to receive report cards more often than the typical three or four times per year (J. F. Wemette, personal communication, 1994). A reporting system that includes multiple reporting tools distributed at different times throughout the school year can address this parental concern. If thoughtfully designed, such multitool systems offer parents, guardians, students, and others precisely the kind of information they want and deserve.

Tools for a Comprehensive Reporting System

The list of reporting tools that can be included in a school or school district's reporting system is extensive. In fact, advances in communication technology make the number and variety of options available to educators virtually unlimited. The reporting systems most highly regarded by parents typically include a mix of traditional and more modern reporting tools. Some of the tools most commonly used are listed in the box below and described in detail in the following pages.

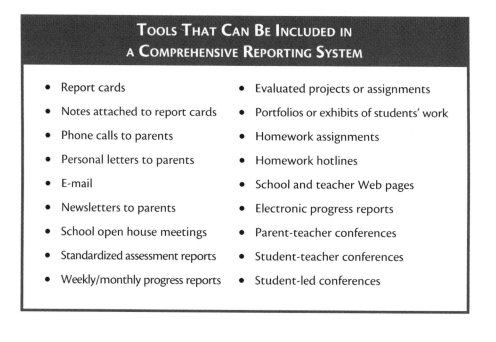

TOOLS THAT CAN BE INCLUDED IN A COMPREHENSIVE REPORTING SYSTEM

- Report cards
- Notes attached to report cards
- Phone calls to parents
- Personal letters to parents
- E-mail
- Newsletters to parents
- School open house meetings
- Standardized assessment reports
- Weekly/monthly progress reports

- Evaluated projects or assignments
- Portfolios or exhibits of students' work
- Homework assignments
- Homework hotlines
- School and teacher Web pages
- Electronic progress reports
- Parent-teacher conferences
- Student-teacher conferences
- Student-led conferences

Report Cards

Report cards form the foundation of nearly every comprehensive reporting system. If the primary purpose of the report card is to communicate information to parents about teachers' judgments of students' achievement and performance in school, then parents' perspectives need to be considered throughout the process of developing the report card. In addition, parents' input should be sought and their concerns specifically addressed when planning report card revisions. For report cards to serve as an effective communication tool, parents must understand all of the information included in the report card and know precisely what it means (Wiggins, 1994). They also must be able to interpret that information correctly and use it appropriately to guide improvement efforts when needed.

If, however, the primary purpose of the report card is to communicate information to students for self-evaluation, then it is students who must be able to understand and accurately interpret the information it includes. This, in turn, means that students' perspectives must be considered in the report card development process and their input sought when planning revisions.

Whatever purpose is selected, we always recommend that purpose be clearly stated on the report card itself. It should be printed in a highlighted box on the top of the report card or otherwise prominently displayed on the first page. This can be done on traditional paper report cards and on digital report cards; the purpose can be announced at the beginning of a video report card. Clearly stating the purpose helps everyone know what the report card represents, the intended audience, and how the included information should be interpreted and used.

Notes Attached to Report Cards

The manner in which a principal interacts with students and the things students subsequently tell their parents about the school greatly affect parents' perceptions of the school and their relationships with educators. One way many principals have found to strengthen their relationships with students and parents is to attach a short, personal note to each student's report card (see Figure 9.1). In some cases, the notes are intended for the parents. More often, however, they are addressed to students. These notes serve two purposes. First, they express the principal's interest in each student's learning progress.

Figure 9.1	Example of a Report Card Note From the Principal

> *Great job in math, Chris!*
> *Next time, let's try to*
> *bring up those marks in*
> *social studies!*

Second, they allow principals to recognize students' accomplishments and to offer encouragement for improvement.

In our interviews with parents and students, we were surprised to find how much they value and appreciate these small notes. Many parents told us that the note is the first thing they read on the report card and that the notes are always saved. Teachers told us that they, too, read the notes and deeply appreciate the principal's personal interest in their students. Although preparing such notes requires time and commitment on the part of principals, they are an effective communication tool that reinforces positive home-school relations (Giba, 1999).

Phone Calls to Parents

Phone calls are one of the easiest and most efficient means of communication between educators and parents. Of all reporting tools, however, phone calls are probably the most underutilized and misused. In our surveys with parents, for example, we discovered that over 60 percent indicated they "feared" phone calls from school. When we investigated this unexpected response in follow-up interviews, parents clarified what they meant. They told us they feared phone calls from school because they received a call for only one of two reasons: their child misbehaved or did something wrong, or their child was sick or hurt. Is it any wonder that parents fear phone calls from school if these are the only reasons educators call them?

Many teachers have started making regular phone calls to parents and, in the process, have discovered countless benefits. Most begin by checking school records to determine with whom their students are living and make special note when surnames differ. Next they notify parents during an open house meeting or in a special note sent home of their intention to call once a month or every other month. Most tell students of their plans as well. Typically, teachers emphasize to parents that they have no set agenda for the call. Rather, they simply want to hear parents' concerns and answer any questions parents might have. Finally, the teachers set aside a time each week to make the calls (Gustafson, 1998).

ONE TEACHER'S EXPERIENCE WITH PHONE CALLS

A middle school's faculty with whom we worked decided to initiate a "Phone Home Program" where every teacher agreed to call the parents or guardians of three students each week. During these calls, teachers informed parents of classroom events, reported on students' recent learning progress, and inquired about questions or concerns that parents might have.

One first-year teacher misinterpreted the plan and began the school year by making three phone calls each night! When the principal observed this beginning teacher's class during the third week of school, he was delighted to find that this teacher had no classroom management problems, no student behavior problems, and 100 percent completion rates on most homework assignments. When asked how she was able to curtail problems that typically plague first-year teachers, she replied simply, "I've talked to all my kids' parents, and they're helping me."

This teacher went on to relate the following conversation she'd had with Jason, a student who had been a challenge to his former teachers.

Jason came into class frowning one morning and indignantly asked his teacher, "You called my mom last night, didn't you?"

"Yes, Jason, I did," replied the teacher.

"Why'd you do that? I haven't done anything wrong."

"No you haven't, Jason, and that's just what I told your mother. In fact, I told her that you've been doing very well and that I thought this was going to be a really great year for you."

"You really told her that, huh?"

"Yes, I did."

(Pause)

"You know, she won't let me watch television now until I finish my homework."

"We talked about that, too."

(Pause)

"Are you going to be talking with my mom again?"

"I'm sure I will, Jason. I told your mother that I plan to call each month. And I'm certain I'll have some good things to tell her about how you're doing."

(Pause)

"This year's sure going to be different, isn't it?"

"Yes, Jason, I think it will . . ."

Teachers report that some weeks they complete the calling in 10 to 15 minutes, with the majority of calls resulting in messages left on answering machines or voice mail. Other weeks, however, every call is answered by a parent eager to talk. Most teachers begin the conversation

with an open-ended statement such as, "Hi, this is Ms. Hartman. I'm
____'s teacher at Walsh. I'm making my regular phone call and wanted
to know if you have any questions or if there is anything you would like
to talk about." Teachers find that parents generally take it from there.

Regular phone calls to parents help teachers keep up-to-date on
their students' lives. Without them, for example, the teacher might
not know that one quiet girl often had late assignments because she
was competing in gymnastics, that a boy's father was taking over cus-
tody, that several fourth-grade girls were picking on another girl at
recess, or that a beloved grandfather had recently died. Regular calls
also give parents the opportunity to check on the information their
children bring home from school (Gustafson, 1998).

ONE PRINCIPAL'S EXPERIENCE WITH PHONE CALLS

An elementary school principal we know uses her cell phone to communicate to
parents what she calls "The Good News." She carries her phone with her as she
observes teachers' classes, visits the cafeteria, walks the hallways, and supervises
the playground. When she sees a student performing well in class, assisting a
classmate, or helping to improve the school, she immediately calls that student's
parent or guardian on her phone and announces, "Hello, this is Ms. Johnson, the
principal at Judd Elementary School. I just saw Tonya ..." After explaining what
she observed and complimenting the child, she hands the phone to the child so
that he or she can talk briefly with their parent or guardian. Everyone leaves with
a big smile.

When asked about calls to parents concerning student problems, Ms. Johnson
explains, "Those I save for after school. Often I have to think more carefully about
what I'm going to say and what strategies I'm going to recommend. When I see a
child doing something wonderful, however, I want to let their parents know
about that right away. And I never have to weigh my words. Plus, I think it means
more to the child."

The principal's phone calls have completely altered the culture of this school.
Parent involvement and participation in school events is at an all-time high, and
parents' regard for Ms. Johnson and the school staff is exceptionally positive. It's
a small thing, but it has made a big difference.

Phone calls can also be used to inform parents of special events
and to invite their participation. Such events might include classroom
celebrations, choir performances, science fairs, or open house meetings. Receiving a call not only reminds parents of the event but tells
them it is important enough that someone took the time to contact

them. And once having promised to be there, parents are likely to keep their promise (Kirschenbaum, 1999).

Nearly all teachers tell us, however, that the first phone call is always the most difficult. Time and again, we have heard stories of parents answering the phone and, upon learning the call is from their child's teacher, ask, "What did he do now?" Automatically, they assume something must be wrong. After discovering the nature of the call, parents often express a sense of relief and usually end the call by adding, "I'm really glad you called." Making regular phone calls to parents takes time and dedication on the part of teachers. Most teachers tell us, however, that the benefits far outweigh the costs.

Personal Letters to Parents

Personal letters to parents allow teachers to model honest communication by notifying parents when their child has done exceptionally well or by informing parents as soon as academic or behavioral problems arise. Letters that report good news should congratulate the child and emphasize the quality and effort displayed in their work. Letters that identify problems should make suggestions to parents as to how the problem might be addressed and stress the teacher's willingness to work with parents toward a solution. This approach keeps parents informed and demonstrates that the teacher feels it is important to share children's successes, as well as their difficulties, with parents (Kreider & Lopez, 1999).

E-mail

Nearly all teachers today have access to e-mail through their schools. Likewise, most parents and guardians today have personal computers in their homes or at work with e-mail services that they access daily. E-mail, therefore, provides an easy and highly efficient way for teachers and parents to communicate directly with each other.

In addition to its ease of use, e-mail offers several advantages over other forms of communication.

- Unlike phone calls, e-mail is not time bound. Both teachers and parents can send and respond to e-mail messages at any time that suits their schedules.
- Because of the response notification options in most e-mail programs, it is easy to determine if a message has been received and when.

- E-mail provides a permanent record of correspondence to which teachers and parents can refer should questions about notification or past discussions ever arise.

In the same way they use personal letters, teachers can use e-mail to notify parents when their child has done exceptionally well or to inform parents of academic difficulties or behavioral problems. Most teachers inform parents or guardians of their openness to e-mail correspondence by including their e-mail address in introductory materials sent home at the beginning of the school year. They also make a point of sharing their e-mail address during open house meetings and at parent-teacher conferences.

Newsletters to Parents

When it comes to fostering communication between school and home, many teachers and parents indicate that conventional forms of communication are more effective than newer ones, such as Web sites and hotlines (Langdon, 1999). Among the more conventional forms, both teachers and parents consider newsletters to be one of the most effective.

Newsletters provide parents and others with everyday details about the school. Newsletters can describe upcoming events, thank parents by name for their assistance, announce student award winners in each class, and provide ideas for specific learning activities parents can do at home with their children. Some newsletters include profiles of new teachers or staff members, and many include a special column by the principal (Kirschenbaum, 1999). Parents often assist in the preparation of newsletters, which are typically distributed once each month. Even though electronic formats may not be preferred, budget constraints have compelled many schools to reduce the cost of distributing newsletters by using electronic versions. When they do, however, most find it more effective to send the newsletter by e-mail to individual parents and guardians, rather than simply posting the newsletter on the school Web site. In this way, they ensure that every parent or guardian who has the technology receives a copy.

In addition to regular newsletters, many schools distribute an attractive calendar and handbook to parents at the beginning of each school year. The calendar notes school events, indicates when interim reports and report cards will be distributed, encourages parents' involvement, and offers detailed suggestions on how parents can support their child's education at home (Kirschenbaum, 1999). The handbook offers information about the school and staff members, describes school policies, and indicates where and how parents can find more details.

School Open House Meetings

A school open house is a brief meeting, usually held in the evening, where parents are invited to the school to visit their child's classrooms and meet with the teachers. Open house meetings are often parents' first opportunity to meet their child's teachers and the teachers' first opportunity to interact with parents.

Because open house meetings tend to be brief and rarely involve detailed discussions about individual students, most teachers regard them casually and spend little time preparing for them. Parents, on the other hand, attach great importance to open house meetings. A *Phi Delta Kappan* poll showed, for example, that nearly 90 percent of parents consider school open house meetings to be the most effective communication device for gathering information about the school and their child's teacher (Langdon, 1999).

To make the most of school open houses, teachers should keep in mind what parents most want to know about their child's teachers. Our evidence shows clearly that parents want to know that

1. their child's teachers are competent; and

2. those teachers care about their child as an individual (see Guskey & Bailey, 2001).

Teachers who focus on communicating these two things to parents at open house meetings create a positive impression among parents and do much to ensure parents' cooperation and assistance throughout the school year.

The manner in which teachers address these two issues is vitally important. In our informal interviews and discussions with parents, we learned, for example, that few parents judge teachers' competence based on years of experience or degrees earned. So to say to parents, "I have been teaching for 17 years and have 2 master's degrees," fails to impress them. Instead, parents and guardians want to know what the teacher has planned for the class, what learning goals have been set, and how the teacher intends to help students reach those goals.

Parents appreciate hearing about special projects, classroom procedures, and tips on how they can help at home.

We also learned that if teachers begin their conversations with parents or guardians by opening a grade book, either in booklet form or on a computer screen, parents are left with the impression that the teacher does not really know their child. In other words, parents reason that "if you cannot say anything about my child before you have to refer to your grade book, then you do not know my child!" This is not to imply that teachers should never refer to records of students' performance in discussions with parents. In fact, examples of students' work provide an excellent basis for conversations. When beginning those discussions, however, teachers must communicate to parents that they know their child and recognize positive attributes of the child.

Perhaps most important, parents want to know that the teacher is personable, approachable, and willing to make special efforts to help students learn. Teachers who convey this in their discussions with parents not only open pathways to better communication, they also facilitate a better working partnership between school and home.

Standardized Assessment Reports

Most schools and school districts today administer some form of standardized tests or assessments each year to gain additional information about students' academic achievement and performance. Because these assessments typically must be sent off to be scored, results are generally not available to teachers, students, or their parents until several months after the tests are administered. The results from assessments given in the spring of the year, for example, may not be returned to the school until the fall, after students have been promoted to the next grade and are enrolled in classes with new teachers.

Students' scores on standardized assessments are usually compared to score distributions obtained from a "national sample" of students who are of similar age or at the same grade level. These comparative results are typically expressed in percentiles, stanines, normal curve equivalents, or some other standardized score. Test manufacturers prepare score summaries for each student, along with brief descriptions of what the scores mean. These summaries then become a part of students' permanent school files, and they may be sent home to parents, who interpret the scores as depicting how their child ranks among age-mates or classmates across the entire state, province, or nation.

Of all reporting tools, standardized assessment reports are probably the most frequently misinterpreted. The statistical procedures often used to generate students' scores (e.g., item response theory models) confuse school counselors and bewilder most parents. Even seemingly simple conveyances such as "grade equivalents" are almost always misunderstood (Hills, 1983). Complicating matters further is the fact that most standardized assessments are not well aligned with the curriculum being taught and, hence, tend to be an inadequate measure of how well students have learned (Barton, 1999). For these reasons, standardized assessment reports typically require detailed explanation from school personnel and extensive parent training. Such efforts not only help parents interpret the reports and scores more accurately, they also help avoid serious misinterpretations and misuse.

Weekly/Monthly Progress Reports

Another reporting tool that many school staffs use to inform parents about what is going on in school and how they can become involved is weekly or monthly progress reports. In some cases, these are short checklists or mini report cards that give parents and guardians a brief summary of students' learning progress between report cards. Others are designed simply to inform parents about the curriculum standards and teachers' expectations for students. The best reports offer parents specific hints on what they can to at home to help.

An example of one such report is illustrated in Figure 9.2. Teachers complete this form and distribute it to students to take home to their parents or guardians on the first day of each month. It informs parents about the curriculum standards to be addressed during the coming month, as well as the planned learning goals. Equally important, it offers parents specific suggestions about how they might help at home. Most teachers find that completing a form such as this takes relatively little time and effort. Still, it is deeply appreciated by parents and frequently leads to significant improvements in student learning. Remember, however, the information included in such reports must be clear, specific, and expressed in parent-friendly language. If parents do not understand the information in the form, they will not be able to use it appropriately.

Figure 9.2 Example of a Monthly Class Report

Morton Middle School **Parent Information & Involvement Form** *Teacher* _____   *Class* _____
During the next month, the topics and ideas we will be studying are:
Our goal in studying these topics and ideas is for students to be able to:
Parents can help at home by:

Evaluated Projects or Assignments

Evaluated projects and assignments represent a highly effective means for teachers to communicate learning goals and expectations to parents. But the form of this evaluation information makes a difference. Projects or assignments that come home with only a single grade or mark at the top of the page provide neither students nor their parents with much useful information. Although it may communicate the teacher's overall appraisal of the student's achievement or performance, it offers no guidance for improvement.

Parents who want to become more involved in their child's learning need guidance and direction from educators, and particularly their child's teacher, as to how they can help. Evaluated assignments or assessments that include specific comments from the teacher, along with clear suggestions for improvement, offer parents that needed guidance. Projects or papers accompanied by explicit scoring rubrics similarly provide parents with a clear description of what the teacher expects and the criteria by which students' work is evaluated. With this information, parents can make sure their efforts at home are well aligned with what the teacher expects at school.

Portfolios or Exhibits of Students' Work

Another efficient and highly effective way of sharing information about students' achievement and performance with parents is to assemble evaluated samples of students' work in a portfolio. Portfolios are simply collections of evidence on student learning that serve three major purposes:

1. To display students' work around a theme

2. To illustrate the process of learning

3. To show growth or progress (Davies, 2000)

Some portfolios are specific to a class or subject area, while others combine students' work across several subjects (Robinson, 1998). Teachers at all levels report that parents are enthusiastic about the use of portfolios as a reporting tool, and parents often indicate they learn more from the portfolio than they do from the report card (Balm, 1995).

Most schools use portfolios in conjunction with report cards to clarify the marks or grades included in the report card. In some schools, however, portfolios serve to inform parents about students' learning on a more regular and ongoing basis. One school with which we are familiar, for example, uses "Friday Folders" to keep parents abreast of their children's performance. A collection of evaluated papers, assignments, and assessments, along with notes from teachers and notices of school events, are included in this permanent folder and sent home each Friday. As such, it becomes a regular school routine. Parents sign the folder each week and record any comments or questions they might have. Students then return the folder to their teacher when they come to school the following Monday.

Exhibits of students' work represent yet another good way to communicate information about students' achievement. The athletic and fine arts departments in schools have long scheduled sporting events, concerts, and plays for parents and interested community members to attend. These events communicate important and meaningful information about "what students can do" to those who watch or listen. Exhibits designed expressly for the purposes of communicating how well students perform in academic tasks can do the same (Brookhart, 1999).

To make the best use of portfolios and exhibits of students' work, teachers must be able to articulate the qualities of good work and help students learn to recognize these qualities in their own work. Teachers also must teach their students how to select the examples to exhibit and how to articulate the reasons for their selections. These important assessment-related skills help students become more thoughtful judges of their own work and lead to higher levels of student performance.

Homework Assignments

Most teachers see homework as a way to offer students additional practice on what they learned in class and to extend students' involvement in learning activities. Many consider homework an opportunity for students to review academic skills and to explore topics of special interest through reports and independent projects. But homework is also an excellent way for teachers to communicate with parents. It provides a means for teachers to let parents know what is being emphasized in class, what is expected of students, and how students' work will be evaluated (Cooper, Robinson, & Patall, 2006).

Students' engagement in homework is closely related to measures of achievement and academic performance at the high school level, although this relationship has more to do with the quality of the homework in which students engage than simply the quantity of work or the amount of time they spend doing it. At the elementary level, however, the relationship between homework and performance in school is much more modest. In the elementary grades, homework serves best to inform parents of what students are doing in school and to involve parents in students' learning tasks (Cooper, 2007).

Homework assignments at the elementary level, therefore, should be designed specifically so that parents and students can work together. For example, an assignment might involve questions that students are to ask their parents or guardians, issues that students and parents are to explore together, or a procedure for students to complete and then have their parents check. Experiences such as these give parents the opportunity to become involved in their children's schoolwork, to encourage good work habits, and to emphasize the importance of learning.

Homework Hotlines

To facilitate completion of homework assignments, many schools develop "homework hotlines." The simplest hotlines permit students and their parents to telephone the school, follow a series of simple instructions, and then hear a recorded message from the teacher describing the homework assignment for that day. Some teachers simply describe the assignment and the due date in their message. Others specify the goal of the assignment, offer suggestions for completion, and outline the criteria by which the assignment will be evaluated. These messages allow students to check on assignments and clarify those of which they are unsure. They also permit students who are absent from school to get a head start on their makeup work.

In other schools, homework hotlines are actually staffed by teachers or teaching assistants who offer direct assistance to students on their homework assignments. Students who get stuck on some aspect of an assignment can call the hotline and get immediate help. They need not wait until their next class to ask a question or to get the assistance they need. Although setting up homework hotlines requires additional expense and effort on the part of educators, the service offers a variety of benefits to both students and their parents.

School and Teacher Web Pages

As schools become increasingly sophisticated in their use of technology, more are establishing their own Web pages. Some school Web pages simply offer information about the school, administrators, and faculty; school policies; and the time and dates of special events.

Others include information about various programs of study and about each course or class within the program. In addition, many teachers develop their own Web pages for parents and students to access (Johnson, 2000). On their Web pages, teachers typically offer descriptions of their classes, information about established learning standards or goals, grading criteria or scoring rubrics for particular class projects, and schedules of assignments. In some cases, these descriptions are regularly updated to include information about daily homework assignments and special class events.

Another important advantage of school and teacher Web pages is that they can offer the opportunity for two-way communication. Most Web pages are combined with e-mail systems that list the e-mail address of each school administrator, teacher, and staff member. Parents who have questions or concerns can correspond with their child's teacher directly and need not worry about interrupting the teacher's busy schedule. Teachers, in turn, can respond to parents' questions and concerns at a time convenient to them. Furthermore, e-mail allows teachers time to think about their response, include pertinent information, offer suggestions or recommendations, and then keep a record of the communication. Although most schools report that few parents correspond with teachers or staff members via e-mail, those who do find it a very useful form of communication.

Electronic Progress Reports

Computerized grading programs and electronic progress reports rank among the best-selling computer software available to educators today. They appeal to teachers primarily because they simplify record-keeping tasks. The spreadsheet formats and database management systems included in these programs make it easy for teachers to enter and precisely tally large amounts of numerical information (Huber, 1997; Vockell & Fiore, 1993). They are particularly well suited to the point-based grading systems of middle and high school teachers, who often record numerical data on the performance of more than 100 students each week.

Most electronic progress reports also present educators with a wide range of grading and record-keeping options. Some simply help teachers to keep more detailed records on students' learning progress (Eastwood, 1996). Others allow teachers to present summaries of students' achievement and performance in a variety of different formats, including computer displays, online reports, and even digital portfolios. Still other programs actually perform grading tasks. The simplest of these scan, mark, and analyze assessments composed of true/false, matching, and multiple-choice items. Exciting advances have been made, however, in the use of computers to evaluate and grade students' essays, compositions, and other writing samples (Page & Petersen, 1995; Wresch, 1993).

For all their advantages, however, computerized grading programs and electronic progress reports also have their shortcomings. First, most are based on highly traditional grading models, which perpetuate practices that we know to be ineffective (O'Conner, 2007). Rather than being created on the basis of best practices in grading and reporting, they are built around the grading procedures most commonly used.

Second, none of the computerized reporting systems that we know allows teachers to record, or parents to distinguish, the difference between *formative evidence,* gathered from students strictly for the purpose of checking on understanding and guiding instructional revisions, and *summative evidence,* gathered for the purpose of determining a grade or mark. This lack of difference fosters the belief among some teachers, as well as many parents and students, that "everything counts" in judging learning success and determining students' grades. The important distinction between feedback designed to foster improvements in teaching and learning and evaluative evidence used to appraise students' cumulative level of knowledge and skill is lost.

Suppose, for example, that a teacher administers an assessment instrument provided by a publisher or testing company that is poorly constructed or poorly aligned with what the teacher taught and the instructional activities in which students engaged. As might be expected, all students perform poorly on this assessment, but then their low marks are recorded in the electronic progress report to which parents have access. Although the teacher may subsequently recognize that the problem resides with the assessment and not with students, parents naturally interpret the mark as an indication of their child's poor academic performance, perhaps due to lack of effort or inadequate preparation. In actuality, the mark was more a reflection of the poor quality of the assessment device than anything having to do with the students!

Such systems also perpetuate the belief that the more pieces of "evidence" you have, the more accurate the grade, even though all measurement experts know that the quality and purpose of the evidence matters most. Two good sources of evidence on student achievement and performance are much better than 20 poor ones.

So while it is a good idea for parents to have access to high-quality information about what their children are doing in school and how well they are performing in relation to clearly articulated learning goals or standards, teachers must be sure to help parents understand the difference between formative (feedback) evidence gathered to improve learning and summative evidence gathered to quantify achievement or evaluate learning progress. Otherwise, the information presented in an electronic progress report has the potential to be sorely misinterpreted and sadly misused (Guskey, 2007).

Parent-Teacher Conferences

Parent-teacher conferences hold special promise as a reporting tool because they involve communication that is both interactive and highly individualized. Teachers can select different pieces of information or even different themes to discuss for different students (Brookhart, 1999). Conferences also offer teachers the opportunity to discuss a wide range of school-related but nonacademic aspects of learning, such as attendance and tardy rates, class participation, attentiveness, social interactions, and class behavior (Nelson, 2000). But as with other forms of reporting, teachers rarely receive preservice training or professional development on how to prepare for these face-to-face encounters with parents and guardians (Little & Allan, 1989).

Poorly planned parent-teacher conferences can be a frustrating experience for both parents and teachers alike. In our interviews with parents, for example, many expressed occasional disappointment with parent-teacher conferences. Some said that the time allotted for the conference was too short to get a clear picture of how their child was doing. Others related stories of having to stand in long lines to have only a few minutes with the teacher. Teachers expressed different but equally serious frustrations. Several described spending hours preparing for conferences and then having only a few parents show up. The parents who did show up often were not the ones with whom the teacher really hoped to speak. Still other teachers told of the difficulties they encountered in dealing with angry and disgruntled parents.

When parent-teacher conferences are well planned, however, they can be key to developing positive working relationships between parents and teachers. To aid in that process, we have included a series of procedural recommendations for planning and conducting effective parent-teacher conferences in Figure 9.3. These recommendations are based on information gleaned from our interviews with parents and teachers. They are divided in the table among things to do before the conference, during the conference, and then after the conference (see Bernick, Rutherford, & Elliott, 1991).

Figure 9.3	Recommendations for Effective Parent-Teacher Conferences

Suggestions for Effective Parent-Teacher Conferences		
Before the conference . . .	*During the conference . . .*	*After the conference . . .*
• Encourage parents to review student work at home, note concerns or questions, and bring those to the conference.	• Provide child care, refreshments, and transportation, if needed.	• Provide parents with a telephone number and schedule of specific times so they may call you with concerns.
• Schedule times that are convenient for both working and nonworking parents.	• Show multiple samples of student work and discuss specific suggestions for improvement.	• Follow up on any questions or concerns raised during the conference.
• Notify parents well ahead of scheduled conference times.	• Actively listen and avoid the use of educational jargon.	• Plan a time to meet again, if necessary.
• Provide staff development for new teachers on the purpose for conferences, preparation, and scheduling.	• Communicate expectations and describe how parents can help.	• Encourage parents to discuss the conference with their child.
• Consider alternative locations, such as churches or community centers, for parent convenience.	• Develop a system for ongoing communication with each parent that recognizes parents as partners.	• Ask parents for a written evaluation of the conference and encourage them to make suggestions.
• Print conference schedules and materials in multiple languages, if necessary.	• Provide resources or materials that parents might use at home to strengthen students' skills.	• Debrief with colleagues to look for ways to improve future conferences.

Parent-teacher conferences also are most efficient and effective when they focus on the following four issues:

1. What is the student able to do?

2. What areas require further attention or skill development?

3. What help or support does the student need to be successful?

4. How is the student doing in relation to established learning standards for students in a similar age range or grade level? (Davies, 1996)

With careful planning and organization, parent-teacher conferences can be both informative and productive. They are an effective way to build positive, collaborative relationships between parents and teachers and should be part of every school's comprehensive reporting system.

Student-Teacher Conferences

Another highly effective but often neglected conference form is the student-teacher conference (Neil, 1987). Like parent-teacher conferences, student-teacher conferences require careful planning and organization. In particular, if the conferences are held during class time, teachers must ensure that students not involved in the conference are engaged in meaningful learning activities. Student-teacher conferences also have their own dynamics and require different approaches to communication about academic work. Nevertheless, they provide for both students and teachers a form of one-to-one, interpersonal communication that cannot be achieved through other formats.

Discussions during student-teacher conferences should focus on the qualities of good work and students' current work in relation to those qualities. Work samples can be reviewed with specific suggestions for improvement. Teachers should express their positive expectations for students' learning and behavior, along with their willingness to help students in efforts to improve. And most important, teachers should actively listen to students to determine how they might be most helpful to the students.

Some teachers conduct student-teacher conferences twice per year, while others schedule conferences with students at the beginning of each marking period. The latter regular schedule of conferences allows teachers to review students' immediate past work while setting improvement goals for forthcoming instructional units and marking periods.

Student-Led Conferences

A highly effective conference form is student-led conferences. In the typical parent-teacher or student-teacher conference, teachers lead the discussion regarding students' learning progress. In contrast, in a student-led conference, the student is responsible for leading the discussion and reporting on learning to parents. The teacher serves primarily as facilitator and observer (Bailey & Guskey, 2001).

Most teachers organize student-led conferences so that several conferences (typically four) are conducted simultaneously in the classroom, with family groups seated far enough apart to allow privacy. The teacher then circulates among family groups, stopping long enough to make pertinent comments and answer questions. Students direct the conversation during the conference, focusing on the work samples they have included in their conference portfolio and on their performance in relation to expected learning goals or standards.

The real power in student-led conferences comes from students taking responsibility for reporting on what they have learned (Shulkind, 2008). To prepare for this responsibility, however, students must be given regular opportunities to evaluate and reflect on the quality of their work. They also must be given guidance in how to organize their work thoughtfully in a portfolio and how to explain their work to their parents or guardians. In other words, students must be actively involved in all aspects of the reporting process.

Despite the need for attention to these preparation responsibilities, we find that teachers at all levels support the use of student-led conferences. Most indicate that the necessary preparation does not require an inordinate amount of instructional time. Plus, preparation tasks blend well with regular classroom routines as a way to promote student accountability. In addition, many teachers consider student-led conferences an extremely efficient way to meet and talk with the parents of their students.

Student-led conferences also are an effective means of promoting parent involvement (Goodman, 2008). Schools that have implemented student-led conferences consistently report dramatic increases in parent attendance at conferences (Little & Allan, 1989).

Through our surveys and interviews with parents, we have learned that they, too, regard student-led conferences very highly. One parent of an elementary student said, "I didn't know my son could speak so well about his work. When I ask him about what he did in school, he usually responds, 'Nothing, really.' But he really does know what he's doing!" Parents of high school students similarly expressed appreciation for all of the preparation and reflection that went into the portfolio of the student's work. Many told us that they especially liked having their son or daughter present to talk about concerns and to ask questions during the conference.

There are many ways to organize student-led conferences, and teachers vary in their format preferences. Important factors to consider when designing a specific format include the age and number of students involved, the flexibility of any previously established school district schedule for conference times, the amount of time available for student preparation, the comfort level of all participants with the concept of student-led conferences, and the specific goals for reporting student learning. It is also important, again, to consider purpose and context in choosing a format.

Student-led conferences are a highly effective way to communicate directly and authentically with parents (Tuinstra & Hiatt-Michael, 2004). When students direct the reporting process, information is communicated in a form everyone can understand and use. As learning becomes increasingly complex from kindergarten through high school, the portfolio becomes a detailed reporting tool that demonstrates students' growth and progress over time. Reviewing the portfolio during the conference becomes a learning experience for everyone involved. As such, student-led conferences are an especially important part of a comprehensive reporting system.

Guidelines for Better Practice

We now turn briefly to a few general guidelines for better practice. As we have stressed from the beginning, most teachers try hard to be fair in their grading and reporting policies and practices. They inform students of the components that will be used in grading and how those components will be weighed or combined. Nevertheless, grading practices vary considerably from teacher to teacher, especially in the perceived meaning of grades and in the factors considered in determining grades (Brookhart, 1994). Furthermore, few teachers have thought deeply about how they grade or seriously considered the potential impact of their grading policies and practices on students.

To develop and implement better grading policies and practices, we need to become more thoughtful about what we do. We need to make better use of the significant knowledge base on grading and reporting that has been assembled over the last century. We also must become more conscientious about applying that knowledge. The following guidelines are offered to help educators at all levels in that process.

Begin With a Clear Statement of Purpose

Many of the dilemmas we face with regard to grading and reporting can be resolved if we are clearer about our purpose. Grading and reporting today are an integral part of teaching and learning at every level of education. But as we have shown, not all educators agree on the purpose of grading or on the intended outcomes. As a result, grading and reporting policies and practices tend to be fragmented, ambiguous, and generally confusing to students, to parents, and to many teachers.

Distinguish the *formative* and *summative* purposes of grading and reporting. As we describe in Chapter 3, most of a teacher's grading and reporting tasks are actually formative in nature; that is, they are designed to offer students prescriptive feedback on their performance. Only occasionally must teachers synthesize that information to assign a cumulative, summative grade to students' achievement and performance (Bloom, Hastings, & Madaus, 1971). By keeping this distinction in mind and by using more thoughtful ways to combine the various sources of information to determine summative grades, teachers can emphasize their role as advocates for students while still fulfilling their evaluation responsibilities.

Recognize that no single reporting tool can serve all reporting purposes well. Improvements in grading and reporting will be best accomplished, therefore, through the development of comprehensive reporting systems. Reporting systems include multiple reporting tools, each designed to fit a specific, well-defined purpose. They communicate multiple types of information to multiple audiences in multiple formats. Such a comprehensive reporting system will serve educators' diverse communication needs far better than any single reporting device.

Provide Accurate and Understandable Descriptions of Student Learning

At all levels of education, teachers must be able to identify what they want their students to learn, what evidence they will use to verify that learning, and what criteria will be used to judge that evidence. These decisions form the basis for all standards-based report cards. They are also the foundation of all grading and reporting.

Decide whether to report on aspects of students' learning apart from evidence on achievement or academic performance. For example, is it important to consider information about students' work habits, effort, or other process criteria? Should information about the amount of improvement or progress criteria be included as well? If information on these types of learning criteria is considered significant in the reporting process, it should be reported separately from evidence on achievement or performance. As we have emphasized in earlier chapters, it is far better to offer multiple grades or marks on different aspects of students' learning than to combine all aspects into a single symbol with fine gradations.

Consider how best to communicate the information. If the primary audience for the information is parents or students, we must ensure that the information is free of jargon and complex technical language. It should be explicit and precise and relate to clearly defined learning standards or goals. Most important, it should communicate students' strengths and what they have achieved, identify any shortcomings or areas of weakness, and recommend practical suggestions for making improvements.

Remember that reporting involves two-way communication. Not only must the information be understood by the audience for whom it is intended, procedures must be in place for questions or concerns to be expressed and addressed. Effective grading and reporting is far more a challenge in effective communication than simply a process of documenting student achievement.

Use Grading and Reporting to Enhance Teaching and Learning

Educators today are becoming increasingly skilled in measurement and assessment techniques. Many use a variety of authentic assessment formats and score students' performance with carefully constructed rubrics (Arter & McTighe, 2001). At the same time, however, their efforts to communicate the results of those assessments to parents, guardians, and other interested persons are often undeveloped and inadequate. Few teachers today have thoroughly considered the consequences of their grading policies and practices or explored possible alternative procedures. As a result, they persist in the use of unsound grading practices that can have profoundly negative effects on students' attitudes, confidence, achievement, self-concept, motivation, and future education (Stiggins, Frisbie, & Griswold, 1989). How teachers grade is a serious matter and one that needs serious attention.

The changes required to eliminate these harmful effects are relatively small and seldom require a significant amount of extra work. A standards-based report card is an important step in that change process. To gain positive outcomes from these changes, however, grading and reporting systems must provide more opportunities for success, more detailed feedback to students and parents, more corrective instruction and specific direction for making improvements, and more positive encouragement. In essence, grades must provide an accurate and understandable description of students' achievement, performance, and progress in learning. Grades are harmful only if they misinform or mislead or are based on factors that have nothing to do with learning.

Parents consistently tell us that they want to know more about how their children are doing in school. Most are willing to become more involved in their children's education but are highly dependent on the school and, especially, their child's teacher for guidance as to how to do so. Information that lets them know what is expected of their children, how their children are performing in relation to carefully articulated standards for learning, and how parents can assist in the process is particularly helpful. A carefully designed standards-based report card offers precisely that information. When the information included in the report card is supported by teachers' records, observations, and samples of students' work, the communication is even more effective. Information that students develop, reflect upon, and then report to their parents and others is better still. Such practices adhere to important principles of honesty and fairness and help ensure that grading and reporting systems are true enhancements to teaching and learning processes.

Conclusion

Grading and reporting is an inherently subjective process. It involves one group of human beings (teachers) making judgments about the performance of another group of human beings (students) and trying to communicate summaries of those judgments to a third group of humans (parents and guardians). But as we have stressed throughout this book, being subjective does not mean that grades or marks lack credibility or are indefensible. Rather, it means that grading and reporting will always be an exercise in professional judgment. Standards-based report cards provide parents, students, and other interested persons with the means to interpret the professional judgments teachers have made.

If those professional judgments are to be meaningful and accurate, teachers must continuously reflect on their purpose in grading. They must constantly review what information they want to communicate, who is the primary audience for that information, and what result they hope to accomplish. If grades and marks are to present information to parents about the adequacy of students' achievement and performance, then the evidence used in determining those grades and marks must relate directly to what students have learned and can do. Other factors related to students' work habits, behaviors, or learning progress, while important, must be reported separately. To include these factors as part of a single grade misrepresents students' learning attainments. Distinguishing achievement from process is the principal advantage of standards-based grading.

Above all else, grading and reporting require careful planning, thoughtful judgment, and a clear focus on purpose. They also require a profound sense of fairness, excellent communication skills, and an overriding concern for students. Such qualities are necessary to ensure grading practices that provide high-quality information on student learning, regardless of the method employed. They also ensure that grading and reporting will be a positive and beneficial aspect of students' learning experiences in school.

References

Adelman, C. (1999). *Answers in the tool box: Academic intensity, attendance patterns, and bachelor's degree attainment.* Washington, DC: Office of Educational Research and Improvement, U.S. Department of Education.

Airasian, P. W. (2001). *Classroom assessment: Concepts and applications* (4th ed.). New York: McGraw-Hill.

Allen, J. D. (2005). Grades as valid measures of academic achievement of classroom learning. *The Clearing House, 78*(5), 218.

Allen, J. D., & Lambating, J. (2001, April). *Validity and reliability in assessment and grading: Perspectives of preservice and inservice teachers and teacher education professors.* Paper presented at the annual meeting of the American Educational Research Association, Seattle, WA. (ERIC Document Reproduction Service No. ED453167)

Allison, E., & Friedman, S. J. (1995). Reforming report cards. *Executive Educator, 17*(1), 38–39.

American Council on the Teaching of Foreign Languages. (1996). *Standards for foreign language learning: Preparing for the 21st century.* Lawrence, KS: Allen Press.

Americans With Disabilities Act of 1990, 42 U.S.C. § 12101 *et seq.*

Arter, J., & McTighe, J. (2001). *Scoring rubrics in the classroom.* Thousand Oaks, CA: Corwin.

Austin, S., & McCann, R. (1992, March). *"Here's another arbitrary grade for your collection": A statewide study of grading policies.* Paper presented at the annual meeting of the American Educational Research Association, San Francisco. (ERIC Document Reproduction Service No. ED343944)

Azwell, T., & Schmar, E. (Eds.). (1995). *Report card on report cards: Alternatives to consider.* Portsmouth, NH: Heinemann.

Bailey, J. M., & Guskey, T. R. (2001). *Implementing student-led conferences.* Thousand Oaks, CA: Corwin.

Bailey, J. M., & McTighe, J. (1996). Reporting achievement at the secondary level: What and how. In T. R. Guskey (Ed.), *Communicating student learning: 1996 yearbook of the Association for Supervision and Curriculum Development* (pp. 119–140). Alexandria, VA: Association for Supervision and Curriculum Development.

Baker, E. T., Wang, M. C., & Walberg, H. J. (1995). The effects of inclusion on learning. *Educational Leadership, 52*(4), 33–35.

Balm, S. S.-M. (1995). Using portfolio assessment in a kindergarten classroom. *Teaching and Change, 2*(2), 141–151.

Barnes, S. (1985). A study of classroom pupil evaluation: The missing link in teacher education. *Journal of Teacher Education, 36*(4), 46–49.

Baron, P. A. B. (2000, April). *Consequential validity for high school grades: What is the meaning of grades for senders and receivers?* Paper presented at the annual meeting of the American Educational Research Association, New Orleans, LA. (ERIC Document Reproduction Service No. ED445051)

Barton, P. (1999). *Too much testing of the wrong kind; too little of the right kind in K–12 education.* Princeton, NJ: Educational Testing Service.

Bennett, R. E., Gottesman, R. L., Rock, D. A., & Cerullo, F. (1993). Influence of behavior perceptions and gender on teachers' judgments of students' academic skill. *Journal of Educational Psychology, 85*(2), 347–356.

Bernick, R., Rutherford, B., & Elliott, J. (1991). *School and family conferences in the middle grades.* Washington, DC: Office of Educational Research and Improvement (OERI), U.S. Department of Education.

Bloom, B. S. (Ed.) (with Englehart, M. D., Furst, E. J., Hill, W. H., & Krathwohl, D. R.). (1956). *Taxonomy of educational objectives: The classification of educational goals; Handbook 1. The cognitive domain.* New York: McKay.

Bloom, B. S. (1976). *Human characteristics and school learning.* New York: McGraw-Hill.

Bloom, B. S., Hastings, J. T., & Madaus, G. F. (1971). *Handbook on formative and summative evaluation of student learning.* New York: McGraw-Hill.

Bloom, B. S., Madaus, G. F., & Hastings, J. T. (1981). *Evaluation to improve learning.* New York: McGraw-Hill.

Board of Education v. Rowley, 458 U.S. 176 (1982).

Boothroyd, R. A., & McMorris, R. F. (1992, April). *What do teachers know about testing and how did they find out?* Paper presented at the annual meeting of the National Council on Measurement in Education, San Francisco.

Brennan, R. T., Kim, J., Wenz-Gross, M., & Siperstein, G. N. (2001). The relative equitability of high-stakes testing versus teacher-assigned grades: An analysis of the Massachusetts Comprehensive Assessment System (MCAS). *Harvard Educational Review, 71*(2), 173–216.

Brookhart, S. M. (1991). Grading practices and validity. *Educational Measurement: Issues and Practice, 10*(1), 35–36.

Brookhart, S. M. (1993). Teachers' grading practices: Meaning and values. *Journal of Educational Measurement, 30*(2), 123–142.

Brookhart, S. M. (1994). Teachers' grading: Practice and theory. *Applied Measurement in Education, 7*(4), 279–301.

Brookhart, S. M. (1999). Teaching about communicating assessment results and grading. *Educational Measurement: Issues and Practice, 18*(1), 5–13.

Brookhart, S. M. (2008). Feedback that fits. *Educational Leadership, 65*(4), 54–59.

Brookhart, S. M. (2009). *Grading* (2nd ed.). Upper Saddle River, NJ: Pearson Merrill Prentice-Hall.

Brookhart, S. M., & Nitko, A. J. (2008). *Assessment and grading in classrooms.* Upper Saddle River, NJ: Pearson Education.

Bursuck, W. D., Munk, D. D., & Olson, M. M. (1999). The fairness of report card grading adaptations: What do students with and without disabilities think? *Remedial and Special Education, 20,* 84–92.

Bursuck, W. D., Polloway, E. A., Plante, L., Epstein, M. H., Jayanthi, M., & McConeghy, J. (1996). Report card grading and adaptations: A national survey of classroom practices. *Exceptional Children, 62*(2), 301–318.

Cameron, J., & Pierce, W. D. (1994). Reinforcement, reward, and intrinsic motivation: A meta-analysis. *Review of Educational Research, 64*(3), 363–423.

Cameron, J., & Pierce, W. D. (1996). The debate about rewards and intrinsic motivation: Protests and accusations do not alter the results. *Review of Educational Research, 66*(1), 39–51.

Carlberg, C., & Kavale, K. A. (1980). The efficacy of special versus regular class placement for exceptional children: A meta-analysis. *Journal of Special Education, 14,* 296–309.

Chastain, K. (1990). Characteristics of graded and ungraded compositions. *Modern Language Journal, 74*(1), 10–14.

Chrispeels, J., Fernandez, B., & Preston, J. (1991). *Home and school partners in student success: A handbook for principals and staff.* San Diego, CA: San Diego City Schools Community Relations and Integration Services Division.

Cizek, G. J., Fitzgerald, S. M., & Rachor, R. E. (1996). Teachers' assessment practices: Preparation, isolation, and the kitchen sink. *Educational Assessment, 3*(2), 159–179.

Conley, D. T. (2000, April). *Who is proficient: The relationship between proficiency scores and grades.* Paper presented at the annual meeting of the American Educational Research Association, New Orleans, LA. (ERIC Document Reproduction Service No. ED445025)

Cooley, W. W. (1997). "The vision thing": Educational research and AERA in the 21st century; Part 1: Competing visions of what educational researchers should do. *Educational Researcher, 26*(4), 18–19.

Cooper, H. (2007). *The battle over homework: Common ground for administrators, teachers, and parents* (3rd ed.). Thousand Oaks, CA: Corwin.

Cooper, H., Robinson, J. C., Patall, E. A. (2006). Does homework improve academic achievement? A synthesis of research 1987–2003. *Review of Educational Research, 76*(1), 1–62.

Corcoran, T., Fuhman, S. H., & Belcher, C. L. (2001). The district role in instructional improvement. *Phi Delta Kappan, 83*(1), 78–84.

Cowan, N. (2000). The magical number 4 in short-term memory: A reconsideration of mental storage capacity. *Behavioral and Brain Sciences, 24,* 87–185.

Cross, L. H., & Frary, R. B. (1996, April). *Hodgepodge grading: Endorsed by students and teachers alike.* Paper presented at the annual meeting of the National Council on Measurement in Education, New York. (ERIC Document Reproduction Service No. ED398262)

D'Agostino, J. V., & Welsh, M. E. (2007, April). *Standards-based progress reports and standards-based assessment score convergence.* Paper presented at the annual meeting of the American Educational Research Association, Chicago.

Davies, A. (1996). *Student-centered assessment & evaluation.* Merville, British Columbia, Canada: Classroom Connections International.

Davies, A. (2000). Seeing the results for yourself: A portfolio primer. *Classroom Leadership, 3*(5), 4–5.

Donahue, K., & Zigmond, N. (1990). Academic grades of ninth-grade urban learning disabled students and low-achieving peers. *Exceptionality, 1*(1), 17–27.

Doran, G. T. (1981). There's a S.M.A.R.T. way to write managements' goals and objectives. *Management Review, 70*(11), 35–36.

Eastwood, K. W. (1996). Reporting student progress: One district's attempt with student literacy. In T. R. Guskey, (Ed.), *Communicating student learning: 1996 Yearbook of the Association for Supervision and Curriculum Development* (pp. 65–78). Alexandria, VA: Association for Supervision and Curriculum Development.

Ebel, R. L. (1979). *Essentials of educational measurement* (3rd ed.). Englewood Cliffs, NJ: Prentice Hall.

Epstein, J. L. (1995). School/family/community partnerships: Caring for the children we share. *Phi Delta Kappan, 76*(9), 701–712.

Esty, W. W., & Teppo, A. R. (1992). Grade assignment based on progressive improvement. *Mathematics Teacher, 85*(8), 616–618.

Etscheidt, S. K. (2006). Progress monitoring: Legal issues and recommendations for IEP teams. *Teaching Exceptional Children, 38*(3), 56–60.

Fan, X., & Chen, M. (1999). Parent involvement and students' academic achievement: A meta-analysis. *Educational Psychology Review, 13*(1), 1–22.

Feldmesser, R. A. (1971, February). *The positive functions of grades.* Paper presented at the annual meeting of the American Educational Research Association, New York. (ERIC Document Reproduction Service No. ED049704)

Floyd, L. (1998). Joining hands: A parental involvement program. *Urban Education, 33*(1), 123–135.

Frary, R. B., Cross, L. H., & Weber, L. J. (1993). Testing and grading practices and opinions of secondary teachers of academic subjects: Implications for instruction in measurement. *Educational Measurement: Issues and Practice, 12*(3), 23–30.

Freedman, M. K. (2005). *Grades, report cards, etc. . . . and the law.* Boston: School Law Pro.

Friedman, S. J. (1998). Grading teachers' grading policies. *NASSP Bulletin, 82*(597), 77–83.

Friedman, S. J., & Frisbie, D. A. (1995). The influence of report cards on the validity of grades reported to parents. *Educational and Psychological Measurement, 55*(1), 5–26.

Friedman, S. J., & Manley, M. (1992). Improving high school grading practices: Experts vs. practitioners. *NASSP Bulletin, 76*(544), 100–104.

Friedman, S. J., & Troug, A. J. (1999). Evaluation of high school teachers' written grading policies. *ERS Spectrum, 17*(3), 34–42.

Friedman, S. J., Valde, G. A., & Obermeyer, B. J. (1998). Computerized report card comment menus: Teacher use and teacher/parent perceptions. *Michigan Principal, 74*(3), 11–14, 21.

Frisbie, D. A., & Waltman, K. K. (1992). Developing a personal grading plan. *Educational Measurement: Issues and Practices, 11*(3), 35–42.

Garet, M. S., Porter, A. C., Desimone, L., Birman, B. F., & Yoon, K. S. (2001). What makes professional development effective? Results from a national sample of teachers. *American Educational Research Journal, 38*(4), 915–945.

Gersten, R., Vaughn, S., & Brengelman, S. U. (1996). Grading and academic feedback for special education students and students with learning difficulties. In T. R. Guskey (Ed.), *Communicating student learning: 1996 yearbook of the Association for Supervision and Curriculum and Development* (pp. 47–57). Alexandria, VA: Association for Supervision and Curriculum Development.

Giba, M. A. (1999). Forging partnerships between parents and teachers. *Principal, 78*(3), 33–35.

Goodman, A. (2008). Student-led, teacher-supported conferences: Improving communication in an urban school district. *Middle School Journal, 39*(3), 48–54.

Gronlund, N. E. (2000). *How to write and use instructional objectives* (6th ed.). Upper Saddle River, NJ: Merrill.

Gronlund, N. E. (2006). *Assessment of student achievement* (8th ed.). Boston: Pearson/Allyn & Bacon.

Guskey, T. R. (1994a). Making the grade: What benefits students. *Educational Leadership, 52*(2), 14–20.

Guskey, T. R. (1994b). Results-oriented professional development: In search of an optimal mix of effective practices. *Journal of Staff Development, 15*(4) 42–50.

Guskey, T. R. (1994c). What you assess may not be what you get. *Educational Leadership, 51*(6), 51–54.

Guskey, T. R. (Ed.). (1996a). *Communicating student learning: 1996 yearbook of the Association for Supervision and Curriculum Development.* Alexandria, VA: Association for Supervision and Curriculum Development.

Guskey, T. R. (1996b). Reporting on student learning: Lessons from the past—Prescriptions for the future. In T. R. Guskey (Ed.), *Communicating student learning: 1996 yearbook of the Association for Supervision and Curriculum Development* (pp. 13–24). Alexandria, VA: Association for Supervision and Curriculum Development.

Guskey, T. R. (1999). Making standards work. *The School Administrator, 56*(9), 44.

Guskey, T. R. (2001a). Helping standards make the grade. *Educational Leadership, 59*(1), 20–27.

Guskey, T. R. (2001b). High percentages are not the same as high standards. *Phi Delta Kappan, 82*(7), 534–536.

Guskey, T. R. (2002a). Computerized gradebooks and the myth of objectivity. *Phi Delta Kappan, 83*(10), 775–780.

Guskey, T. R. (2002b). *How's my kid doing? A parent's guide to grades, marks, and report cards.* San Francisco: Jossey-Bass.

Guskey, T. R. (2004). The communication challenge of standards-based reporting. *Phi Delta Kappan, 86*(4), 326–329.

Guskey, T. R. (2005). Five key concepts kick off the process: Professional development provides the power to implement standards. *Journal of Staff Development, 26*(1), 36–40.

Guskey, T. R. (Ed.). (2006a). *Benjamin S. Bloom: Portraits of an educator.* Lanham, MD: Rowman & Littlefield Education.

Guskey, T. R. (2006b). "It wasn't fair!" Educators' recollections of their experiences as students with grading. *Journal of Educational Research and Policy Studies, 6*(2), 111–124.

Guskey, T. R. (2006c). Making high school grades meaningful. *Phi Delta Kappan, 87*(9), 670–675.

Guskey, T. R. (2007, Spring). Efficacy of online reporting. *Alberta Assessment Consortium Communiqué,* p. 2. Available June 26, 2009, at http://www.aac.ab.ca/AACCommunique/nlspring07.html

Guskey, T. R. (2009a). Closing the knowledge gap on effective professional development. *Educational Horizons, 87*(4), 224–233.

Guskey, T. R. (Ed.). (2009b). *Practical solutions for serious problems in standards-based grading.* Thousand Oaks, CA: Corwin.

Guskey, T. R., & Anderman, E. M. (2008). Students at bat. *Educational Leadership, 66*(3), 8–14.

Guskey, T. R., & Bailey, J. M. (2001). *Developing grading and reporting systems for student learning.* Thousand Oaks, CA: Corwin.

Guskey, T. R., & Huberman, M. (Eds.). (1995). *Professional development in education: New paradigms and practices.* New York: Teachers College Press.

Guskey, T. R., & Jung, L. A. (2006). The challenges of standards-based grading. *Leadership Compass, 4*(2), 6–10.

Guskey, T. R., Smith, J. K., Smith, L. F., Crooks, T., & Flockton, L. (2006). Literacy assessment, New Zealand style. *Educational Leadership, 64*(2), 74–79.

Guskey, T. R., & Yoon, K. S. (2009). What works in professional development? *Phi Delta Kappan, 90*(7), 495–500.

Gustafson, C. (1998). Phone home. *Educational Leadership, 56*(2), 31–32.

Haladyna, T. M. (1999). *A complete guide to student grading.* Boston: Allyn & Bacon.

Hall, K. (1990). *Determining the success of narrative report cards.* Unpublished manuscript.

Handler, B. R. (2003, April). *Special education practices: An evaluation of educational environmental placement trends since the regular education initiative.* Paper presented at the Annual Meeting of the American Educational Research Association, Chicago.

Hargis, C. H. (2003). *Grades and grading practices: Obstacles to improving education and to helping at-risk students* (2nd ed.). Springfield, IL: Charles C Thomas.

Hattie, J., & Timperley, H. (2007). The power of feedback. *Review of Educational Research, 77*(1), 81–112.

Henderson, A. T., & Berla, N. (1994). *A new generation of evidence: The family is critical to student achievement.* Washington, DC: National Committee for Citizens in Education.

Heritage, M. (2007). Formative assessment: What do teachers need to know and do? *Phi Delta Kappan, 89*(2), 140–145.

Hills, J. R. (1983). Interpreting grade-equivalent scores. *Educational Measurement: Issues and Practice, 2*(1), 15, 21.

Hills, J. H. (1991). Apathy concerning grading and testing. *Phi Delta Kappan, 72*(7), 540–545.

Hiner, R. (1973). The cultural function of grading. *Clearing House, 47*(6), 356–361.

Hoover-Dempsey, K. V., Walker, J. M. T., Sandler, H. M., Whetsel, D., Green, C. L., Wilkins, A. S., et al. (2005). Why do parents become involved? Research findings and implications. *Elementary School Journal, 106*(2), 105–130.

Huber, J. (1997). Gradebook programs: Which ones make the grade? *Technology Connection, 4*(1), 21–23.

Hunt, P., Farron-Davis, F., Beckstead, S., Curtis, D., & Goetz, L. (1994). Evaluating the effects of placement of students with severe disabilities in general education versus special classes. *Journal of the Association for Persons with Severe Handicaps, 19,* 200–214.

Individuals With Disabilities Education Act, 20 U.S.C § 1400–1491 (1997).

Individuals With Disabilities Education Improvement Act, 20 U.S.C § 1400–1482 (2004).

Johnson, D. (2000). Teacher Web pages that build parent partnerships. *Multi Media Schools, 7*(4), 48–51.

Joyce, B. (1993). The link is there, but where do we go from here? *Journal of Staff Development, 14*(3), 10–12.

Jung, L. A. (2009). The challenges of grading and reporting in special education: An inclusive grading model. In T. R. Guskey (Ed.), *Practical solutions for serious problems in standards-based grading* (pp. 27–40). Thousand Oaks, CA: Corwin.

Jung, L. A., & Guskey, T. R. (2007). Standards-based grading and reporting: A model for special education. *Teaching Exceptional Children, 40*(2), 48–53.

Kain, D. L. (1996). Looking beneath the surface: Teacher collaboration through the lens of grading practices. *Teachers College Record, 97*(4), 569–587.

Kirschenbaum, H. (1999). Night and day: Succeeding with parents at School 43. *Principal, 78*(3), 20–23.

Kovas, M. A. (1993). Make your grading motivating: Keys to performance based evaluation. *Quill and Scroll, 68*(1), 10–11.

Kreider, H. M., & Lopez, M. E. (1999). Promising practices for family involvement. *Principal, 78*(3), 16–19.

Langdon, C. A. (1999). The fifth Phi Delta Kappa poll of teachers' attitudes toward the public schools. *Phi Delta Kappan, 80*(8), 611–618.

Lieberman, A. (1995). Practices that support teacher development: Transforming conceptions of professional learning. *Phi Delta Kappan, 76*(8), 591–596.

Linn, R. L. (1983). Testing and instruction: Links and distinctions. *Journal of Educational Measurement, 20*(2), 179–189.

Linn, R. L., & Gronlund, N. E. (2000). Grading and reporting. In *Measurement and assessment in teaching* (8th ed.; pp. 377–404). Upper Saddle River, NJ: Prentice-Hall.

Little, A. W., & Allan, J. (1989). Student-led parent-teacher conferences. *Elementary School Guidance and Counseling, 23*(3), 210–218.

Lomax, R. G. (1996). On becoming assessment literate: An initial look at preservice teachers' beliefs and practices. *Teacher Educator, 31*(4), 292–303.

Marzano, R. J. (1999). Building curriculum and assessment around standards. *The High School Magazine, 6*(5), 14–19.

Marzano, R. J. (2000). *Transforming classroom grading.* Alexandria, VA: Association for Supervision and Curriculum Development.

Marzano, R. J., & Kendall, J. S. (1995). *The systematic identification and articulation of content standards and benchmarks: Update.* Washington, DC: U.S. Government Printing Office.

McMillan, J. H. (2001). Secondary teachers' classroom assessment and grading practices. *Educational Measurement: Issues and Practice, 20*(1), 20–32.

McMillan, J. H., Myran, S., & Workman, D. (2002). Elementary teachers' classroom assessment and grading practices. *Journal of Educational Research, 95*(4), 203–213.

McMillan, J. H., & Nash, S. (2000, April). *Teacher classroom assessment and grading practices decision making.* Paper presented at the annual meeting of the National Council on Measurement in Education, New Orleans.

Mid-Continent Research for Education and Learning (McREL). (2007). *Content knowledge: A compendium of standards and benchmarks for K–12 education* (4th ed.). Denver, CO: Author. Retrieved December 2007 from http://www.mcrel.org/standards-benchmarks/

Miller, G. A. (1956). The magical number seven, plus or minus two: Some limits on our capacity for processing information. *Psychological Review, 63,* 81–97.

Miller, M. D., Linn, R. L., & Gronlund, N. E. (2009). *Measurement and assessment in teaching* (10th ed.). Upper Saddle River, NJ: Pearson Education.

Murphy, E. J. (2006). The "last mile" in standards-based reform: Conducting a match study linking teacher-certification tests to student standards. *Phi Delta Kappan, 87*(9), 700–704.

National Academy of Science. (1996). *National science education standards.* Washington, DC: National Committee on Science Education Standards and Assessment, National Research Council.

National Assessment of Educational Progress (NAEP). (2008). *The NAEP glossary of terms.* Retrieved June 26, 2009, from http://nces.ed.gov/nationsreportcard/glossary.asp

National Center on Secondary Education and Transition. (2005, June). *Key provisions on transition: IDEA 1997 compared to H.R. 1350 (IDEA 2004).* Retrieved June 26, 2009 from http://ncset.org/publications/related/ideatransition.asp

National Commission on Teaching and America's Future. (1996). *What matters most: Teaching for America's future.* New York: Author.

National Council for the Social Studies. (1994). *Curriculum standards for social studies.* Silver Springs, MD: Author.

National Council of Teachers of English. (1996). *Standards for the English language arts.* Urbana, IL: Author

National Council of Teachers of Mathematics. (1989). *Curriculum and evaluation standards for school mathematics.* Reston, VA: Author.

National Council of Teachers of Mathematics. (2000). *Principles and standards for school mathematics.* Washington, DC: National Council of Teachers of Mathematics. Retrieved June 28, 2009, from http://standards.nctm.org

Natriello, G., & Dornbusch, S. M. (1984). *Teacher evaluation standards and student effort.* New York: Longman.

Natriello, G., Riehl, C. J., & Pallas, A. M. (1994). *Between the rock of standards and the hard place of accommodation: Evaluation practices of teachers in high schools serving disadvantaged students.* Baltimore, MD: Center for Research on Effective Schooling for Disadvantaged Students, Johns Hopkins University.

Nava, F. J. G., & Loyd, B. H. (1992, April). *An investigation of achievement and nonachievement criteria in elementary and secondary school grading.* Paper presented at the annual meeting of the American Educational Research Association, San Francisco.

Neil, L. R. (1987). Individual student-teacher conferences: Guiding content revision with sixth graders. *Writing Center Journal, 7*(2), 37–44.

Nelson, K. (2000). Measuring the intangibles. *Classroom Leadership, 3*(5), 1, 8.

Norman, R. L., & Buckendahl, C. W. (2008). Determining sufficient measurement opportunities when using multiple cut scores. *Educational Measurement: Issues and Practice, 27*(1), 37–46.

O'Connor, K. (2007). *A repair kit for grading: 15 fixes for broken grades.* Portland, OR: Educational Testing Service.

O'Connor, K. (2009). *How to grade for learning K–12* (3rd ed.). Thousand Oaks, CA: Corwin.

O'Neill, J., & Conzemius, A. (2005). *The power of SMART goals: Using goals to improve student learning.* Bloomington, IN: Solution Tree.

Ornstein, A. C. (1994). Grading practices and policies: An overview and some suggestions. *NASSP Bulletin, 78*(559), 55–64.

Page, E. B., & Petersen, N. S. (1995). The computer moves into essay grading: Updating the ancient test. *Phi Delta Kappan, 76,* 561–565.

Pardini, P. (1997). Report card reform. *School Administrator, 54*(11), 19–20, 22–25.

Peckron, K. B. (1996). Beyond the A: Communicating the learning progress of gifted students. In T. R. Guskey (Ed.), *Communicating student learning: 1996 yearbook of the Association for Supervision and Curriculum Development* (pp. 58–64). Alexandria, VA: Association for Supervision and Curriculum Development.

Polloway, E. A., Epstein, M. H., Bursuck, W. D., Roderique, T. W., McConeghy, J. L., & Jayanthi, M. (1994). Classroom grading: A national survey of policies. *Remedial and Special Education, 15,* 162–170.

Reedy, R. (1995). Formative and summative assessment: A possible alternative to the grading-reporting dilemma. *NASSP Bulletin, 79*(573), 47–51.

Rehabilitation Act of 1973, 29 U.S.C. § 701 *et seq.*

Ring, M. M., & Reetz, L. (2000). Modification effects on attributions of middle school students with learning disabilities. *Learning Disabilities Research & Practice, 15*(1), 34–42.

Robinson, D. (1998). Student portfolios in mathematics. *Mathematics Teacher, 91*(4), 318–325.

Sarason, S. (1990). *The predictable failure of educational reform.* San Francisco: Jossey-Bass.

Schafer, W. D. (1991). Essential assessment skills in professional education of teachers. *Educational Measurement: Issues and Practice, 10*(1), 3–6, 12.

Seeley, M. M. (1994). The mismatch between assessment and grading. *Educational Leadership, 52*(2), 4–6.

Senge, P. M. (1990). *The fifth discipline.* New York: Doubleday Currency.

Shafer, S. (1997). *Writing effective report card comments.* New York: Scholastic.

Shulkind, S. B. (2008). New conversations: Student-led conferences. *Principal Leadership, 9*(1), 54–58.

Shuster, C., Lynch, T., & Polson-Lorczak, M. (1996, April). *A study of kindergarten and first grade report cards: What are young children expected to learn?* Paper presented at the annual meeting of the American Educational Research Association, New York. (ERIC Document Reproduction Service No. ED400289)

Shute, V. J. (2008). Focus on formative feedback. *Review of Educational Research, 78*(1), 153–189.

Silva, E. (2009). Measuring skills for the 21st century. *Phi Delta Kappan, 90*(9), 630–634.

Silva, M., Munk, D. D., & Bursuck, W. D. (2005). Grading adaptations for students with disabilities. *Intervention in School and Clinic, 41,* 87–98.

Sirotnik, K. A. (2002). Promoting responsible accountability in schools and education. *Phi Delta Kappan, 83*(9), 662–673.

Smith, J. K. (2003). Reconsidering reliability in classroom assessment and grading. *Educational Measurement: Issues and Practice, 22*(4), 26–33.

Stiggins, R. J. (1989). Inside high school grading practices: Building a research agenda. *Educational Measurement: Issues and Practice, 8*(2), 5–14.

Stiggins, R. J. (1991). Relevant classroom assessment training for teachers. *Educational Measurement: Issues and Practice, 10*(1), 7–12.

Stiggins, R. J. (1993). Teacher training in assessment: Overcoming the neglect. In S. L. Wise (Ed.), *Teacher training in measurement and assessment skills* (pp. 27–40). Lincoln, NE: Buros Institute of Mental Measurements.

Stiggins, R. J. (1999). Evaluating classroom assessment training in teacher education programs. *Educational Measurement: Issues and Practice, 18*(1), 23–27.

Stiggins, R. J. (2008a). Report cards: Assessments for learning. Chapter 11 in *Student-involved assessment for learning* (5th ed.; pp. 267–310). Upper Saddle River, NJ: Merrill/Prentice Hall.

Stiggins, R. J. (2008b). *Student-involved assessment for learning* (5th ed.). Upper Saddle River, NJ: Merrill/Prentice Hall.

Stiggins, R. J., Frisbie, D. A., & Griswold, P. A. (1989). Inside high school grading practices: Building a research agenda. *Educational Measurement: Issues and Practice, 8*(2), 5–14.

Stiggins, R., & Knight, T. (1997). *But are they learning? A commonsense parent's guide to assessment and grading in schools.* Portland, OR: Assessment Training Institute.

Tomlinson, T. (1992). *Hard work and high expectations: Motivating students to learn.* Washington, DC: Office of Educational Research and Improvement, U.S. Department of Education.

Trumbull, E. (2000). Why do we grade—and should we? In E. Trumbull & B. Farr (Eds.), *Grading and reporting student progress in an age of standards* (pp. 23–43). Norwood, MA: Christopher-Gordon.

Trumbull, E., & Farr, B. (Eds.). (2000). *Grading and reporting student progress in an age of standards.* Norwood, MA: Christopher-Gordon.

Truog, A. L., & Friedman, S. J. (1996, April). *Evaluating high school teachers' written grading policies from a measurement perspective.* Paper presented at the annual meeting of the National Council on Measurement in Education, New York.

Tuinstra, C., & Hiatt-Michael, D. (2004). Student-led parent conferences in middle schools. *School Community Journal, 14*(1), 59–80.

Tyler, R. W. (1949). *Basic principles of curriculum and instruction.* Chicago: University of Chicago Press.

Vockell, E. L., & Fiore, D. J. (1993). Electronic gradebooks: What current programs can do for teachers. *Clearing House, 66*(3), 141–145.

Waldron, N. L. (1998). The effects of an inclusive school program on students with mild and severe learning disabilities. *Exceptional Children, 64,* 395–405.

Waltman, K. K., & Frisbie, D. A. (1994). Parents understanding of their children's report card grades. *Applied Measurement in Education, 7*(3), 223–240.

Walvoord, B. E., & Anderson, V. J. (1998). *Effective grading: A tool for learning and assessment.* San Francisco: Jossey-Bass.

Welsh, M. E., & D'Agostino, J. (2009). Fostering consistency between standards-based grades and large scale assessment results. In T. R. Guskey (Ed.), *Practical solutions for serious problems in standards-based grading* (pp. 75–104). Thousand Oaks, CA: Corwin.

Wiggins, G. (1994). Toward better report cards. *Educational Leadership, 52*(2), 28–35.

Wiggins, G. (1996). Honesty and fairness: Toward better grading and reporting. In T. R. Guskey (Ed.), *Communicating student learning: 1996 yearbook of the Association for Supervision and Curriculum Development* (pp. 141–176). Alexandria, VA: Association for Supervision and Curriculum Development.

Wiggins, G., & McTighe, J. (2005). *Understanding by design* (2nd ed.). Alexandria, VA: Association for Supervision and Curriculum Development.

Wiles, C. A. (1992). Investigating gender bias in the evaluations of middle school teachers of mathematics. *School Science and Mathematics, 92*(6), 295–298.

Willingham, W. W., Pollack, J. M., & Lewis, C. (2002). Grades and test scores: Accounting for observed differences. *Journal of Educational Measurement, 39*(1), 1–37.

Wormeli, R. (2006). *Fair isn't always equal: Assessing and grading in the differentiated classroom.* Portland, ME: Stenhouse.

Wresch, W. (1993). The imminence of grading essays by computer—25 years later. *Computers and Composition, 10*(2), 45–58.

Yoon, K. S., Duncan, T., Lee, S. W., Scarloss, B., & Shapley, K. L. (2007). *Reviewing the evidence on how teacher professional development affects student achievement* (Issues and Answers Report, REL 2007–No. 033). Washington, DC: U.S. Department of Education, Institute of Education Sciences, National Center for Education Evaluation and Regional Assistance, Regional Educational Laboratory Southwest. Retrieved June 26, 2009, from http://ies.ed.gov/ncee/edlabs/regions/southwest/pdf/REL_2007033.pdf

Index

CORWIN
A SAGE Company

The Corwin logo—a raven striding across an open book—represents the union of courage and learning. Corwin is committed to improving education for all learners by publishing books and other professional development resources for those serving the field of PreK–12 education. By providing practical, hands-on materials, Corwin continues to carry out the promise of its motto: **"Helping Educators Do Their Work Better."**